Community Matters

A FACING HISTORY AND OURSELVES APPROACH TO ADVISORY

People make choices. Choices make history.

Copyright © 2019 by Facing History and Ourselves, Inc. All rights reserved.

Facing History and Ourselves® is a trademark registered in the US Patent & Trademark Office.

Facing History and Ourselves
16 Hurd Road
Brookline, MA 02445
www.facinghistory.org

1 2 3 4 5 6 7 8 9 10

ISBN 978-1-940457-44-4

TABLE OF CONTENTS

Introduction to *Community Matters*:
A Facing History and Ourselves Approach to Advisory **1**

Best Practices for Advisors **3**

Making Space for Mini-Conferences **5**

Fostering a Reflective and Supportive Community **7**

    A. Contracting in a Facing History and Ourselves Advisory 8

    B. Journaling in a Facing History and Ourselves Advisory 9

    C. Opening Routines for Advisory Meetings 12

    D. Closing Routines for Advisory Meetings 15

Getting Started: Navigating the Activities **17**

Sample Advisory Meeting Maps for the Opening Weeks **19**

Section 1: Welcome to Advisory! (Activities 1–15) **21**

Section 2: Exploring Identity: Who Am I? (Activities 16–28) **65**

Section 3: Understanding Community (Activities 29–37) **115**

Section 4: Membership and Belonging: Who Are "We"? Who Are "They"?
(Activities 38–52) **141**

Section 5: Case Study: Ostracism and Bullying (Activities 53–63) **205**

Section 6: Choosing to Participate (Activities 64–69) **265**

Appendix: Designing Your School's Advisory Program **291**

    Placing Advisory in the Master Schedule 291

    Coordinating and Sustaining the Advisory Program 292

    Deciding Who Will Serve as an Advisor 292

    Establishing Advisory Meeting Spaces 293

    Providing Materials for Advisors 293

    Grouping the Students into Advisories 293

    Planning Advisory Meetings: Consistency versus Tailoring 294

    Advisory as a Go-To Structure When Troubling Events or Crises Arise 295

Introduction to *Community Matters: A Facing History and Ourselves Approach to Advisory*

Advisory works to help schools establish safe and inclusive communities where students learn to listen to diverse viewpoints and make their voices heard. Advisories serve as student-centered spaces, facilitated by a trusted adult, where honest questioning, discussion, and social and academic growth can occur; where students build understanding and empathy, break down stereotypes, and find and build their voices; and where they develop the skills necessary for academic and community success. A school-wide advisory program with these characteristics can help lay the foundation for a community centered on equity and justice.

Advisory supports adolescents' social and developmental needs by helping them better understand themselves as learners, peers, and members of the broader communities in which they live. Furthermore, advisory creates space outside of academic classes where students can develop a trusting relationship with an adult in school and can wrestle with the social and academic questions they face—questions that, when left unanswered, can impede their ability to learn and thrive.

Built on a foundation of social-emotional learning, *Community Matters: A Facing History and Ourselves Approach to Advisory* provides one year's worth of activities and materials for grades 8–10. Social–emotional learning (SEL) is an integral part of young people's success in school, which depends not only on academic achievement but also on students' ability to engage respectfully and responsibly with others. At its core, SEL helps students and adults to develop the fundamental competencies for life effectiveness, including handling oneself, one's relationships, and one's work effectively and ethically. Principles of SEL can also be used as a framework for improving schools with a focus on creating caring learning communities with respectful, supportive relationships among students and adults.

Adolescence is a time when two tasks take on special importance: determining our own individual identity and figuring out where and how we belong. *Community Matters* supports and challenges young people who are beginning to see themselves as unique individuals with a desire to belong. The activities are grouped into six sections that align with Facing History and Ourselves' scope and sequence (visit facinghistory.org to learn more about our scope and sequence). Advisees begin with the foundational tasks of learning each other's names and establishing group norms. Then they embark on an exploration of their identities by examining how the relationship between the individual and society plays out in their lives. They pay close attention to the similarities and differences between their "real" and their online identities. Next, advisees reflect on why we all have a tendency to arrange ourselves into "in" groups and "out" groups. They apply this theme of membership and belonging to a real-life case study, which challenges them to consider the factors that can lead to ostracism and bullying, as well as the roles that people play when they witness or become aware of ostracism, bullying, and cyberbullying. In the final section, advisees explore different ways of participating in the world around them in order to help them realize that even though they are young, they still have the power to shape their communities through their choices and actions.

In addition to the themes of identity, membership, belonging, and participation addressed in this guide, some schools may wish to include other important topics in their advisory programs, such as personal and academic goal-setting, time management, stress management, and college and career prep. For information, activities, and resources to help incorporate these important topics into your school's advisory program alongside *Community Matters*, we recommend the following resources:

- *The Advisory Guide: Designing and Implementing Successful Advisory Programs in Secondary Schools* by Rachel Poliner and Carol Miller Lieber
- *Teaching the Whole Teen: Everyday Practices that Promote Success and Resilience in School and Life* by Rachel Poliner and Jeffrey Benson

Best Practices for Advisors

Advisory requires a paradigm shift in how adults think about their role in a school and their relationship to content. In traditional classrooms, teachers usually choose the content and deliver the material for students to learn. In advisory, the goals and roles are different. The adult's role is to facilitate community development, listen to and mentor students, and create spaces for reflection and discussion. The content is student-centered: What issues are students facing in school? How can advisory support all students in overcoming those obstacles, succeeding in school, and developing their voices? In this rich environment, advisees explore and expand their sense of who they are as individuals and what it means to be a contributing part of their school community.

To help create this student-centered learning environment, advisors should keep in mind the following keys to leading a successful advisory group:

Students are at the heart of advisory.

Students are the curriculum. The focus of your time together should be on helping them do their best in school, helping them consider their futures, helping them make good choices, and helping them be part of a supportive group. School climate and peer culture are also key focus areas for advisory—shaping a climate and peer culture to be physically safe, socially safe, and emotionally safe. The best emotional states for learning are comfortable and curious, not vigilant and defensive.

Relationships are the primary source of authority.

The primary source of authority comes from advisor relationships with their advisees—showing they care, getting to know them as individuals, becoming a trusted adult. Most advisories are not graded or offer only a small portion of a credit, so advisees participate because they have a voice in what is happening, get academic and emotional support, and learn about themselves and others, not because there are threats of low grades and non-credit. As teachers and administrators take on the role of advisor, it is important for the adults to build trusting relationships with their advisees while at the same time establishing and maintaining professional boundaries.

Leadership and ownership are shared.

Advisory should involve advisee leadership and a sense of shared ownership of the space and meeting time. Advisors should look for opportunities for advisees to run rituals and routines, suggest topics for discussion, or take on leadership roles in planning and implementing group projects.

Advisees are known and celebrated as unique individuals.

One of the roles of an advisor is to know each advisee well. To accomplish this goal, there are some simple but important practices to follow, including

- learning advisees' names and pronouncing them correctly,
- greeting advisees by name at the outset of every advisory meeting,
- knowing advisees' strengths, extracurricular activities, and hobbies,
- establishing a mini-conferencing routine, even if it is for two minutes with each advisee, as a regular part of advisory,
- and, if possible, having a few minutes of informal individualized conversation with each advisee each month about a topic other than academics.

Routines and rituals help create community.

Routines and rituals establish community, provide a structure for the group to follow, and help advisory feel different from academic classes.

- **Routines** are recurring strategies used during advisory meetings. Opening and closing routines mark the beginning and ending of each advisory meeting. Routines are also used to structure written reflections, to facilitate small-group and whole-group discussions, to relieve stress, and to guide goal setting and mini-conferences.
- **Rituals** provide opportunities to build connection and community by marking special occasions, such as holidays, school vacations, benchmarks (registering to vote, getting a driver's license, taking exams for the first time, the end of the year), and accomplishments (academic, extracurricular, or out-of-school). For example, your advisory group can develop a spirit-boosting ritual that they perform before a group member has a big game or performance.

The more that your advisory uses rituals and routines, the more your advisees will know how to participate in activities, take on leadership roles during meetings, and feel ownership of the space.

Advisory is an inclusive and welcoming space.

In order to improve their social skills and contribute in a positive way to the overall school climate, advisees have to talk with one another, not just with you, their advisor. For most advisory group purposes, the advisor should try to arrange the chairs, desks, or tables into a circle, square, or arc. Sitting in rows greatly impedes interaction. For small-group discussions, advisees should arrange their seats into small islands so that group members are close together and facing one another. Pairs might sit side by side in their chairs or on the floor to facilitate quieter conversations. You can start the year (and revisit when needed) by asking for advisee input on room design and establish a routine where they move the chairs safely, quietly, and quickly at the outset of the meeting, between activities, and before leaving for their next class.[1]

---

[1] Rachel Poliner, a national leader and author for advisory programs, wrote this section.

Making Space for Mini-Conferences

The Goal of Mini-Conferences in Advisory

One key reason for implementing a school-wide advisory program is to provide time and space for mini-conferencing between advisors and individual advisees on a regular basis. Advisees can benefit from individualized conversations with an adult in the building who may or may not be their teacher and who has a good sense of the whole student—their academic program, strengths, areas for growth, personal interests, and home life. These short one-to-one conversations help advisees develop a growth mindset, self-management skills (reflecting on and improving learning habits), and interpersonal skills (self-advocacy with teachers). They also offer an opportunity to address equity issues—what some advisees might have noted earlier as "skills or moves or tricks that some kids know how to do to be successful at school" but that are a mystery to other students.

Since advisors focus on the advisee as a whole, not how they are doing in just one class, they might notice slumps sooner than specific academic teachers might notice them, hear about stress building up or complications with friends or at home, or be able to help advisees connect what they are learning to a passion they have mentioned in advisory. Mini-conferencing also fosters a greater sense of connection between each advisee and their advisor—a key protective factor for school success and healthy development.

For more information about how to implement mini-conferences, suggested activities, and goal-setting templates, we recommend Rachel Poliner and Carol Miller Lieber's *The Advisory Guide: Designing and Implementing Effective Advisory Programs in Secondary Schools.*

Best Practices for Mini-Conferences

- Sit next to the advisee or across a corner of a desk (a partnership position), not directly across (an opposition position).
- Introduce to the whole group a template that they will use repeatedly. Review or briefly brainstorm the kinds of responses that fit each prompt.
- Set SMART goals. If your advisees do not have experience setting SMART goals, you can provide models. For example, "Getting a better grade in math" or "Arriving to first period on time" are too vague. A more specific and time-bound version of the first goal could be "For the next three weeks, I will meet with my math teacher on Tuesdays for 30 minutes during my free period. I will write the meeting in my planner and set a reminder on my phone."
- Prepare coaching questions to help advisees understand their own learning process. What steps have you tried? What was the impact? What else could you try? If advisees need to ask a teacher for an extension or a retest, have them role-play their request with you first. Then offer suggestions of your own.

What do other advisees do during mini-conferences?

Group projects or certain routines can be worthwhile, self-running, and able to create just enough noise to give the mini-conference some privacy. You might also invite advisees to choose (appropriate) background music if they are working on a project.

A few options to consider as one-time projects:

- During the first round of mini-conferences (see Activity 16, which can be done anytime in the opening weeks of the school year), have advisees make their advisory folders, where they will store their activity handouts, goal-setting sheets, and journals. Provide basic art supplies so that advisees can personalize these. Pocket folders work well because advisees can store journals in one side pocket and papers in the other.
- If you have space, have the advisory group make an advisory mural that represents them to be hung in the room or outside in the hall.

A few options to consider as ongoing routines:

- Choose a couple of prompts (better yet, have advisees create a routine for choosing the prompts) for discussion in trios, with a fun template for writing or drawing their responses.
- Gather and use puzzles and brainteasers from online, print, and game sources. Advisees can manage the process and get good mental exercise. Word games may be easy for some advisees but challenging for others. Advisees might have opposite reactions to Sudoku puzzles. Vary the puzzles and brainteasers so that everyone has time with exercises that stretch their normal ways of thinking. You can chat as a group and/or with individual advisees about how they manage frustration with puzzles and brainteasers and how that connects to the way they manage frustration in classes.[2]

---

[2] Rachel Poliner, a national leader and author for advisory programs, wrote this section.

Fostering a Reflective and Supportive Community

We believe that a Facing History and Ourselves advisory ought to be a microcosm of democracy—a place where explicit rules and implicit norms protect everyone's right to speak; where different perspectives can be heard and valued; where advisees take responsibility for themselves, each other, and the group as a whole; and where each member has a stake and a voice in collective decisions. This section of the introduction to *Community Matters* includes descriptions of four strategies with some suggested activities to help foster a reflective and supportive advisory community that invites questioning, collaboration, and problem-solving: contracting, journaling, opening routines, and closing routines.

Two ways in which you can create a strong foundation for a reflective advisory are by incorporating advisory contracts and advisory journals into your routines. Even if you already incorporate both of these elements into your regular classroom, we recommend taking a moment to refresh yourself by reading the sections that follow, **Contracting in a Facing History and Ourselves Advisory** and **Journaling in a Facing History and Ourselves Advisory**, which will help you consider how these strategies can serve as effective tools to help foster civil discourse in your advisory group. For additional thoughts about your role in this process, consult the resource Fostering Civil Discourse: A Guide for Classroom Conversations, available at facinghistory.org/advisory-media.

In addition to journaling and contracting, beginning and ending each advisory meeting with a short opening and closing routine can help create a space that is welcoming and feels different from "regular class." By taking five minutes at either end of each advisory meeting to take the pulse of the group and to weave in fun opportunities for interaction or quiet reflection, you can help to set a tone for the meeting that invites participation and sharing.

A: Contracting in a Facing History and Ourselves Advisory

Contracting is the process of openly discussing with your advisees expectations about how members of the group will treat each other. It is an effective strategy for making your advisory a reflective community that values the unique contributions of its members, honors different perspectives, and engages in shared decision-making. These types of communities are usually created through deliberate nurturing from advisees and advisors who have shared expectations about how group members will treat each other. The instructions below describe how to discuss advisory norms and then draft and agree to a formal contract of behavior.

Advisees should create their advisory contract in the first two to three weeks of the school year, after they have had an opportunity to learn each other's names, play some interactive games, and understand the purpose of advisory at their school. The first activity in **Section 1: Welcome to Advisory!** offers a detailed explanation of contracting, as well as a number of ways that advisors can develop advisory contracts with their groups.

Advisory contracts are not static documents. Advisory groups should revisit their contracts periodically throughout the year. Good times to revisit, and possibly revise, the contract include:

- Before and/or after reading or viewing a challenging piece of content
- Before engaging in a discussion about a potentially controversial or challenging topic
- When an advisee feels that they, or members of the group, have not lived up to one or more of the expectations on the contract
- At the beginning of each section of *Community Matters* (each section begins with a contracting activity that fosters reflection, promotes discussion, and invites revision)

B: Journaling in a Facing History and Ourselves Advisory

A journal is an instrumental tool for helping advisees develop their ability to critically examine their surroundings from multiple perspectives and to make informed judgments about what they see and hear. Many advisees find that writing or drawing in a journal helps them process ideas, formulate questions, and retain information. Journals make learning visible by providing a safe, accessible space for your advisees to share thoughts, feelings, and uncertainties. Journals also help to nurture a sense of community and offer a way for advisees to process their thinking before sharing their ideas and questions in pairs, small groups, or circle discussions. Frequent journal writing also helps advisees become more fluent in expressing their ideas in writing or speaking. Below, we describe some of the many ways you can use journals as an effective learning tool in your advisory sessions.

Questions to Consider Before Using Journals in Advisory

1. **What sort of notebook should advisees use for their journals?**
   Because advisees will be writing in their journals throughout *Community Matters,* and at times they will reflect on past entries, it is important that they always have their journals with them during the advisory meeting. You can use exam "blue books" or have advisees staple together 15 to 20 sheets of lined paper (they can design a cover) that will serve as their advisory journals. These types of journals are cheaper than spiral notebooks or composition books and easier to store in pocket folders along with advisory handouts and readings.

2. **Are journal entries public or private?**
   Advisees are entitled to know in advance of each writing opportunity if the entry is private or if they will be sharing their ideas with a partner or with the group as a whole. Some advisors might want to collect advisee journals periodically to better understand their advisees' thinking and engagement with the material. You might collect their journals once a term and only read a few pages that the advisee selects and marks with a sticky note. If you are reading their journals, you can establish a rule that if advisees wish to keep information in their journals private, they should fold the page over or remove the page entirely. Or you might never collect their journals and instead listen in on or join small-group discussions.

3. **How should journal content be shared?**
   Advisees are often best able to express themselves when they believe that their journal is a private space, and, as explained above, it is important that they always know in advance of writing the purpose and audience for each entry. At the same time, we encourage you to provide multiple opportunities for advisees to voluntarily share ideas and questions they have recorded in their journals. Some advisees may feel more comfortable reading directly from their journals than speaking "off the cuff"

in discussions, while others will prefer speaking more generally about the ideas and questions they explored in writing rather than reading aloud from the page.

4. What is appropriate content for journals?

At Facing History, we believe that the purpose of journal writing is to provide a space where advisees can connect their personal experiences and opinions to the concepts they are exploring in advisory. Therefore, some material that is appropriate to include in personal diaries or a blog may not be appropriate to include in advisory journals, and it is important for advisors to help advisees make this distinction. To avoid uncomfortable situations, many advisors find it helpful to clarify topics that are not suitable material for journal entries. Also, as mandated reporters, advisors should explain that they are required by law to take certain steps, such as informing a school official, if advisees reveal information about possible harm to themselves or another student. Advisees should be made aware of these rules, as well as other guidelines you might have about appropriate journal writing content.

5. What forms of expression can be included in a journal?

Students learn and communicate best in different ways. The journal is an appropriate space to respect different learning styles. Some of your advisees may wish to sketch their ideas, for example, rather than record thoughts in words. Other advisees may feel most comfortable responding in concept webs and lists, as opposed to prose. When you introduce the journal to advisees, you might brainstorm different ways that they can use it to express their thoughts.

Suggestions for How to Use Journals in Advisory

Once you settle on the expectations for journal writing in your advisory, there are many possible ways that you can have advisees record ideas in their journals. Here are some examples:

1. **Advisor-selected prompts:** One of the most common ways that advisors use journals is by asking advisees to respond to a particular prompt, such as a question or quotation. This writing often prepares advisees to participate in an activity, helps them make connections between the themes of an activity and their own lives, or provides an opportunity for advisees to make meaning of ideas in a reading or film. In many of the advisory activities, you will find suggested prompts for journal writing.

2. **Brainstorming:** The journal is an appropriate place where advisees can freely list ideas related to a specific word or question. To activate prior knowledge before they encounter new material, you might ask advisees to brainstorm everything they know about a concept or an event. As a strategy for reviewing material, you might ask them to brainstorm ideas they remember about a topic.

3. **Freewriting:** Freewriting is open, no-format writing. Freewriting can be an especially effective strategy when you want to help advisees process particularly sensitive or provocative material. Some advisees respond extremely well to freewriting, while

others benefit from more structure, even if that means a loosely framed prompt such as, "What are you thinking about after watching/reading/hearing/discussing this material? What does this text/scenario remind you of?"

4. **Creative writing:** Many advisees will enjoy writing poems or short stories that incorporate the themes addressed in a particular activity, video, or reading. To stimulate their work, some advisees benefit from ideas that structure their writing, such as a specific poem format or an opening line for a story (for example: "I could not believe my eyes when I walked down the hall and saw . . . ").

5. **Drawings, charts, and webs:** Advisees do not always have to express their ideas in words. At appropriate times, encourage them to draw their feelings or thoughts. They can also use symbols, concept maps, Venn diagrams, tables, and other graphic organizers to record information.

6. **Vocabulary:** Advisees can use their journals as a place to keep their working definitions of terms, noting how those definitions change over time. The back section of their journals could be used as a glossary, the place where they record, review, and revise key definitions.

7. **Structured sharing:** While there will be times when some advisees will not want to publicly share thoughts from their journals, most of the time they are eager to have the opportunity to select something from their journals to share with a small group or the larger group in a discussion. At these times, you should let advisees know in advance that what they wrote will be shared with the group. Another way to share is with a pass-around, where journals are "passed around" from one advisee to the next. Advisees read the page that is opened (and only that page!) and then write about connections they see in their own lives, things they have seen or read, current events, or moments in history.

C: Opening Routines for Advisory Meetings

Advisees are more likely to participate when advisory feels like a supportive community. Remember that the goal of advisory is to create a space where students can find support, have a voice, and feel comfortable. Opening routines can help set a welcoming and inclusive tone, especially if they're used repeatedly and involve advisee input and, eventually, leadership. Opening routines can be playful, personal, and reflective, and they can be done in small groupings or as a full group. It's the tone and repeated use that helps to shape the advisory atmosphere.

Choose an opening routine for each advisory session that will help set the energy level that the day's meeting needs or that connects to the topic, piquing curiosity.

1. **Connection Circles**

    This routine can be used for lighthearted community building or in a more serious way, to check on everyone's perspective on a group decision or current topic. The questions below can be used once or multiple times over the course of the year, with advisees working in pairs, trios, or in full-group Wraparounds. You might also use the Concentric Circles strategy for this opening routine. Visit facinghistory.org/advisory-media to learn about the Wraparound and Concentric Circles teaching strategies.

    - Who is a leader you admire and why?
    - What is your wildest career fantasy?
    - If you were a street sign, what would you be? Why?
    - If you could meet anyone from history, who would it be?
    - Where do you feel most like yourself?
    - What is one goal you hope to accomplish this year?
    - What are some highs and lows from your time at school so far?
    - What's something healthy or helpful you did in the last day?
    - How were you an upstander this week? (This is an example of a go-round question to use once "upstander" has been introduced.)
    - What was the most helpful mistake you made this week?
    - Which classmate did you learn something from this week?
    - "I feel mostly _____ because _____."
    - "The main thing on my mind right now is _____."
    - What is something you did really well last week?
    - What's a choice you made recently? If given another chance, would you do anything different?

2. Take a Stand!

This routine uses the Barometer strategy (visit facinghistory.org/advisory-media to learn about this teaching strategy). Create a list of statements to which advisees are likely to have a wide array of reactions, from "Yes! I strongly agree!" to "Nope! I strongly disagree," from "I can't wait!" to "Never," or another pair of opposing labels. For community-building purposes, a few interesting and varied questions will provide an opportunity for advisees to interact with one another. To use the "Take a Stand!" opening routine to pique interest in a topic that you will be discussing during the advisory session, write a few statements or choose one or more quotations that relate to the topic and will prompt a range of responses.

- Explain the Barometer format to the group and then facilitate the activity. Because this is a warm-up routine, you might only use one to three statements before digging into the main activity for the session.

- Sample "take a stand" statements:
  - I'd much rather see a movie in a theater than stream it.
  - Rainy weather is better than sunny weather.
  - It's important to get to know different kinds of music.
  - Individual sports are better than team sports.

- To foster advisee leadership and sense of ownership over the space, ask an advisee to run the exercise next time. They can also write statements on index cards for the group to use in future opening routines.

3. Mindfulness Minute

Sometimes the most supportive opening (and/or closing) routine provides a chance for everyone to catch their breath and feel calm. Here are four options that use the different senses:

- Take a deep breath, paying attention to your breathing: how it enters, flows through, and leaves your body. Take a second breath that is slower and more conscious. Take a third breath that is even slower and more conscious. Continue slow, conscious breathing for the remainder of the minute.

- Listen to the noises in the room for 20 seconds. Then listen for noises outside the room, in the hallway and other rooms, for 20 seconds. Then listen for noises outside the school for 20 seconds.

- For one minute, look at something really carefully—all the parts of a pencil or pen, shades of light on a book or desk, how an ant or spider moves, the nuances of a poster, the dust in the air.

- Choose a simple action, like raising your hand or standing up and sitting down. Do it in super slow motion. Be aware of what your body is doing to prepare for the movement, and what different parts of your body are doing for each tiny segment of the movement.[3]

---

3 Adapted from Rachel Poliner and Jeffrey Benson, *Teaching the Whole Teen: Everyday Practices That Promote Success and Resilience in School and Life* (California: Corwin, a Sage Company, 2017), 152–53.

To foster advisee leadership and sense of ownership over the space, ask an advisee to run the exercise next time, choose which option the group will use, research new options, and/or make up their own opening mindfulness routine.

4. Notable Quotable

Quotations are excellent resources to provoke thought and prompt conversation. There will be many occasions in advisory when a quotation about community, courage, success, failure, fear, feeling like an outsider or insider, or another topic can serve to open the advisory meeting effectively. To foster advisee leadership and a sense of ownership over the advisory space, after you have facilitated the "notable quotable" routine a few times, ask for volunteers to run the activity next time or to choose a new quotation from a favorite book or website. This activity can be used as an opening or closing routine.

- In all cases, project/pass out and read aloud the quotation, give time for advisees to think, and then ask advisees to share reflections in small groups or with the whole group. The following sentence starters can help advisees respond to a quotation:
  - The quotation made me think of/about . . .
  - The speaker/writer is trying to encourage . . .
  - I wonder what the speaker/writer meant by . . .
  - Parts I agree with are . . . Parts I don't understand are . . . Parts I'd challenge are . . . Parts that raise questions for me are . . .
  - The quotation relates to my personal experience because . . .

5. Fist to Five

This quick activity helps you take the pulse of the room and can be used as an opening or closing routine. You can also use it during an advisory to check for understanding, assess advisees' confidence with the material, or seek general consensus.

- For an opening routine, after advisees have entered the room and are seated in a circle, pose a question and have them respond by holding up a fist or one, two, three, four, or five fingers. The fist, which represents zero, marks the low end of the scale ("I don't understand," "I'm not feeling well," "I don't feel confident"), and the five marks the high end ("Great," "I'm excited," "I've got it!"). Some examples of "fist to five" questions include:
  - "Fist to five, how are you feeling on this Monday?" (after the assembly, on this Friday, in light of learning about . . . , etc.)
  - "Fist to five, how do you feel about your time management last night?"
  - "Fist to five, how do you feel about your understanding of the bystander effect?"
  - "Fist to five, how ready are you to start our first activity?"
  - "Fist to five, how well do you understand the instructions for the next activity?"

D: Closing Routines for Advisory Meetings

Closing routines can serve as a transition from advisory back to academic classes, help advisees summarize or reflect on something from the session, and offer a connection or preview to the next advisory. You can vary how you implement the closing routine. Advisees might be in pairs, trios, or sitting in a circle. At times, you might choose to have your advisees write their responses on an exit card, sticky note, or index card with or without their names. Alternatively, closing routines can be verbal activities with no writing.

Repeating a closing routine will help advisees internalize the behavior, which will lead to more meaningful reflections. Furthermore, once they have internalized the routines, they can have a voice in choosing which one they would like to do at the end of a meeting.

1. **Maintain and Modify**

    Make a routine of asking the following questions:
    - What helped us function well as an advisory today that we should maintain?
    - What's something we should modify so we can improve?

2. **Revisit the Contract**

    After your group creates its advisory contract, you might read aloud the contract and then pose one or more of the following questions to celebrate high-functioning days or reflect on challenging days.
    - How well did we demonstrate our contract today?
    - What examples can you give from this session of a member of our group honoring our contract?
    - What needs some attention? How might we make it better in the next session?

    At the end of a week, quarter, or term, you might revisit the contract to determine whether or not it needs to be revised before moving forward.

    > "We've had these guidelines for _____ now. Are there any we need to clarify? Add? Demonstrate better?"

3. **Grab a Goal**

    Ask advisees to think about a goal they would like to set. It might be an academic goal or a personal goal, one related to school or not related to school. Consider prompting them to help them establish their goals:
    - This week I will . . .
    - This week I am going to try . . .

- In the next advisory meeting, I will . . .
- My goal in _____ is to _____. To achieve my goal, I need to . . . [4]

4. Give and Get

Make a routine of asking the following questions, where "got" could be something like had fun, got information, or got help with a challenge. "Gave" could be something like helped someone, participated fully, offered an idea, or gave full attention when listening.

- What's something you got today in our advisory?
- What's something you gave?

5. One-Word Wraparounds

Close advisory sessions with one-word Wraparounds (visit facinghistory.org/advisory-media to learn about this teaching strategy), which are very fast go-rounds in a circle. For example, after giving advisees time to think, prompt them to say a word to describe how they're feeling about their day or a word to describe how they are feeling about an upcoming event like the weekend, homecoming, exams, etc.

6. Closing Challenge

Offer a challenge for advisees to do over the course of the next week. Check in about the "closing challenge" during opening or closing routines in the upcoming week.

Some possible challenges might include:

- Invite someone new to sit next to you in the cafeteria.
- Introduce yourself to your guidance counselor, homeroom teacher, coach, principal, etc.
- "Like" someone's social media post in your advisory or at your school and add a positive comment.
- Invite someone you don't know well to be on your team in PE or in your group in a class.[5]

---

4 Rebecca Alber, "6 Opening and Closing Routines for New Teachers," *Edutopia*, August 17, 2016, accessed July 3, 2018, https://www.edutopia.org/blog/6-opening-and-closing-routines-new-teachers-rebecca-alber.
5 Rachel Poliner, a national leader and author for advisory programs, contributed to this section.

Getting Started: Navigating the Activities

Advisory is an intentional group, one that works at being an effective group for all members and provides a safe place for building skills, getting support, giving support, and doing short activities through larger projects—fun though serious. Therefore, advisory starts with fostering comfort and bonds, establishing a sense of "groupness," and building a group culture that supports learning. The activities in *Community Matters: A Facing History and Ourselves Approach to Advisory* are developed to promote that sense of community because adolescents are best able to share ideas, take risks, and help each other when they feel a sense of belonging and safety in a given environment.

The 68 activities in *Community Matters* are not intended to be taught in sequential order in 68 consecutive advisory meetings. They are grouped into six sections, and each section starts with an overview and suggestions for how to navigate the activities. There is information about which activities fit well together and which ones are foundational to this Facing History program and should not be skipped.

It is important to remember that *Community Matters* is designed to be used alongside advisory activities that support academic and personal goal-setting, study skills, time management, college and career counseling, and other skills and habits of mind that your advisees need in order to feel successful both in and outside of school.

Navigating the Activities in Sections 1–6

- **You can find all videos, teaching strategies, and other online resources referenced throughout this curriculum at facinghistory.org/advisory-media.**
- The six sections of the advisory program are aligned with the following components of Facing History's scope and sequence: the individual and society, membership and belonging, a central case study, and choosing to participate.
- Each section includes detailed activity plans with clearly stated purposes, notes to the advisor, materials, and a suggested procedure that advisors can implement as written or adapt for their own groups.
- The "approximate time" for each activity is an estimate. The reality depends on the size of the advisory group and the amount of time the advisor devotes to reflective writing and discussions.
- The activities do not include opening and closing routines, so advisors should add an opening and a closing routine that fits the needs of their group to each activity.

Advisory Folders and Journals

Because the activities in the first section of *Community Matters* can be ordered and combined in different ways, it is hard to know when your group will get its first handout or respond to its first journal prompt. You should be prepared to distribute journals and folders to each advisee in the opening days of the year. It is up to you to decide how to store them. Advisees will need their folders and journals in every meeting after the first week or two. Because reflection is at the heart of *Community Matters*, advisees will revisit their journal responses and handouts over the course of the year. It is important that they keep their advisory materials together so they can fully engage in the writing activities and discussions.

- You can set the expectation that advisees bring their folders and journals, along with a pen or pencil, to each meeting.
- Alternatively, you might collect the folders and journals at the end of each meeting to store in your classroom or office.
- Or, if possible, you can set aside a space in the advisory room where they can store their materials. Because journal responses can be personal, it is important that the space is secure and other students can't access the folders and journals between meetings.

The Advisory Community-Building Project (Section 6)

Community Matters culminates with a final project that invites advisees to work collaboratively to benefit their school community. Since the themes of community, membership, and participation are at the heart of this advisory program, and all of the activities direct energy toward this final project, **we recommend that you start by reading "Advisory Community-Building Project Guidelines" on page 269 so you can familiarize yourself with the project.**

You can introduce the project to your group in the fall and invite them to record ideas on a piece of chart paper or in their journals so they can make ongoing connections between the advisory activities and content, their experiences at school, and their school's culture. You may find that you don't need brainstorming activities at the end of the year because your advisees have been generating ideas for their project all along. Some groups might get excited about organizing a school-based project earlier in the year, and the activities and resources in Section 6: Choosing to Participate can help get them started.

Sample Advisory Meeting Maps for the Opening Weeks

How your school decides to organize advisory activities depends in large part on how often advisory meets each week, the length of each meeting, and the size the groups. These sample meeting maps are for the opening weeks of the school year. Note that many of the activities in the "Welcome to Advisory!" section of *Community Matters* are short games and get-to-know-you activities that are designed to be combined with one another. **Most activities in Sections 2–6 are designed to take 30–40 minutes. Advisors should add their own opening and closing routines to start and end each advisory meeting throughout the year.**[6]

Sample Meeting Map: 50-Minute period

Meeting	Meeting Outlines
Meeting 1	Opening Routine: Activity 2: Welcome to Advisory! Activity 5: MeUUMe Activity 10: Advisory Bingo School Administrative Tasks Closing Routine: One-Word Wraparound
Meeting 2	Opening Routine: Fist to Five Activity 6: Concentric Questions Activity 4: Get to Know the Advisor Activity 3: What Is Advisory? Closing Routine: Give and Get
Meeting 3	Opening Routine: Quote of the Day Activity 9: This Is Better than That! Activity 1: Develop an Advisory Contract Closing Routine: Fist to Five
Meeting 4	Opening Routine: Connection Circles Activity 1: Develop an Advisory Contract (continued) Activity 11: Birthday Line-Up Closing Routine: Revisit the Contract (questions)
Meeting 5	Opening Routine: Mindfulness Minute Activity 4: Get to Know the Advisor (additional questions not answered in Meeting 2) Activity 14: Checking In on the Opening Days Closing Routine: Grab a Goal

---

[6] Rachel Poliner, a national leader and author for advisory programs, contributed to this section.

Sample Meeting Map: 40-Minute period

Meeting	Meeting Outlines
Meeting 1	Opening Routine: Activity 2: Welcome to Advisory! Activity 5: MeUUMe School Administrative Tasks Closing Routine: One-Word Wraparound
Meeting 2	Opening Routine: Fist to Five Activity 6: Concentric Questions Activity 4: Get to Know the Advisor Closing Routine: Give and Get
Meeting 3	Opening Routine: Quote of the Day (quote about names) Activity 7: Lines and Circles Activity 3: What Is Advisory? Closing Routine: Maintain and Modify
Meeting 4	Opening Routine: Mindfulness Minute Activity 1: Develop an Advisory Contract Closing Routine: Give and Get
Meeting 5	Opening Routine: Fist to Five Activity 1: Develop an Advisory Contract (continued) Closing Routine: Revisit the Contract (questions)
Meeting 6	Opening Routine: Connection Circles Activity 13: Dear Advisory Closing Routine: One-Word Wraparound
Meeting 7	Opening Routine: Quote of the Day (quote about goals) Activity 14: Checking In on the Opening Days Closing Routine: Grab a Goal

SECTION 1:
Welcome to Advisory!

ACTIVITIES

Develop an Advisory Contract

Welcome to Advisory!

What Is Advisory?

Get to Know the Advisor

MeUUMe (Name Game)

Concentric Questions

Lines and Circles

Like Peanut Butter and Jelly

This Is Better than That!

Advisory Bingo

Birthday Line-Up

60-Second Interview

Dear Advisory

Checking In on the Opening Days

How Can I Support You?

Purpose	Materials	Abridged Advisor Notes

1: Develop an Advisory Contract — 2 x 30 min — page 26

Establish norms and expectations for how the group will treat each other, communicate, and problem-solve.	Journals Chart paper and markers	This activity is a key component of building community and developing the norms that will allow advisees to take risks, grapple with challenging content, and engage in civil discourse. We recommend that your advisees start the process of contracting in their third or fourth meeting, after they have learned each other's names and played community-building games. If you have not already done so, read more about Contracting in section A of Fostering a Reflective and Supportive Community on page 8. This activity includes a journal response. If you have not introduced journaling in a prior meeting, plan to set aside time to do so before your advisees write their first entry.

2: Welcome to Advisory! — 10 min — page 30

Welcome advisees, introduce the advisor, and offer a brief explanation of the rationale of the advisory program.	None	Start the year with this activity. Arrange the chairs or desks in a circle or arc before the start of the advisory meeting. Your introduction should be inviting and short so you can move on to name games and community-building activities.

3: What Is Advisory? — 20 min — page 32

Identify common experiences in school—the good and the bad. Understand the role advisory plays in helping advisees navigate these experiences.	None	Pair this activity with one or two get-to-know-you games in the first or second advisory session of the year.

4: Get to Know the Advisor — 15 min — page 34

Forge a strong advisor-advisee relationship by allowing advisees to learn about what makes their advisor a unique individual and discover commonalities with their advisor.	Index cards	Include this activity in one of the first three advisory meetings, if possible. You can combine it with one or more get-to-know-you games or community-building activities.

5: MeUUMe (Name Game) — 15 min — page 35

Learn the proper pronunciation of names and start to build a positive group culture where advisees feel and are known.	None	MeUUMe includes paired introductions between every advisory member, which can feel more inviting than group games for students who are shy.

6: Concentric Questions — 15 min — page 37

Learn each other's names and start to build a positive group culture where advisees feel known and are known.	None	This is a fun, low-threat, low-vulnerability activity that doesn't require any special knowledge or skills. This activity uses the Concentric Circles teaching strategy, which you can learn about at facinghistory.org/advisory-media.

7: Lines and Circles — 20 min — page 39

Learn each other's names and start to build a positive group culture where advisees practice collaboration and get to know one another.	None	This is a fun, low-threat, low-vulnerability activity that doesn't require any special knowledge or skills.

8: Like Peanut Butter and Jelly — 15 min — page 41

Learn each other's names and start to build a positive group culture where advisees feel known and valued.	HANDOUT: **Role Cards for Like Peanut Butter and Jelly**	English Language Learners may need additional support to understand their role and find their partner. Circulate during the activity to help as needed until you are confident that everyone has an idea of the pair they are looking for.

Section 1: Welcome to Advisory!

Purpose	Materials	Abridged Advisor Notes
9: This Is Better than That!		20 min — page 44
Learn each other's names and start to build a positive group culture where advisees practice collaboration and get to know one another.	None	This is a fun, low-threat, low-vulnerability activity that doesn't require any special knowledge or skills.
10: Advisory Bingo		15 min — page 46
Reinforce the importance of learning and using each other's names. Create a positive group culture where advisees feel and are known. Discover common interests and experiences across the group.	HANDOUT: Advisory Bingo HANDOUT: Advisory Bingo (Blank)	Advisory bingo invites advisees to practice writing each other's names and builds community by acknowledging both shared and unique talents and interests. This activity involves a handout that advisees might want to keep. If you have not passed out folders for advisory handouts, you should build in time to do so before or after the game.
11: Birthday Line-Up		15 min — page 50
Create a positive group culture where advisees feel and are known. Initiate the conversation about rituals and what the group would like to celebrate, and how, over the course of the year.	None	In this activity, it is up to the advisor to establish the parameters for upcoming birthday celebrations. It is important that whatever ritual you establish, it is inclusive of every advisee in the group.
12: 60-Second Interview		20 min — page 52
Practice names and start to learn more about each other in paired conversations, which can feel safer than large-group discussions for many advisees. Create a positive group culture where advisees feel and are known. Discover common interests and experiences across the group.	HANDOUT: 60-Second Interview	If you use the Concentric Circles strategy (visit facinghistory.org/advisory-media to learn about this teaching strategy) to pair advisees for their interviews, have them arrange their desks in two circles facing each other so they can sit during the interviews to facilitate note-taking on the interview handout.
13: Dear Advisory		30 min — page 55
Celebrate the unique qualities that each advisee brings to the group and learn about each other's areas of expertise.	Lined paper or journals	This activity can also be done as a way of asking for and receiving advice within the advisory group throughout the year. Have your advisees write problems or challenges that they are facing on individual index cards. Then collect the cards, read them out loud one by one, and have the group discuss possible solutions or next steps.
14: Checking In on the Opening Days		30 min — page 57
Learn about issues advisees are having (follow up with one-on-one conversations). Get a pulse on how advisees are understanding school culture. Start to develop norms for participation.	HANDOUT: Peaks and Valleys	Include this activity in the first two weeks of the school year, if possible. Modify the first part of the activity, "School Basics," if your advisees are not new to the school building. At the beginning of the year, use pairs and trios to encourage sharing among the group and to provide space for quieter students who might not yet feel comfortable answering personal questions in a larger group. Ask the group to problem-solve before offering your own ideas.
15: How Can I Support You?		30 min — page 61
Foster advisee-advisor relationships and a sense of community within the group. Encourage self-advocacy by inviting advisees to articulate the ways in which the advisor can support them.	HANDOUT: How Can I Support You?	Include this activity in the second or third week of the school year, if possible. The final reflective discussion introduces a routine for closing advising meetings that involve group collaboration. You might choose to use this routine over the course of the year or develop your own set of reflection questions with your advisees that you revisit after group-work activities.

Welcome to Advisory!

ACTIVITIES 1–15

OVERVIEW

The materials in the opening section of *Community Matters: A Facing History and Ourselves Approach to Advisory* have been developed to create a welcoming environment and promote a sense of community. Advisees are best able to share ideas, take risks, and help each other when they feel a sense of trust and belonging in a given environment. In addition to a number of low-risk name games, there are several activities that provide meaningful ways for advisees to reflect on their identities and introduce themselves to their peers. The process of learning about their peers can break down stereotypes and help build trust among the group. For example, advisees who assume they do not have anything in common with their peers may learn that they share an interest in the same music or that they have been through a similar experience. The activities, discussions, and reflections at the end of the section are designed to help advisees start to consider what it means to be part of a community and how to respond to challenges that may arise within the group. The goal of this opening section of *Community Matters* is to launch your advisory program in a way that feels welcoming, inclusive, and exciting to your school community.

NAVIGATING THE ACTIVITIES

The activities in this section can be broken into three categories: getting to know each other, starting the school year, and creating group norms. They are designed to stand alone in shorter advisory meetings or be combined for longer ones (see **Sample Advisory Meeting Maps for the Opening Weeks** on page 19).

- Activity 1: Develop an Advisory Contract is an important step in any Facing History program for creating a reflective and inclusive community, and your group will re-visit its advisory contract over the course of the year. While contracting is set as the first activity to help highlight its importance, you should not contract in the first advisory meetings. Wait until your advisees play some name games, understand the purpose of advisory, and start to get acquainted with each other.

- For Activities 2–15, you should work with your advisory coordinator to choose which ones you will include in the opening weeks of the school year and how you will combine them with each other and with school-specific activities like touring the building, assigning lockers, or maintaining an academic planner.

- The number and type of introductory activities and games you play with your group will depend on how well your advisees know each other, how well they know you, and how well you know them. It is important that advisees don't just know each other's names; they also need to be able to pronounce them correctly.

ACTIVITY 1

Develop an Advisory Contract

Purpose: Establish norms and expectations for how members of the group will treat each other, communicate, and problem-solve.

> **APPROXIMATE TIME:**
> 2 x 30 minutes
>
> **MATERIALS:**
> Advisory journal
> Chart paper and markers

ADVISOR NOTES:

1. **When to Contract with Your Group**

   This activity is a key component of building community and developing the norms that will allow advisees to take risks, grapple with challenging content, and engage in civil discourse. We recommend that your advisees start the process of contracting in their third or fourth meeting, after they have learned each other's names and played some community-building games. Before leading this session, you should familiarize yourself with the Contracting strategy, which is explained in **Contracting in a Facing History and Ourselves Advisory** on page 8.

2. **Introduce and Explain Journaling to Your Advisees**

   Advisees will reflect in their journals during this meeting. If you have not introduced journaling to your group, prepare to do so in advance by first reading **Journaling in a Facing History and Ourselves Advisory** on page 9. It is important that your advisees understand the purpose of journal writing, as well as how entries will or will not be shared. Exam "blue books" work well for advisory journals since they are small and inexpensive and advisees can store them in their advisory folders (see Advisor Notes in Activity 10: Advisory Bingo for tips about advisory folders).

3. **Pacing This Activity**

   Because there are so many topics to cover in the opening weeks of advisory, such as name and introductory games, getting to know the advisor, and administrative tasks, you might find that you need two to three advisory sessions to complete the contracting process. Natural breaks in the activity occur after advisees have journaled and defined *contracting* and worked in small groups to create their list of norms, and after the group has voted to decide on the norms it commits to upholding during activities and discussions.

PROCEDURE:

1. **Pass Out and Explain the Purpose of Advisory Journals**

2. **Reflect on Group Participation**
   - Ask advisees to respond in their journals to the following questions. Let them know that they will be sharing their ideas with a partner. Project or read aloud the following prompts one at a time.
     - Identify when you have felt comfortable sharing your ideas and questions in a class. What happened in those moments to help you feel comfortable?
     - Identify when you have had ideas or questions but have not shared them. Why not? What was happening at those moments?
   - Then have advisees turn and talk with a partner, sharing their reflections about when they felt comfortable and uncomfortable sharing their ideas in a group.

3. **Brainstorm Advisory Group Expectations**
   - Explain to the group that they will be working together to develop an advisory contract. A contract implies that all parties have a responsibility to uphold the agreement.
   - Ask them to define *contract* and share their ideas about the purpose of contracts and the types of things they can protect. You might also define and discuss the term *norm*: a principle of right action binding upon the members of a group and serving to guide, control, or regulate proper and acceptable behavior.[1]
   - Divide advisees into small groups of three or four and ask them to come up with three norms that they feel are important for everyone in the group to follow in order to foster a safe and inclusive environment. They can write their three ideas in their journals or on chart paper that you hang on the wall.

4. **Discuss Advisory Norms and Expectations**
   - Ask each group to present its list of norms. Then ask advisees to look for places where they can consolidate like ideas. Have an advisee read their new list out loud and discuss whether or not the groups feel like they have captured the norms that they think are important to uphold in advisory.
   - Then start to finalize the list by asking advisees to write their names alongside norms and expectations that they think are important (or use sticky notes), or use "Stand Up/Sit Down" or "Cross the Line" from Activity 3: What Is Advisory? to allow advisees to explain their rationale for why they think an idea should or should not be included.

---

[1] "Norm," Merriam-Webster.com, accessed June 23, 2018.

Section 1: Welcome to Advisory!

5. Create and Sign the Contract

- After the group has agreed to its norms and expectations, have one or more advisees record the information on a large piece of chart paper and then ask everyone to sign their names. Hang the contract on the wall (or bring it to each advisory meeting to post if you are in a space such as the library or a conference room where you are not allowed to keep it hanging).

- Let advisees know that they will revisit and reflect on the contract over the course of the year, before and after challenging conversations and at the start of each section of *Community Matters*.

6. Reflect on the Process of Creating the Contract

Sit in a circle for a closing discussion about the activity and how the advisees felt about the way they worked together to create their contract. You might draw from the following questions:

- What process did your small group use to come up with your three or four norms? What do you think worked well in your small group? How do you think you could do better the next time you work in a small group?

- What process did our whole group use to come up with our contract? What do you think worked well in the process? How do you think we could do better the next time we work on a project in a whole group?

EXTENSIONS:

The following activities offer ideas for additional ways for your group to develop its advisory contract.

1. Reflect on a List of Norms

- If you think your group would benefit from starting the contracting conversation in a more concrete way, you can share a list of norms that other Facing History classrooms and advisories have developed. Ask advisees to discuss what they think about the following norms. Which ones do they think would help their group create a safe, respectful, productive learning environment?

    - Listen with respect. Try to understand what someone is saying before rushing to judgment.

    - Make comments using "I" statements.

    - If you do not feel safe making a comment or asking a question, write the thought in your journal. You can share the idea with your advisor first and together come up with a safe way to share the idea.

    - If someone says an idea or question that helps your own learning, say thank you.

- If someone says something that hurts or offends you, do not attack the person. Acknowledge that the comment—not the person—hurt your feelings and explain why.
- Put-downs are never okay.
- If you don't understand something, ask a question.
- Think with your head and your heart.
- Share the talking time—provide room for others to speak.
- Do not interrupt others while they are speaking.
- Write thoughts in your journal if you don't have time to say them during class.
- Journal responses do not have to be shared publicly.

• Then invite advisees to edit the list by deleting, revising, or adding to it.

2. **Discuss Possible Scenarios**

   Another way to help advisees develop a contract is to have them envision what they would like to have happen during certain scenarios. Scenarios can be drawn from advisees' own experiences. They might include situations such as these:

   - When we have an idea or question we would like to share, we can . . .
   - When we don't feel comfortable sharing an idea out loud, we can . . .
   - When someone says something that we appreciate, we can . . .
   - When someone says something that feels confusing, we can . . .
   - When someone says something that feels offensive, we can . . .
   - To make sure all advisees have the opportunity to participate in a small- or whole-group discussion, we can . . .
   - If we read or watch something that makes us feel sad or angry, we can . . .
   - To show respect for the ideas of others, we can . . .

ACTIVITY 2

Welcome to Advisory!

Purpose: Welcome advisees, introduce the advisor, and offer a brief explanation of the rationale of the advisory program.

APPROXIMATE TIME: 10 minutes

MATERIALS: NONE

ADVISOR NOTES:

1. Create a Welcoming Space

Arrange the chairs or desks in a circle or arc before the start of the advisory meeting. Your introduction should feel inviting and be kept short so you can move on to one or more name games and community-building activities.

2. The Importance of Correct Pronunciation

An important step when creating a welcoming community is insisting on the correct pronunciation of everyone's name. If you struggle to pronounce an advisee's name correctly, spend a few minutes with them outside of the meeting to practice. They might feel uncomfortable having their name at the center of focus in the group, especially if they don't know the others well. It can help to write the advisee's name phonetically in your attendance book. Modeling correct pronunciation will set the tone and expectation for the group as a whole.

PROCEDURE:

1. Greet Advisees at the Door

Welcome each advisee as they enter the room as you would a guest to your home. If you don't already know their names or nicknames, ask them to say the name they would like to be called and repeat it back to practice the pronunciation, and then introduce yourself.

2. Introduce Yourself Briefly to the Group

3. Provide a Simple Rationale for the Advisory Group

You might use or adapt one of the following examples of advisory rationales, or your school may develop a rationale that aligns with its mission:

- Advisory is meant to be a supportive place to help you do well in school, learn about yourself, support each other, and have good conversations about meaningful topics. Advisory isn't graded. We'll be together for two years. I'm glad that I'll have two years to get to know you and support you. (Applies to a single-grade group that loops for two years.)

- Our advisory group is your home base for the next four years. It's where we'll problem-solve about school issues, talk about topics in school and in the world, set goals for this week and the next ten years, and figure out how to achieve those goals. Advisory comes with a quarter credit, based mostly on participating well; we'll talk more about that later. We're going to see each other through thick and thin; I'm going to support you from now till you graduate. (Applies to a single-grade high school group that loops for four years.)

- Welcome to our new advisory group members! Our group has members from all grades so we can welcome you into our school culture. We're a supportive place, with no grades involved, for problem-solving and having good conversations about meaningful topics. I'm here as a facilitator for the group and an advocate for each of you. (Applies to a mixed-grade high school group that loops for four years.)

ACTIVITY **3**

What Is Advisory?

Purpose: Identify common experiences in school—the good and bad. Understand the role that advisory plays in helping advisees navigate these experiences.

APPROXIMATE TIME: 20 minutes

MATERIALS: NONE

ADVISOR NOTES:

Choose an Opening Routine that Encourages Community Building

The first part of this activity can be done as an opening routine. You can read about each strategy in more detail in **Opening Routines for Advisory Meetings** on page 12.

- **Cross the Line:** Everyone stands in a row, imagining a line in front of them. Or you can place a long piece of masking tape on the floor to serve as the line. You will read a prompt, and anyone who thinks that prompt relates to them should step over the line for a couple of seconds and then step back.

- **Stand Up/Sit Down:** Everyone starts in a seated position. You will read a prompt, and anyone who thinks that prompt relates to them should stand up for a couple of seconds and then sit back down.

PROCEDURE:

1. **Stand Up/Sit Down or Cross the Line**

   - Tell advisees that they will be responding to a series of prompts by either crossing a line or standing up and sitting back down (choose the strategy before the advisory meeting begins).

   - Establish the following guidelines:

     - Everyone decides for themselves whether to cross the line (or stand up); there's no pointing or commenting, "Hey, you're confused every day; cross the line!"

     - For each prompt, notice briefly who has had the experience, who has not, and what experiences are especially common for your group.

     - Explain that you, the advisor, will step over or stand up for every prompt because you've experienced all the prompts and you want everyone to know that nobody will ever be crossing over or standing up by themselves. (Remember, you're still building a sense of safety in the group, which is accomplished with lots of little steps like this one.)

- Ask advisees to cross the line (or stand up) if they have had any of the following experiences. Cross the line (stand up) if . . .
    - You've ever felt confused about something at school and didn't know who to ask.
    - You've ever felt like kids at school really don't know you.
    - You've ever felt like adults at school don't really know you.
    - You've felt like school is overwhelming and stressful.
    - You've felt like there are skills or tricks that some kids know how to do to be successful at school.
    - You wish that there were a place at school to talk about things that matter to you.
    - You think kids put each other down at school.
    - You wish kids treated each other better at school.
    - You wish there was an adult at school you could talk to.

2. **Debrief the Activity**
   - Move into a circle to debrief the activity. Explain to the group that advisory is a place to get help with all those experiences. When advisories work well, advisees have an adult and peers who know them well, support them, problem-solve together, improve the school culture, support everyone's success, and talk about issues.
   - Explain your role as the advisor: "So, I'll do my best to be a good listener, help you problem-solve, and occasionally I will nag—so you can feel safe, do well in school, and think about who you are and want to become. To foster the best group environment, I'll ask for your input and for your help running some group advisory meetings, and I'll encourage all of us to reflect on how we are doing as a group."
   - Let the group know how often and for how long they will be meeting over the course of the year, and provide an overview of some of the big questions (see below) that they will be exploring together through activities and conversation. Also let them know that they will be meeting one-on-one with you in short mini-conferences to set and revisit goals and get support. They will learn more about mini-conferences in the upcoming weeks.
       - Who am I? What factors shape my identity?
       - How do peer pressure, conformity, and fear affect the decisions we make about how we treat others?
       - What factors can divide a community or break it apart? How can members of a community help it rebuild and become stronger?

ACTIVITY 4

Get to Know the Advisor

Purpose: Forge a strong advisor-advisee relationship by allowing advisees to learn about what makes their advisor a unique individual. Discover commonalities that are shared between adults and teens in the group.

APPROXIMATE TIME: 30 minutes

MATERIALS: Index Cards

ADVISOR NOTES:

Place This Activity in the First Week of the Advising

Try to include this activity in one of the first three advisory meetings, if possible. You might combine it with one or more get-to-know-you or community-building activities.

PROCEDURE:

1. **Develop Questions to Ask the Advisor**

   - Explain to advisees that they will have a chance to get to know you as a person. They will be writing interview questions that you will answer in this meeting and in future meetings. Remind them that questions should be appropriate and that you will not answer ones that are inappropriate. If you feel like it is necessary, give a few examples of topics that you don't feel comfortable discussing.

   - Have advisees move into groups of three, and then pass out a small stack of index cards to each group. You might have advisees count off to create random groups. The groups should talk about what they want to know about you and write one question (legibly!) on each index card.

2. **Interview the Advisor**

   - Collect the index cards and pick a few to answer in this meeting. Feel free to offer a few bits of information about yourself that advisees did not ask, particularly things they might feel a connection with or things they might be curious to ask you more about.

   - Tell advisees that you will answer more of their questions in upcoming advisory meetings.

ACTIVITY 5

MeUUMe[1] (Name Game)

Purpose: Learn the proper pronunciation of names and start to build a positive group culture where advisees feel and are known.

APPROXIMATE TIME: 15 minutes

MATERIALS: NONE

ADVISOR NOTES:

Choose "Get to Know You" Activities with Care

Name games can be anxiety-producing for many students, especially games that put them on the spot to think of something clever, require them to remember and recall new information, or involve a coordination challenge such as catching a ball. When meeting a new group of peers, what many adolescents desire most is to fit in and not stand out by saying or doing the "wrong" thing. For this reason, we recommend that you choose get-to-know-you activities that are fun, low-threat, low-vulnerability, and don't require any special knowledge or skill, while at the same time providing opportunities for advisees to meet each other in pairs and small groups. In these less threatening situations, your advisees will be more likely to engage in authentic and meaningful conversations, while at the same time retaining what they are learning about their peers.

PROCEDURE:

1. **Explain How the Game Works**

   - Instruct advisees to stand in a straight line. There should be room for the line to grow from one end. It might need to round corners in the small space during the activity.
   - The first advisee in line (e.g., Bao) turns to the second person (e.g., Amara) and follows the name process of "Me-You-You-Me" (MeUUMe) as outlined:
     - Bao says his own name: Bao
     - Amara says her own name: Amara
     - Bao says Amara's name: Amara
     - Amara says Bao's name: Bao
   - Bao then moves on to the third person in the line, the fourth, and so on.
   - After the first person has passed by, the second person starts by addressing the third person, and so on. The first person joins the end of the line, and the game finishes when the last person from the original line has had their turn at introducing themselves to each person in the group.

---

[1] "Icebreakers and Name Games," Orange County Department of Education, accessed May 30, 2019, https://ocde.us/EducationalServices/STEMandHumanities/AVID/Documents/icebreakers.pdf.

- Encourage your advisees to maintain eye contact when introducing themselves to their partner. It is good practice for interviews!
- Tell your advisees that if they forget the order of the introduction, they should think of the name of the game: MeUUMe, or Me, You, You, Me. You might want to write "MeUUMe" on the board to help them remember the pattern.

ACTIVITY **6**

Concentric Questions

Purpose: Learn each other's names and start to build a positive group culture where advisees feel known and are known.

APPROXIMATE TIME: 15 minutes

MATERIALS: NONE

ADVISOR NOTES:

1. **Choose "Get to Know You" Activities with Care**

   Name games can be anxiety-producing for many students, especially games that put them on the spot to think of something clever, require them to remember and recall new information, or involve a coordination challenge such as catching a ball. When meeting a new group of peers, what many adolescents desire most is to fit in and not stand out by saying or doing the "wrong" thing. For this reason, we recommend that you choose get-to-know-you activities that are fun, low-threat, low-vulnerability, and don't require any special knowledge or skill, while at the same time providing opportunities for advisees to meet each other in pairs and small groups. In these less threatening situations, your advisees will be more likely to engage in authentic and meaningful conversations, while at the same time retaining what they are learning about their peers.

2. **Familiarize Yourself with the Concentric Circles Teaching Strategy**

   This activity uses the **Concentric Circles** teaching strategy, which you can learn about at facinghistory.org/advisory-media. If there isn't room for advisees to form a circle in your classroom, have them form two parallel lines.

PROCEDURE:

1. **Explain How the Concentric Questions Activity Works**

   - Before asking your advisees to move into two concentric circles, explain that they will introduce themselves and have short paired conversations that respond to questions you will provide. Each advisee will have 30 seconds to answer the question (or longer if you prefer, as long as both circles have equal time).

   - Have the group form two concentric circles facing each other, and explain that after each round, one of the circles will move in a clockwise direction so that everyone is with a new partner for the next round. Advisees should start each round by introducing themselves to each other and end each round by thanking their partners.

   - After one time around the circle, you can challenge your advisees to start the next loop by saying, "Hi, _____ (name)" if they remember the name of the individual across the circle from them. Alternatively, you can mix them up and create two new circles so they meet with some new advisees for the second round. Repeat the process until you run out of questions or are ready to move to the next activity.

2. **Play the Game**

   Choose from the following set of questions, or create your own. Then project or say one question per round.

   - Who was your childhood favorite character from a book, show, or film, and why?
   - What makes you laugh?
   - If you could run the school cafeteria for a week, what would you serve?
   - If you could travel anywhere in the world, where would you go?
   - If you could be a character in a movie—any kind of movie—who would you be, and why?
   - What is something that you would like to learn how to do?
   - If you could only eat one meal or food for the rest of your life, what would it be?
   - What's the nicest thing anyone has done for you?
   - If you could visit any time in history, when would it be?
   - What would you do with your Saturday if the Internet went down (everywhere) for 24 hours?
   - Where do you see yourself in five years?

ACTIVITY **7**

Lines and Circles

Purpose: Learn each other's names and start to build a positive group culture where advisees practice collaboration and get to know one another.

> **APPROXIMATE TIME:** 20 minutes
>
> **MATERIALS:** NONE

ADVISOR NOTES:

1. **Choose "Get to Know You" Activities with Care**

   Name games can be anxiety-producing for many students, especially games that put them on the spot to think of something clever, require them to remember and recall new information, or involve a coordination challenge such as catching a ball. When meeting a new group of peers, what many adolescents desire most is to fit in and not stand out by saying or doing the "wrong" thing. For this reason, we recommend that you choose get-to-know-you activities that are fun, low-threat, low-vulnerability, and don't require any special knowledge or skill, while at the same time providing opportunities for students to meet each other in pairs and small groups. In these less threatening situations, your advisees will be more likely to engage in authentic and meaningful conversations, while at the same time retaining what they are learning about their peers.

2. **Similarities with Activity 11: Birthday Line-Up**

   One instruction commonly used with "Lines and Circles" is for students to line up according to their birthdays. That particular instruction is not included in this activity because it is used in the "Birthday Line-Up" activity later in this section, to help the advisory group discuss the routines it will establish to celebrate special life events and achievements.

PROCEDURE:

1. **Explain How the Game Works**
   - After clearing a space in the center of the room, ask advisees to stand together in the center. Tell them that without talking, making noise, or writing, they need to line up or form small groups based on the instructions you provide.
   - After the group is in a line or small groups, they can break their silence and introduce themselves to the people around them.

2. **Play the Game**
   - Give the instruction for the first round, and remind advisees that they need to complete the task while remaining silent. Once they are in their lines, they can

break their silence and introduce themselves to the person next to them (have someone at one end start the pairings). If they realize they have made a mistake in the order, they should rearrange themselves.

- Line up in alphabetical order by first name.
- Line up in alphabetical order by last name.
- Line up by shoe size from smallest to largest.

• Then have advisees form groups based on the following categories. Remind them that they need to remain silent while completing the task. Once they are in their groups, they can break their silence and introduce themselves, as well as share something about themselves related to the topic. For example, for favorite food, they might talk about their favorite brand of this food item or recipe or restaurant.

- Get into groups by favorite food.
- Get into groups by favorite game or sport to watch or play.
- Get into groups by favorite school subject.

3. Debrief the Activity

- Have the group sit in a circle and discuss the following questions together:
  - Who discovered something surprising about a group member? Let's hear a few.
  - Who discovered something you have in common with a group member? Let's hear a few.
  - How did it feel to have to complete a task without being able to communicate? What does this activity suggest about communication in our advisory group?

ACTIVITY 8

Like Peanut Butter and Jelly

Purpose: Learn each other's names and start to build a positive group culture where advisees feel known and valued.

> **APPROXIMATE TIME:** 15 minutes
>
> **MATERIALS:**
> HANDOUT
> Role Cards for Like Peanut Butter and Jelly

ADVISOR NOTES:

1. **Choose "Get to Know You" Activities with Care**

   Name games can be anxiety-producing for many students, especially games that put them on the spot to think of something clever, require them to remember and recall new information, or involve a coordination challenge such as catching a ball. When meeting a new group of peers, what many adolescents desire most is to fit in and not stand out by saying or doing the "wrong" thing. For this reason, we recommend that you choose get-to-know-you activities that are fun, low-threat, low-vulnerability, and don't require any special knowledge or skill, while at the same time providing opportunities for students to meet each other in pairs and small groups. In these less threatening situations, your advisees will be more likely to engage in authentic and meaningful conversations, while at the same time retaining what they are learning about their peers.

2. **Support English Language Learners**

   English Language Learners may need additional support to understand their role and find their partner. Circulate during the activity to help as needed until you are confident that everyone has an idea of the pair they are looking for.

3. **Prepare Materials in Advance**

   For this activity, you will need one copy of the handout **Role Cards for Like Peanut Butter and Jelly** that you cut along the dotted lines.

PROCEDURE:

1. **Explain How the Game Works**

   - Pass out one role card from the **Role Cards for Like Peanut Butter and Jelly** handout to each advisee and tell them not to show it to anyone. Then let them know that this game has two objectives: find the person whose role pairs with their own and start to get to know that individual.

   - Explain that in order to find their partner, they need to circulate and ask "yes" or "no" questions. For example, they might ask, "Are you a candy bar?" They can ask one "yes" or "no" question and then move to a new advisee. They should not stay with one person and keep asking questions until they figure it out.

- Once they find their match, the pair should move off to the side and sit down for a conversation in which they introduce themselves and learn three new things that they do not know about their partner. Let them know that they will be introducing their partner and sharing what they learn with the group.

2. **Play "Like Peanut Butter and Jelly"**

    - Instruct your advisees to start mingling. Circulate to make sure they are only asking "yes" and "no" questions. As they move to sit together, remind pairs that they should introduce themselves and learn three new things about each other.

    - Once everyone has finished their conversations, have the group move into a circle. Advisees should reveal their roles (if the group doesn't know), introduce their partner to the group, and share one thing they learned about their partner.

    - End the activity by taking the same risks your advisees did and sharing three things about yourself that they probably don't know about you.

HANDOUT

Role Cards for Like Peanut Butter and Jelly

Directions: Before the advisory meeting, cut along the dotted lines to make role cards for each advisee.

Salt	Pepper
Fork	Knife
Circle	Square
Jupiter	Mars
Batman	Wonder Woman
Ocean	Lake
Yellow	Green
Ford	Chevrolet
Elephant	Giraffe
Airplane	Train
Soccer	Volleyball
Coca-Cola	Sprite

ACTIVITY 9

This Is Better than That!

Purpose: Learn each other's names and start to build a positive group culture where advisees practice collaboration and get to know one another.

> **APPROXIMATE TIME:** 20 minutes
>
> **MATERIALS:** NONE

ADVISOR NOTES:

Choose "Get to Know You" Activities with Care

Name games can be anxiety-producing for many students, especially games that put them on the spot to think of something clever, require them to remember and recall new information, or involve a coordination challenge such as catching a ball. When meeting a new group of peers, what many adolescents desire most is to fit in and not stand out by saying or doing the "wrong" thing. For this reason, we recommend that you choose get-to-know-you activities that are fun, low-threat, low-vulnerability, and don't require any special knowledge or skill, while at the same time providing opportunities for students to meet each other in pairs and small groups. In these less threatening situations, your advisees will be more likely to engage in authentic and meaningful conversations, while at the same time retaining what they are learning about their peers.

PROCEDURE:

1. **Explain How the Game Works**

   - Divide your advisory into groups of three and give your advisees time to introduce themselves to each other. Position the groups as far apart from one another as possible so they can't overhear each other's conversations. Provide each group with paper and writing utensils as needed.

   - Explain that you will list four objects on the board and then give the groups a problem to solve. Group members have three minutes to discuss how each object could help them solve the problem and then to rank the objects from 1 to 4, most to least useful.

   - After each round, you can change groups so advisees work with different peers, or keep the same groups to maintain momentum.

2. **Play the Game**

   - Round 1

     - Write the names of the following four objects on the board: marshmallow, paperclip, basketball, and bunsen burner.

- Reveal the first problem: You are an astronaut, and your spaceship lost power on its return trip from Mars.
- After three minutes, have each group share its ranking and provide a justification for its decisions. Encourage groups to ask each other questions and to notice similarities and differences in their rankings.

• Round 2
- Write the names of the following four objects on the board: skateboard, blow dryer, coconut, and hammock.
- Reveal the second problem: You're stranded on a desert island, and you see a ship passing in the distance.
- After three minutes, have each group share its ranking and provide a justification for its decisions. Encourage groups to ask each other questions and to notice similarities and differences in their rankings.

• Round 3
- Write the names of the following four objects on the board: spare car tire, stapler, trumpet, and tent.
- Reveal the third problem: It's a zombie apocalypse!
- After three minutes, have each group share its ranking and provide a justification for its decisions. Encourage groups to ask each other questions and to notice similarities and differences in their rankings.

ACTIVITY **10**

Advisory Bingo

Purpose: Reinforce the importance of learning and using each other's names. Create a positive group culture where advisees feel and are known. Discover common interests and experiences across the group.

> **APPROXIMATE TIME:** 20 minutes
>
> **MATERIALS:**
> - HANDOUT Advisory Bingo
> - HANDOUT Advisory Bingo (Blank)

ADVISOR NOTES:

1. **Create Advisory Folders**

   Advisees will receive their first *Community Matters* handout in this meeting. It is important that advisees have a place to store their advisory handouts, notes, and journals because they will be revisiting, revising, and reflecting on what they have written over the course of the year. If you don't already have a system in place to help advisees store their materials, we suggest that your school provide the following items:

   - Pocket or manila folder for handouts
   - Exam "blue book," or 20 pages of lined paper stapled together, for a journal that can be stored in the advisory folder

   If you have not passed out folders for advisory handouts, you should build in time in this meeting to do so before or after Advisory Bingo. Explain to advisees the purpose of their advisory folder, where it will be stored between meetings, and who has access to the folder's contents.

2. **Choose a Version of Advisory Bingo**

   There are two versions of the handout **Advisory Bingo**, one with completed boxes and one that is blank. For groups where the advisees already know each other well, such as a group of seniors in a small school, you might ask them to brainstorm ideas to write on the blank handout. Or you might use the blank handout to create your own version of Advisory Bingo that would work well for your group.

PROCEDURE:

1. **Explain How the Game Works**
   - Distribute your chosen version of the **Advisory Bingo** handout and explain to advisees that this activity is not a race to finish first. The purpose of the activity is to keep learning names, as well as to hear each other's stories and find connections and shared interests.

Community Matters: A Facing History and Ourselves Approach to Advisory

- Instruct advisees to circulate and ask each other whether they match a category on the bingo chart. When they find someone who is a match, the advisee should write that person's name (it is important that advisees write the names so they can practice the spelling). Then advisees should ask a follow-up question that relates to the category on the bingo chart. For example, if a partner speaks more than one language, the advisee might ask how they learned that language or how to say something (appropriate) in it.
- Unless your advisory group is very small, advisees should only use a peer's name once on their bingo chart.

2. **Debrief Advisory Bingo**

   Instruct the group to sit in a circle and debrief the activity using one or more of the following prompts:
   - Who discovered something surprising about a group member? Let's hear a few.
   - Who discovered something you have in common with a group member? Let's hear a few.
   - What do you want to know more about?

3. **Extend the Activity with an Additional Prompt**
   - You can extend the activity with the prompt, "Just by looking at me, you wouldn't know . . . " Give a half-minute to think of something, and then go around the circle and have advisees introduce themselves in a **Wraparound** (visit facinghistory.org/advisory to learn about this teaching strategy), offering this new characteristic, hobby, accomplishment, or experience.
   - Then ask them: What else would you like to know?
   - Ask if a couple of advisees want to make a new bingo sheet using the blank handout to use on another day—which you will check to make sure all items are school-appropriate.

HANDOUT

Advisory Bingo

Find one person who fits the criteria for each box and write their name there. Then ask a follow-up question that relates to the topic in the box before moving on to another person.

B	I	N	G	O
Someone who is fluent in a language other than English	Someone who plays a musical instrument	Someone who read three books over the summer	Someone who has been involved in student government	Someone who went to a concert in the past year
Someone who has more than three siblings	Someone who likes to play video games	Someone who has acted in a school or community play	Someone who traveled out of state in the past year	Someone who has a pet other than a cat or dog
Someone who has broken a bone	Someone who can recite a favorite quotation	**FREE BOX Your choice of an interesting topic**	Someone whose sibling attends or attended this school	Someone who has always lived in this state
Someone who likes to dance	Someone who moved to this area in the last three years	Someone who has a favorite TV show	Someone who likes to garden	Someone who volunteers outside of school once a month or more
Someone who has a birthday in the same month as you	Someone who plays on a sports team at school or in the community	Someone who's met somebody famous	Someone who has seen all of the movies in the Marvel Universe	Someone who is allergic to one or more foods

HANDOUT

Advisory Bingo (Blank)

Bingo designers: Consider writing prompts so you can find a few things the group has in common, prompts so you find out who can help tutor each other, and prompts to find out who has what hobbies, interests, goals, or anything else you want to know.

B	I	N	G	O
		FREE BOX Your choice of an interesting topic		

ACTIVITY **11**

Birthday Line-Up

Purpose: Create a positive group culture where advisees feel and are known. Initiate the conversation about rituals and what the group would like to celebrate, and how, over the course of the year.

APPROXIMATE TIME: 20 minutes

MATERIALS: NONE

ADVISOR NOTES:

1. **Set Parameters for Celebrating Birthdays**

   In this activity, it is up to the advisor to establish the parameters for upcoming birthday celebrations. It is important that whatever ritual you establish, it is inclusive of every advisee in the group regardless of socioeconomic status, the distance they live from school and their mode of transportation, and allergies. Challenge your advisees to come up with ways to celebrate birthdays that do not involve anyone—including you—having to bake or spend money.

PROCEDURE:

1. **Set Up, Explain, and Play "Birthday Line-Up"**

   - After clearing a space in the center of the room, ask advisees to stand together there. Tell them that without talking, making noise, or writing, they need to line up by birthday month and day.
   - After the group is in a line, have each advisee say their name and then the month and day they were born.

2. **Debrief "Birthday Line-Up"**

   Sit in a circle and choose from the following questions to debrief the activity:

   - Were you successful in lining up according to your birthday days and months? What factors contributed to your success? If you were not successful and made some mistakes, what factors may have gotten in the way of your success?
   - How did the group decide on a strategy to line up? Was everyone involved in the decision-making process, or were decisions about strategy made by a few people? How did you feel during this time?
   - What observations did you make about how the group worked together? What are you proud of in terms of group collaboration and cooperation? What might you have done as individuals and as a group to improve collaboration and cooperation?

3. Discuss How to Celebrate Birthdays

- Involve advisees in the process of deciding how they want to acknowledge and celebrate birthdays this year. Don't forget to include summer birthdays or birthdays that fall during school vacation weeks. Challenge the group to get creative and come up with ideas that don't involve spending money!

- Time allowing, start a discussion about other rituals they might want to put in place this year, such as for before holidays, before or after exams or report cards, or to cheer on advisees before big games, performances, or life events.

ACTIVITY **12**

60-Second Interview

Purpose: Practice names and start to learn more about each other's stories in paired conversations, which can feel safer than large group discussions for many advisees. Create a positive group culture where advisees feel and are known. Discover common interests and experiences across the group.

APPROXIMATE TIME: 20 minutes

MATERIALS:
HANDOUT
60-Second Interview

ADVISOR NOTES:

1. **Modify the Concentric Circles Strategy**

   If you use the **Concentric Circles** strategy to pair advisees for their interviews, have them arrange their desks in two circles facing each other so they can sit during the interviews to facilitate note-taking on the handout. If your room has tables, you can arrange the tables in a circle and have pairs sit on either side of the table. Visit facinghistory.org/advisory-media to learn more about the Concentric Circles teaching strategy.

PROCEDURE:

1. **Explain 60-Second Interviews**

   - Distribute the **60-Second Interview** handout and read aloud the directions.
   - Have advisees pair up. You can count them off or move them into two concentric circles, facing one another.
   - Remind everyone that the information they share with their partners could be shared with the whole group during the final debrief.

2. **Conduct 60-Second Interviews**

   - If your advisees are not in concentric circles (in which case you can assign one circle as A and one circle as B, switching each round so different advisees go first), instruct advisees to choose who will be A and B.
   - Have pairs choose which question from the **60-Second Interview** handout they would like to discuss in this first round.
   - Set a timer for 60 seconds. Instruct Advisee A to begin. They should speak in response to the question they chose. When 60 seconds is up, Advisee B responds to the same prompt.
   - Rotate to new partners two or more times, so advisees speak to at least three people total. Time allowing, you might add additional rounds and use the back of the handout for notes.

3. **Debrief 60-Second Interviews**

    - Sit in a circle and debrief the activity using the **Wraparound** strategy (visit facinghistory.org/advisory-media to learn about this teaching strategy).
    - Instruct advisees to complete this sentence frame for each of the peers they interviewed:
        - The first person I talked to was _____, and one interesting thing I learned was _____.
        - The second person I talked to was _____, and one interesting thing I learned was _____.
        - The third person I talked to was _____, and one interesting thing I learned was _____.
    - Have each advisee read ONE sentence frame in the first Wraparound. Then wrap two more times so everyone has shared something about each one of their interviews.

HANDOUT

60-Second Interview

Directions:

1. With your partner, find a question that interests both of you.
2. Choose who will be A and who will be B.
3. Advisee A talks for 60 seconds about their answer to the question. Advisee B writes down Advisee A's name and at least one interesting point from the interview.
4. When 60 seconds are up, switch, and Advisee B speaks for 60 seconds. Advisee A writes down Advisee B's name and at least one interesting point from the interview.
5. Switch to a new partner, pick a new question for both of you, and repeat the process.

Interview Questions to Choose From:

- What's one place you would like to visit in your lifetime? Why do you want to go there?
- What's one thing you would like to change about your neighborhood that would make it a better place to live?
- What worries you most about the world you live in today?
- Name one thing you could teach someone how to make or how to do.
- What's one thing that you would like to change about your school that would make it a better place for you?
- Describe your family. What is something weird, unusual, or special about one person in your family?

Advisee's name	Interesting thing you want to remember from your interview with this person

ACTIVITY **13**

Dear Advisory

Purpose: Celebrate the unique qualities that each advisee brings to the group and learn about each other's areas of expertise.

> **APPROXIMATE TIME:** 30 minutes
>
> **MATERIALS:** Lined paper or journals

ADVISOR NOTES:

1. **Modify "Dear Advisory" to Give Advice Later in the Year**

   "Dear Advisory" can also be done as a way of asking for and receiving advice within the advisory group throughout the year. Have your advisees write problems or challenges that they are facing on individual index cards. Then collect the cards, read them out loud one by one, and have the group discuss possible solutions or next steps for each.

2. **Encourage Creativity by Providing Choice**

   At the end of this activity, your advisees will be writing a letter to the group in which they share an area of personal expertise. There are many ways that they might want to convey this information: a poem, rap, dialogue, series of cartoon panels, drawing, song, advertisement, reality show application, newspaper article, mural, series of tweets . . . the list goes on. Choice empowers adolescents and leads to buy-in. Take some time to brainstorm ways advisees might craft their letters, and provide these kinds of choices in future activities.

3. **Pacing This Activity**

   If your advisees don't have time to share their "Dear Advisory" letters in their groups, you can collect them or have them store their letters in their folders. In upcoming meetings, you can read one or more letters in your opening or closing routine, or build in time for the groups to reconvene and hear each other's stories.

PROCEDURE:

1. **Explain and Model the "Dear Advisory" Activity**
   - Explain to advisees that they will be learning new things about the members of the advisory group today. They will start by brainstorming a list of ten things they are "experts" in.
   - Start by modeling your list as a way to illustrate the notion of expert as vast and varied.

- Then pass out lined paper or have advisees use their journals to brainstorm a list of ten things they have expertise in. Tell them to skip three or four lines between each item on their list.

2. Share Expert Lists in Groups

- Divide advisees into groups of four and have them sit in a small circle or square.
- Then have them pass their lists to the person on their left. They should read through the list and respond to it by writing a star by the topics they find most interesting, ask questions in the space underneath the items on the list, annotate or comment on topics that they are also experts in, etc.
- Continue to rotate each list within your advisory group until everyone has read and commented on every list and the lists have arrived back with the creators.
- Instruct advisees to look over the notes from their peers and choose one of the ten topics to expand on in a letter to their advisory group that starts with "Dear Advisory" and tells the story of how and why they are an expert in this particular area. Encourage creativity by inviting advisees to write their letter in a different genre (see Advisor Notes).

3. Share "Dear Advisory" Letters

- Once advisees have finished their letters, you can have everyone pass the letters around again and respond in the margins or have advisees read or share their letters (or whatever they created) with the group.
- If time is limited, you can have a couple of advisees share their letters and then collect the rest. In upcoming advisory meetings, have two or three advisees read their letters at the start of the meeting until everyone's letter has been read.

ACTIVITY **14**

Checking In on the Opening Days

Purpose: Learn about issues advisees are having and follow up as needed with one-on-one conversations. Get a pulse on how advisees are understanding school culture.

> **APPROXIMATE TIME:** 30 minutes
>
> **MATERIALS:**
> HANDOUT
> Peaks and Valleys

ADVISOR NOTES:

1. **Where to Place This Activity**

   Try to place this activity in the first two weeks of the year, if possible. This is a good activity to revisit throughout the year—for example, at the beginning or end of a marking period or midway between school vacations, when your advisees might be feeling tired.

2. **Modify "School Basics" as Needed**

   Modify the first part of the activity, "School Basics," if your advisees are not new to the school building. You might challenge older advisees to familiarize themselves with specific spaces in the school or to meet new faculty or staff members. For example, seniors can benefit from meeting the registrar, since they will need to request their transcripts for college and job applications. Freshmen should meet the nurse, the librarian, and the staff member who distributes tardy slips. Everyone in the building should know the names of custodial, maintenance, and kitchen staff members.

3. **Create a Safe Environment that Encourages Sharing**

   At the beginning of the year, use pairs and triads to encourage sharing among the group and to provide space for quieter members who might not yet feel comfortable answering personal questions in a larger group. This "checking in" activity can become a routine in your advisory, and as the group becomes more comfortable with each other, you can shift from small- to whole-group circle share-outs.

4. **Addressing the "Peaks" and the "Valleys" of the Opening Weeks**

   Some of the "peaks" (positive or exciting moments) advisees share might be worth applauding; some of the "valleys" (lows) might be scary, frustrating, or confusing moments and can provide opportunities to problem-solve and support each other. In most cases, ask the group to problem-solve before offering your own ideas.

   - Who has had a similar experience (question, confusion, or frustration)?
   - Who has an idea that might help . . . ?

PROCEDURE:

1. Review School Basics as Needed

As a whole advisory, discuss the questions (or create additional ones) that apply to your group:

- Have you found all of your classes? The bathrooms?
- Does your locker work properly? Does your gym locker work properly?
- What's the most confusing thing about the cafeteria? What's the best/worst food?
- Where is the nurse's office and what are the names of the staff there?
- Where is your counselor's office and what is the counselor's name?
- What are some useful shortcuts to know?
- How can you access your homework online?
- Do your classes seem like the right fit for you? What should you do if they do not feel right?
- Have you figured out how to say all of your teachers' names correctly? Which ones seem challenging?
- Are teachers pronouncing your name correctly? What's a respectful way to explain to them the correct pronunciation of your name?

2. Discuss "Highs," "Lows," and School Culture

- Let advisees know that they will be sharing some highs and lows from the opening days/weeks of the school year.
- Divide the advisees into pairs or groups of three. Distribute the handout **Peaks and Valleys** and have advisees discuss the following questions:
    - What are some highs from your time at school so far (or in the last week)?
    - What are some lows from your time at school so far (or in the last week)?
    - What was surprising or interesting?
    - What was scary, frustrating, or confusing?
    - What does the school culture feel like so far to you? What excites you? What do you think needs to change?
- Move the group into a circle to share ideas from their discussions. Discuss strategies for how they might celebrate each other's highs and help problem-solve when there are lows.
- Collect their handouts so you can analyze them to assess if there are patterns, groups or individuals you may need to check in with one-on-one, or important ideas that they recorded but didn't share in the discussion.

3. **Reflect on the First Weeks of the Year**

    - Depending on how comfortable your group seems to be with sharing with one another, you might ask advisees to close their eyes for this activity so they are not swayed by others' responses.

    - Ask advisees for a "fist-to-five" reaction (showing zero to five fingers to indicate reactions: fist means "not at all," five fingers means "very") on whether school feels welcoming, whether they look forward to attending each day, and whether kids seem friendly.

    - If you see fists or only a few fingers, talk with the whole group or with specific advisees who might need extra support in a mini-conference.

HANDOUT

Peaks and Valleys

Directions: Discuss the following questions and record the key ideas that you want to share with your advisory group and advisor. Your advisor will collect the handout, so if there are things you want your advisor to know but don't want to share out loud with the group, you should write them down.

Group Members' Names:
_____

1. What are some "peaks" from your time at school so far (or in the last few weeks)?

2. What are some "valleys" from your time at school so far (or in the last few weeks)?

3. What was surprising or interesting?

4. What was scary, frustrating, or confusing?

5. What does the school culture feel like so far to you? What excites you? What do you think needs to change?

6. Is there anything else about school culture or how you are feeling this year that we didn't talk about and you want to share?

ACTIVITY **15**

How Can I Support You?

Purpose: Foster advisee-advisor relationships and a sense of community within the group. Encourage self-advocacy by inviting advisees to articulate the ways in which the advisor can support them.

APPROXIMATE TIME: 30 minutes

MATERIALS:
HANDOUT
How Can I Support You?

ADVISOR NOTES:

The Importance of Closing Routines

The final discussion introduces a routine that you can use to close future advisory meetings that have required groups to collaborate. Use this routine with the questions as written or develop your own set of reflection questions with your advisees that they revisit after group work activities over the course of the year.

PROCEDURE:

1. **Reflect on How the Advisor Can Support Advisees**

   - Arrange the group in a circle and explain that you would like to know how you can best support them as their advisor this year.
   - Then pass out the handout **How Can I Support You?**
   - Next, have advisees work individually to respond to the three questions on the handout. Before they start writing, let them know that they will be sharing their ideas in small groups and that you will be collecting the handouts at the end of the meeting.

2. **Collaborate to Create a Group List**

   - Divide advisees into small groups, perhaps counting off to mix up the group. Instruct them to share what they wrote on their handouts.
   - Next, pass out one blank copy of the handout **How Can I Support You?** to each group and have them discuss and then record three ideas in each box that they can all agree on.
   - To debrief, ask for each group to share one idea at a time, round-robin style, while you listen, jot notes, and ask clarifying questions. Offer a summarizing description, such as, "It sounds like you want me to be a good listener, help you problem-solve, and occasionally it's okay for me to nag. Is that a fair summary? That's for each of you as individuals. I also plan to help us function well as a group."

Section 1: Welcome to Advisory!

3. **Reflect on the Group Process**
   - Return to a circle for a closing discussion about the activity and how well the groups felt they worked together to create their shared lists. You might draw from the following questions:
     - What process did your group use to share what you wrote on your handouts?
     - How did your group choose which ideas to include on the group handout and which ideas not to include?
     - What do you think worked well in your group?
     - How do you think you could do better the next time you work in a group?
   - Collect the individual handouts so you have a snapshot of what each advisee values and needs in an advisor this year.

HANDOUT

How Can I Support You?

Directions: Think of someone who is (or was) a good advisor to you in your life. It could be a friend, a relative, someone at school, someone from your religious institution or your job, anybody. Then respond to the questions in the space provided on the chart. You will be sharing your responses in small groups.

Questions	My Ideas
In what ways do/did they support you that have led you to think of them as a good advisor?	
What are/were some their qualities that have made them a good advisor to you?	
What would make me (your current advisor) an effective advisor to you this year?	

SECTION 1

SECTION 2:

Exploring Identity: Who Am I?

ACTIVITIES

Getting to Know Me: Preparing for the First Mini-Conference

What's in a Name?

Dual Identities

Our Names and Our Place in the World

My Identity Chart

Identity Chart Discussion

Bio-Poems

Who Is the Real You?

Real Life vs. Online Identity

Identity and Language

Identity, Family, and Legacy

My Life Road Map

Exploring Identity Final Reflection

Purpose	Materials	Abridged Advisor Notes
16: Getting to Know Me: Preparing for the First Mini-Conference		30+ min page 70
Reflect on interests, concerns, passions, and goals for the first round of individual mini-conferences.	**HANDOUT: Getting to Know Me**	Before conducting your first round of mini-conferences, read "Making Space for Mini-Conferences." Try to conduct your initial round of mini-conferences early in the year so that your first one-on-one interaction with each advisee is not about academic issues or grades.
17: What's in a Name?		40 min page 73
Explore the relationship between our names, our identities, and the societies in which we live.	**HANDOUT: What's in a Name? Gallery Walk Quotations** Colored markers and paper	Before the advisory meeting, prepare the quotations on the What's in a Name? Gallery Walk Quotations handout for a gallery walk (visit facinghistory.org/advisory-media to learn about this teaching strategy). Consider modeling the Sketch to Stretch strategy. You can find examples of this strategy online.
18: Dual Identities		45 min page 76
Explore the broader identities that our names represent and introduce the idea that our identities are made up of many factors, some of which we choose for ourselves and some which are chosen for us.	**READING: Two Names, Two Worlds** **HANDOUT: Navigating Two Worlds**	Familiarize yourself with the our Read Aloud strategies, available at facinghistory.org/advisory-media, and choose one for the reading Two Names, Two Worlds. Some advisees might feel uncomfortable reading an unfamiliar piece out loud, especially one that includes some terms in Spanish, so it is important that advisees have choice about reading. This activity can be divided into two parts for shorter advisory meetings.
19: Our Names and Our Place in the World		30 min page 82
Consider what parts of our identities we choose for ourselves versus the parts that are chosen for us, as well as the impact that labels can have on our identities.	**READING: Orientation Day** **HANDOUT: Orientation Day Graphic Organizer**	If you have more time to devote to this activity, you can find the full version of Jennifer Wang's essay, Names and Identity, at facinghistory.org/advisory-media.
20: My Identity Chart		30 min page 86
Consider the various factors that make up one's identity. Create community and break down stereotypes by sharing identity charts.	**HANDOUT: Starburst Identity Chart** **HANDOUT: Inside–Outside Identity Chart**	Identity charts are a graphic tool that can help students consider the many factors that shape the identities of both individuals and communities (visit facinghistory.org/advisory-media to learn more about this teaching strategy). Before this advisory session, create or start to make your own individual identity chart.
21: Identity Chart Discussion		30 min page 91
Create community, break down stereotypes, and encourage risk taking.	None	In this activity, advisees will use their personal identity charts created in Activity 20: My Identity Chart.
22: Bio-Poems		30 min page 93
Consider factors that shape identity, such as experiences, relationships, hopes, and interests.	**HANDOUT: Bio-Poem Template**	To help your advisees get to know you, share your own bio-poem. You could provide a student example as a model, but it will be more powerful for your advisees if they see you taking the same social and academic risks you are asking of them. Visit facinghistory.org/advisory-media to learn more about the Bio-Poem teaching strategy.

Purpose	Materials	Abridged Advisor Notes
23: Who Is the Real You?		30 min — page 96
Consider other aspects of individual identity and introduce the idea that an online identity might differ from a "real life" identity.	**HANDOUT:** Online-Search Identity Chart **VIDEO:** Online vs. Offline Self: Who Is the Real You? (see y2u.be/SZAkZ4TzSEA)	None
24: Real Life vs. Online Identity		45 min — page 98
Deepen the exploration of online versus "real life" identities by examining how the ways in which individuals present themselves on social media can emphasize some aspects of their identities while minimizing or hiding others.	**READING:** Creating Ourselves Online and in "Real Life" Chart paper and markers	Before the advisory meeting, familiarize yourself with the Gallery Walk and Big Paper strategies, available at facinghistory.org/advisory-media. Copy, cut out, and tape each excerpt from the reading on a separate piece of chart or butcher paper and post them around the room in preparation for the activity.
25: Identity and Language		30 min — page 102
Explore the relationship between identity and language and the decisions we make about how we choose to communicate with others.	**AUDIO:** Lost in Translation (see facinghistory.org/advisory-media) **READING:** Lost in Translation	None
26: Identity, Family, and Legacy		30 min — page 106
Explore the relationship between legacy and identity by examining the extent to which we inherit or receive our identities and how the legacies of older generations can influence our identities.	**HANDOUT:** Social Identity Map **VIDEO:** Condoleezza Rice's Family Matters (see facinghistory.org/advisory-media) **VIDEO:** Deidre Prevett: American Dreams in Muskogee Nation (see facinghistory.org/advisory-media)	There are two short video clips from the documentary film *American Creed* that you can choose from for this activity, or, time allowing, you might show both before having a circle discussion. While the activity is written for Condoleezza Rice's video clip, you can follow the same procedure and use the same questions if you choose to use Deidre Prevett's video clip instead. If you are interested in exploring American identity in greater depth using *American Creed*, visit facinghistory.org/advisory-media to access our collection of *American Creed* educator resources.
27: My Life Road Map		2 x 45 min — page 109
Reflect on key choices that help shape identity and foster community through the sharing of personal stories.	White paper (legal size or larger) Colored markers, pens, and/or pencils **HANDOUT:** Positive-Negative Line Graph (optional)	You will probably need two advisory meetings for this activity. Advisees can brainstorm and create their maps in the first session and then share and discuss their maps in the second session. While this activity is based on the Life Road Maps strategy (visit facighistory.org/advisory-media to learn about this teaching strategy), you can also use the Positive-Negative Line Graph handout for this activity. You can conduct mini-conferences with advisees while the group is creating their life road maps.
28: Exploring Identity Final Reflection		30 min — page 112
Review the overarching themes, questions, journal responses, and work from this section of *Community Matters* and reflect on new understanding and lingering questions.	None	Providing advisees with the time and space to reflect on their learning, growth, and lingering questions allows them to synthesize the material in meaningful ways before being introduced to new themes and concepts.

SECTION 2

Exploring Identity: Who Am I?

ACTIVITIES 16–28

OVERVIEW

Because identity development is a key developmental task of adolescence, it is important for advisory to support adolescents' exploration of who they are and how they fit into the world around them. In this section, advisees engage in this exploration by considering how much of our identities we choose for ourselves versus how much is determined by other influences, such as our families, our culture, and the circumstances of our lives. They will extend this exploration by considering how we create, or re-create, our identities online, and how our online identities compare to our "real life" ones. This comparison will help advisees understand the many factors that can influence how they choose to portray themselves to the world. Advisees will also consider the groups they belong to and how those groups influence their identities and the choices they make. Finally, through their discussions and other activities, advisees will deepen their relationships with each other, break down stereotypes they may have of their peers, and start to develop a sense of identity for their advisory group.

NAVIGATING THE ACTIVITIES

This section of *Community Matters* explores different facets of identity: names, family, language, and online versus "real" identity.

- Activity 16: Getting to Know Me: Preparing for the First Mini-Conference introduces mini-conferences, an important routine explained in **Making Space for Mini-Conferences** on page 5. Try to schedule your first round of mini-conferences in this section of *Community Matters* so you can start to know your advisees one-on-one and establish the routine before the first marking period.

- If you do not have time for all of the activities in this section, try to include at least one identity and name activity (Activities 17–19) to help advisees connect the name games and introductory activities from the first section of *Community Matters* to the theme of identity.

- Activities 20–21, 23–24, and 27–28 are important to include because they introduce key Facing History themes and concepts that prepare advisees for material they will encounter in the upcoming sections of *Community Matters.*

ACTIVITY **16**

Getting to Know Me: Preparing for the First Mini-Conference

Purpose: Reflect on interests, concerns, passions, and goals for the first round of individual mini-conferences.

APPROXIMATE TIME:
30+ minutes

MATERIALS:
HANDOUT
Getting to Know Me

ADVISOR NOTES:

1. **Understand the Purpose and Value of Mini-Conferences**

   Before conducting your first round of mini-conferences, read **Making Space for Mini-Conferences** on page 5 to better understand the value of establishing them as a routine that helps support the academic, social, and personal lives of your advisees.

2. **Build in Time for Mini-Conferences**

   Try to conduct your initial round of mini-conferences early in the year so your first one-on-one interaction with each advisee is not about academic issues or grades. The amount of time it takes to conduct each round of mini-conferences depends on the size of your group and the length of your advisory meeting. Advisors with 7–10 advisees will be able to spend more time in each mini-conference than advisors with 15–20 advisees. Ideally, you will be able to spend three to five minutes with each advisee. While you are mini-conferencing, the others can work in small groups on activities such as bio-poems, life road maps, or discussion of a reading or video. **Making Space for Mini-Conferences** has additional ideas for activities that work well during mini-conferences.

PROCEDURE:

1. **Explain the Purpose of Mini-Conferences**
   - Let your advisees know that in addition to opening and closing routines, mini-conferences are another routine that will help you know them and be able to support them as they strive to reach their goals this year. While they should always feel free to schedule a conference with you or a counselor outside of advisory, you will be building in time during advisory to check in with them about their academic goals, personal goals, and social goals. The first round of mini-conferences provides an opportunity for you to get to know advisees a bit better as individuals.

70 Community Matters: A Facing History and Ourselves Approach to Advisory

- To prepare for the conference, explain to the group that they will each be completing a short questionnaire. Let them know that you will collect it after the conference because there probably won't be time to discuss all of their responses and you want to be able to see the responses to all of the questions.

2. **Prepare for and Conduct Mini-Conferences**
    - Pass out and have advisees complete the handout **Getting to Know Me**.
    - After your advisees have finished their reflections, either start your first round of mini-conferences after the group has settled into a new activity, or have advisees store their handouts in their advisory folders if you plan start mini-conferences in a future meeting.

HANDOUT

Getting to Know Me

Directions: Respond to the following prompts in two to three sentences, giving a brief explanation of your answer. Then put a star by three prompts that you want to talk about in your first mini-conference. If there is time, you and your advisor can talk about more, or you can come back to the other topics in future mini-conferences.

1. A highlight of my summer vacation was . . . because . . .

2. When I have free time on the weekend, you can find me . . .

3. This year, I am most excited about . . . because . . .

4. This year, I am most nervous about . . . because . . .

5. I would describe my personal style as . . . because . . .

6. I would like to learn more about (does not have to be academic) . . . because . . .

7. The best thing about being a student at _____ (school's name) is . . . because . . .

8. The worst thing about being a student at _____ (school's name) is . . . because . . .

9. In order to best support me as my advisor this year, you should know that . . .

ACTIVITY **17**

What's in a Name?

Purpose: Explore the relationship between our names, our identities, and the societies in which we live.

> **APPROXIMATE TIME:**
> 40 minutes
>
> **MATERIALS:**
> HANDOUT
> What's in a Name? Gallery Walk Quotations
>
> Colored markers and paper

ADVISOR NOTES:

1. Before the advisory session, prepare the quotations on the **What's in a Name? Gallery Walk Quotations** handout for a **gallery walk**. Visit facinghistory.org/advisory-media to learn about the Gallery Walk teaching strategy.

2. Consider modeling the Sketch to Stretch strategy by making your own visual for a quotation about names that you share during the advisory session. You can find examples of this strategy online.

PROCEDURE:

1. **Start with a Gallery Walk**

   - Start by inviting your advisees to circulate around the room and read the quotations about names. Let them know that they will have a chance to discuss the quotations in a few minutes.

   - Next, invite advisees to stand by the quotation that most interests them. Perhaps they connect personally with the idea or they aren't quite sure what it means. After everyone is standing by a quotation, have each group take their quotation from the wall and sit together in a circle. Divide groups larger than four into smaller groups or pairs. Students who don't have a group can work alone if they feel passionate about their quotation or join another group.

2. **Sketch to Stretch**

   - To help your advisees explore their quotations in more depth, have them discuss the following questions in their small groups:
     - Why did you choose this quotation?
     - What do you think it means?
     - What ideas about names do you think the writer or speaker wants us to consider? What's worth talking about?
     - What questions does your quotation raise for you?

- Then pass out markers and photocopy paper or chart paper. Explain to the group that they will have seven minutes to create a visual representation that captures the main idea of their quotation. They can incorporate words or phrases from the quotation into their sketch if they wish. Challenge them to use color, symbols, and images and remind them that they are creating a sketch and not a masterpiece!
- After seven minutes, invite volunteers from each group to share their quotation and visual. They can also share highlights from their discussion.

3. **Discuss What's in a Name?**
    - Sit in a circle to discuss the following questions as a group. Remind advisees that they can refer to the name quotations to support their thinking.
        - Are our names the same as who we are?
        - How do our names relate to our identities?
        - In what ways can names be empowering? How can names be limiting?
        - What are some things we can do in our advisory group to make sure that names are always empowering and never limiting? How about in our school?

HANDOUT

What's in a Name? Gallery Walk Quotations

Directions: Before the advisory session, print this handout and cut apart the quotations. Glue or tape each quotation to a piece of paper for the gallery walk.

"If I'm gonna tell a real story, I'm gonna start with my name."
–Kendrick Lamar, *Vulture*

"What's in a name? that which we call a rose / By any other name would smell as sweet."
–William Shakespeare, *Romeo and Juliet*

"Call him Voldemort, Harry. Always use the proper name for things. Fear of a name increases fear of the thing itself."
–J. K. Rowling, *Harry Potter and the Sorcerer's Stone*

"A wife should no more take her husband's name than he should hers. My name is my identity and must not be lost."
–Lucy Stone, nineteenth-century abolitionist and suffragist

"Tigers die and leave their skins; people die and leave their names."
–Japanese proverb

"It is through our names that we first place ourselves in the world. Our names, being the gift of others, must be made our own."
–Ralph Ellison, *The Collected Essays of Ralph Ellison*

"I'd be stupid not to take into consideration that there are certain things people will not consider me for because my name is Lopez. And I know I can do any kind of role. I don't want anybody to say, Oh, she can't pull this off. So those are barriers that you have to overcome."
–Jennifer Lopez

ACTIVITY **18**

Dual Identities

Purpose: Introduce the concept of identity and explore the complex relationship between our names and our identities.

> **APPROXIMATE TIME:**
> 45 minutes
>
> **MATERIALS:**
> **READING**
> Two Names, Two Worlds
> **HANDOUT**
> Navigating Two Worlds

ADVISOR NOTES:

1. **Create an Inclusive and Welcoming Environment for Reading**

   In this activity, advisees will read a poem written by a student reflecting on the relationship between his name and his identity. Before the advisory meeting, think about how you would like your group to read the poem. You might choose a **Read Aloud** strategy, such as "popcorn style." Visit facinghistory.org/advisory-media to learn about the different Read Aloud teaching strategies. Some advisees might feel uncomfortable reading an unfamiliar piece out loud, especially one that includes some terms in Spanish, so it is important that advisees have a choice about reading, especially while you are still building community and establishing your advisory space as welcoming and inclusive.

2. **Pacing This Activity**

   If your advisory meeting is shorter than 45 minutes, you can divide this activity into two parts by completing the concentric circles activity and reading the poem in the first meeting and then discussing the poem and reflecting on it in a journal response in the second meeting.

PROCEDURE:

1. **Explore the Broader Identity a Name Represents**

   - Explain to the group that in this activity, they will be reflecting on how well they think their own name reflects who they are. Then they will use the metaphor of an online search results page to think about the characteristics that make up who they are.

   - Project or write on the board some or all of the following sentence starters, and use the **Concentric Circles** strategy for paired discussions (visit facinghistory.org/advisory-media to learn about this teaching strategy). It is important that your advisees have a choice about what they share, so let individuals choose which sentence stem to start with each round. Have advisees in one circle share for one minute before switching to the other circle. For example, you might ask the outside circle to start and time them for one minute as they respond to the prompt while advisees on the inside circle listen. Then advisees on the inside circle respond to the prompt for one minute.

- I was given my name because . . .
- I like/dislike my name because . . .
- My name is/isn't a good fit for my personality because . . .
- Describe a time when someone made an assumption about you because of your name.
- Describe a time when your name affected your behavior.

2. Read and Discuss "Two Names, Two Worlds"

- Provide advisees with copies of the reading **Two Names, Two Worlds** and the handout **Navigating Two Worlds**. Explain how the group will read the poem together.
- After reading the text, divide advisees into pairs or small groups of three to complete the handout.
- Then choose from the following questions for a circle discussion:
    - What is your favorite line from the poem, and why?
    - What one or two lines from the poem do you most relate to, and why?
    - Who is Jonathan Rodríguez? What are some of the words he uses to describe himself?
    - What do you think Jonathan Rodríguez means when he uses the phrase "two names, two worlds"? What two worlds does his name represent?
    - What are some of the worlds that you move between? In what ways is it easy to move between them? In what ways is it challenging? What are some of the strategies you've developed to help you overcome the challenges?

3. Reflect on Today's Discussion

Ask advisees to complete three to five of the following sentence starters from the poem in their **journals** and then share one with the group in a **Wraparound** format to create a group poem (visit facinghistory.org/advisory-media to learn about these teaching strategies).

- Born in _____ / But raised in _____.
- I'm not the typical . . .
- I get lost in . . .
- I listen to _____ / But don't make me _____.
- I am proud to say: . . .
- I am beginning to appreciate that . . .
- I am beginning to see that . . .
- Join me and . . .

READING

Two Names, Two Worlds

In the poem below, Jonathan Rodríguez reflects on how his name represents his identity.

Hi I'm Jon………..No—Jonathan
Wait—Jonathan Rodríguez
Hold on—Jonathan *Rodríguez*
My Name, Two names, two worlds
The duality of my identity like two sides of the same coin
With two worlds, there should be plenty of room
But where do I fit?
Where can I sit?
Is this seat taken? Or is that seat taken?
There never is quite enough room is there?
Two names, Two worlds
Where do I come from?
Born in the Washington Heights of New York City
But raised in good ol' Connecticut
The smell of freshly mowed grass, autumn leaves
Sancocho, Rice and Beans
The sound from Billy Joel's Piano Keys
And the rhythm from *Juan Luis Guerra*
I'm from the struggle for broken dreams
Of false promises
Of houses with white picket fences
And 2.5 kids
The mountains and *campos de la Republica Dominicana*
And the mango trees
I'm not the typical kid from suburbia
Nor am I a smooth Latin cat
My head's in the clouds, my nose in a comic book
I get lost in the stories and art
I'm kinda awkward—so talkin' to the ladies is hard
I listen to *Fernando Villalona* and *Aventura* every chance I get,
But don't make me dance *Merengue*, *Bachata*
Or *Salsa*—I don't know the steps
I've learned throughout these past years

I am a mix of cultures, a mix of races

"*Una Raza encendida,*

Negra, Blanca y Taina"

You can find me in the parts of a song, *en una cancion*

You can feel my African Roots *en la Tambora*

My *Taino* screams *en la guira*

And the melodies of the lyrics are a reminder of my beautiful Spanish heritage

I am African, Taino and Spanish

A Fanboy, an athlete, a nerd, a student, an introvert

I'm proud to say: *Yo soy Dominicano*

I'm proud to say, I am me

I am beginning to appreciate that I am

Una bella mezcla

I am beginning to see that this world is also a beautiful mix

Of people, ideas and stories.

Is this seat taken?

Or is that seat taken?

Join me and take a seat,

Here we'll write our own stories[1]

---

1 Jonathan Rodríguez, untitled poem.

HANDOUT

Navigating Two Worlds

Directions: Inside the thought bubbles, write examples from the poem to show Jonathan Rodríguez's two identities. Then discuss the questions below with your group. Do not work on Part Two yet. It's for later!

Part One

Discuss the following questions as a group:

1. What do you think Jonathan Rodríguez means when he uses the phrase "two names, two worlds"?

2. What two worlds do you think his name might represent?

3. What advice could you give Jonathan that would help him move between these two worlds?

Part Two

Directions: Respond to the following reflection questions in your journal or in the space below. Then choose some (or all) of the sentence starters from "Two Names, Two Worlds" and write your own identity poem in your journal or on separate paper.

1. What are some of the worlds that you move between?
2. In what ways is it easy to move between them?
3. In what ways is it challenging?
4. What are some of the strategies you've developed to help you overcome the challenges?

My Identity Poem

Title: _____

- Hi, I'm _____.
- Born in _____ / But raised in _____.
- I'm not the typical . . .
- I get lost in . . .
- I listen to _____ / But don't make me _____.
- I am proud to say: . . .
- I am beginning to appreciate that . . .
- I am beginning to see that . . .
- Join me and . . .

ACTIVITY **19**

Our Names and Our Place in the World

Purpose: Consider what parts of our identities we choose for ourselves and what parts are chosen for us, as well as the impact that labels can have on our identities.

> **APPROXIMATE TIME:**
> 30 minutes
>
> **MATERIALS:**
> **READING**
> Orientation Day
>
> **HANDOUT**
> Orientation Day Graphic Organizer

ADVISOR NOTES:

1. **Full Version of Jennifer Wang's Essay**

   If you have more time to devote to this activity, you can find the full version of Jennifer Wang's essay, **Names and Identity**, at facinghistory.org/advisory-media.

PROCEDURE:

1. **Discuss the Relationship between Names and Identity**

   - In their journals or with a partner in a "pair-share" format, ask advisees to respond to the following question:

     > My name is/isn't a good fit for my personality because . . .

     While advisees should be able to keep their responses private, time allowing, ask if any volunteers want to share their thoughts with the group.

   - Then discuss the following question together: *What do our names reveal about our identities?* Consider listing your advisees' ideas on the board to reference later in the session.

2. **Read Aloud a Teenager's Story about Her Name**

   - Pass out the reading **Orientation Day** and **read aloud** Jennifer Wang's story about the tension she feels between her name and her identity (visit facinghistory.org/advisory-media to learn about the Read Aloud teaching strategy).

   - To help advisees engage with the text, ask them to underline or put a star in the margin by places where they can relate to Jennifer's experience. They can also write a question mark in places where her experience raises questions for them.

3. Discuss the Essay in Small Groups

Pass out the handout **Orientation Day Graphic Organizer** and divide your advisory into groups of three. Have advisees share what they starred and questioned in the text and then work together to complete the handout.

Bring the group together in a circle to share from their handouts. Then discuss the following questions as an advisory group:

- What could Wang's teacher have done to make her feel more welcome in the class?
- What could other students have done to make Wang feel like she belonged?
- What is important to know about each other in order to work together as an advisory this year?

READING

Orientation Day

Directions: In this essay, 17-year-old Jennifer Wang, who came to the United States from Beijing, China, when she was seven, reflects on a time when she had to introduce herself to a group of strangers at a new school. As you read, underline the words and phrases that Wang uses to describe her identity.

Something about myself? How do I summarize, in thirty seconds, everything which adds up and equals a neat little bundle called Me? Who am I, and why do I matter to any of you?

First of all, I am a girl who wandered the aisles of Toys "R" Us for two hours, hunting in vain for a doll with a yellowish skin tone. I am a girl who sat on the cold bathroom floor at seven in the morning, cutting out the eyes of Caucasian models in magazines, trying to fit them on my face . . .

While I was growing up, I did not understand what it meant to be "Chinese" or "American." Do these terms link only to citizenship? Do they suggest that people fit the profile of either "typical Chinese" or "typical Americans"? And who or what determines when a person starts feeling American, and stops feeling Chinese?

I eventually shunned the Asian crowds. And I hated Chinatown. . . . I hated the noise, the crush of bodies, the yells of mothers to fathers to children to uncles to aunts to cousins. . . . I hated not understanding their language in depth—the language of my ancestors, which was also supposed to be mine to mold and master.

I am still not a citizen of the United States of America, this great nation, which is hailed as the destination for generations of people, the promised land for millions. . . . I stare blankly at my friends when they mention the 1980s or share stories of their parents as hippies. And I hate baseball.

The question lingers: Am I Chinese? Am I American? Or am I some unholy mixture of both, doomed to stay torn between the two?

I don't know if I'll ever find the answers. Meanwhile, it's my turn to introduce myself . . . I stand up and say, "My name is Jennifer Wang," and then I sit back down. There are no other words that define me as well as those do. No others show me being stretched between two very different cultures and places—the "Jennifer" clashing with the "Wang," the "Wang" fighting with the "Jennifer."[1]

---

1 Jennifer Wang, "Orientation Day," in *YELL-Oh Girls! Emerging Voices Explore Culture, Identity, and Growing Up Asian American*, ed. Vickie Nam (New York: HarperCollins, 2001), 199–200. Reproduced by permission from HarperCollins Publishers.

HANDOUT

Orientation Day Graphic Organizer

Directions: Discuss the following questions and record your ideas in the boxes below.

How do you think it feels to have different parts of your identity fighting against each other? What are some of the factors that can impact how people feel about their identities?

What words or phrases does Wang use to describe her identity?	What words or phrases does Wang use to describe her attitude—how she feels—toward her identity?
What do you think is the most valuable idea in the essay? Why?	What advice could you give Jennifer Wang that would help her move between these two worlds?

How do you think it feels to have different parts of your identity fighting against each other? What are some of the factors that can impact the way people feel about their identities?

ACTIVITY **20**

My Identity Chart

Purpose: Consider the various factors that make up one's identity. Create community and break down stereotypes by sharing identity charts with other advisees.

> **APPROXIMATE TIME:**
> 30 minutes
>
> **MATERIALS:**
> ☐ HANDOUT
> Starburst Identity Chart
>
> ☐ HANDOUT
> Inside-Outside Identity Chart

ADVISOR NOTES:

1. **Understand the Purpose of Identity Charts**

   Identity charts are a graphic tool that can help students consider the many factors that shape the identities of both individuals and communities. To learn more about using the Identity Charts teaching strategy, visit facinghistory.org/advisory-media. In this activity, advisees will use identity charts to analyze the ways they define themselves and the labels that others use to describe them. Sharing their own identity charts with peers can help your advisees build relationships and break down stereotypes. In this way, identity charts can be used as an effective advisory community-building tool.

2. **Model Identity for Your Advisory**

   Before this advisory meeting, create or start to make your own individual identity chart using the template that your advisees will use in the activity. Sharing your chart as a model and speaking about a few factors that make up your identity is an excellent community-building opportunity and a way for your advisees to learn more about you.

3. **Choose an Identity Chart Template**

   In addition to the identity chart provided on our teaching strategy page (visit facinghistory.org/advisory-media to access this teaching strategy), there are two other identity chart templates that you can use for this activity: the **Starburst Identity Chart** or the **Inside-Outside Identity Chart**. Both templates allow advisees to consider the range of factors that make up their identities and how the way others perceive them can differ from their own ideas and feelings about their identities. If you feel like it is too early in the year to talk about perception, which can lead to discussions about stereotyping and discrimination, start with the identity chart example on the website. Students can update their identity charts using the other templates later in the year—for example, to complement activities in **Section 4: Membership and Belonging**.

PROCEDURE:

1. **Reflect on the Factors that Make Up Identity**

    - Explain to advisees that today they will be thinking about the many factors that make up their identities. Start by asking them to respond to the following question in their journals. You might get them started by first writing on the board a few factors that make up your own identity. Think generally at this point (race, age, gender, family identities, faith, etc.).

    - Then ask advisees to make a list in their journal that responds to the following prompt:
        > What factors make up your identity? Write as many as you can think of in a list.

    - Have advisees debrief with a partner, and then, on the board, generate a big list of factors that make up identity.

    - If it doesn't come up in discussion as you generate your group list, prompt students with questions that help them think about the following ideas:
        - Some aspects of our identities are consistent over our lives; others change as we gain skills and have different roles in life.
        - Some feel very central to who we are no matter where we are; others might feel more like background or depend on the situation.
        - Some identities are labels others put on us; others see us as having that identity, but we might not.

2. **Create Personal Identity Charts**

    - Explain to advisees that they will now think about the factors that make up their own identities and represent them in personal identity charts.

    - Project or share a model of your identity chart and tell the story behind a few factors to help your advisees understand how to create their charts and, more important, allow them to get to know you better as an individual and advisor.

    - Distribute the **Starburst Identity Chart** or **Inside-Outside Identity Chart** handout and give advisees time to complete it (see Advisor Notes about selecting an identity chart template). Let the group know that they will be sharing their identity charts with a small group of peers, but if they don't feel comfortable doing so, they can share one or two facets of their identity but keep their chart private.

    - After advisees have had time to create their charts, have them share the charts with a partner. Following the example of how you modeled your own identity chart, encourage advisees to share the story behind one or two of the factors on their charts. Encourage advisees to share with someone they don't know well, create the pairs yourself, or draw names from a hat so advisees are meeting new people in the group through this sharing activity. They can also add ideas to their own charts if their paired discussions spark new thinking.

3. Debrief Group Discussions

- Ask your advisees to move into a circle and share something new or interesting that they learned about a peer's identity.
- Then ask advisees to place their identity charts in their advisory folders, because they will be using them in future activities and mini-conferences.

HANDOUT

Starburst Identity Chart

Directions: Write your name in the circle. At the ends of the arrows pointing outward, write words or phrases that describe what you consider to be key aspects of your identity. At the ends of the arrows pointing inward, write labels that others might use to describe you. Add more arrows as needed.

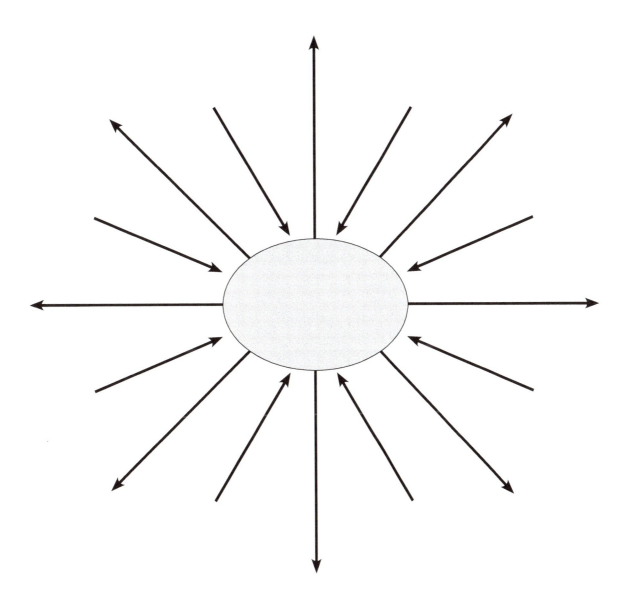

HANDOUT

Inside-Outside Identity Chart

Directions: In the first circle, write words or phrases that describe what you consider to be key aspects of your identity. In the second circle, write labels others might use to describe you. In the overlapping portion, insert any factors that fit into both categories.

What factors make up your identity?

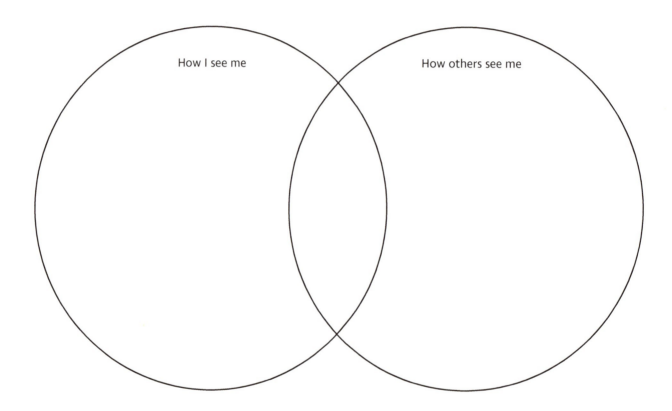

ACTIVITY **21**

Identity Chart Discussion

Purpose: Consider the various factors that make up one's identity. Create community and break down stereotypes by sharing identity charts and discussing identity with other members of the group.

> **APPROXIMATE TIME:** 30 minutes
>
> **MATERIALS:** NONE

ADVISOR NOTES:

1. **Revisit Identity Charts**

   In this activity, advisees will discuss personal identity charts created in Activity 20: My Identity Chart. They do not need to show their charts unless they feel comfortable doing so.

PROCEDURE:

1. **Add to Personal Identity Charts**

   Instruct advisees to review their identity charts from the previous meeting and add any new factors to their charts that they might have considered since the group last met.

2. **Discuss Identity Charts in Concentric Circles**

   - Explain to the group that they will be sharing aspects of their identity charts in **concentric circles** (visit facinghistory.org/advisory-media to learn about this teaching strategy). Let them know that they do not need to show their identity charts to their partners. They can just discuss the questions. Then organize your advisees into two concentric circles.

   - Choose from the following questions to read aloud and/or project. Rotate one of the circles so that advisees have new partners before introducing the next question.
     - If you could pick one part of who you are that best describes you, what would it be and why?
     - What parts of your identity are you pretty sure will be with you forever? Which parts are likely to change?
     - What parts of your identity do you choose for yourself? What parts of your identity do you think are determined by others, by society, or by chance?
     - Whose opinions and beliefs have the greatest effect on how you think about your own identity?

Section 2: Exploring Identity: Who Am I?

- What is an aspect of your identity that helps you overcome tough times? What is the story of a time when that aspect of your identity helped you overcome an obstacle?
- What dilemmas arise when others view you differently than you view yourself?
- What part of your identity is most often misunderstood by other people? How do you deal with it?
- Is that an aspect of your identity that might change in the next year or two? What might cause it to change? Or is there an aspect of your identity that you would like to change, and why?

3. **Debrief Concentric Circles**

Sit in a group circle to debrief the concentric circles activity and discuss the following questions:

- What similarities did you discover between your identity and that of someone in our group?
- What is something interesting that you learned about someone in our group?
- What are some similarities that members of our group share?
- What are some ways in which members of our group are unique?

ACTIVITY **22**

Bio-Poems

Purpose: Consider factors that shape identity, such as experiences, relationships, hopes, and interests.

APPROXIMATE TIME: 30 minutes

MATERIALS:
HANDOUT
Bio-Poem Template

ADVISOR NOTES:

1. **Model the Bio-Poem Format**

   To help your advisees get to know you, create your own bio-poem that you share with the group before they write their own. You could also provide a student example as a model, but it will be a more powerful experience for your advisees if they see you taking the same social and academic risks that you are asking of them. Visit facinghistory.org/advisory-media to access the student example and to learn more about the teaching strategy.

2. **Create Space for Advisee Voice and Choice**

   You can adapt the bio-poem format to include other categories, such as personal heroes, mantras, or beliefs. Allowing advisees to suggest categories that they think should be included in their bio-poems invites participation and ownership.

PROCEDURE:

1. **Brainstorm Ideas for a Bio-Poem in Journals**

   - Tell advisees that they will be creating short poems that explore aspects of their identities. You can share your own bio-poem now or later in the period.
   - Start by having advisees brainstorm ideas for their bio-poems in their journals. Read each category listed below and give them time to list their ideas. Let them know that they don't need to write complete sentences. The purpose of this journal response is to generate as many ideas as possible.

     1. Adjectives that you would use to describe yourself
     2. Relationships in your life (e.g., friend, brother, daughter)
     3. Things you love
     4. Important memories
     5. Things you fear
     6. Accomplishments
     7. Hopes or wishes
     8. Home (location)

2. Advisees Write Their Bio-Poems

- Pass out the handout **Bio-Poem Template**. Let your advisees know that they don't have to follow the order or categories on the template if they have other ideas. Some of your advisees will need this structure, while others will find it too restrictive.

- Give advisees time to draft their own poems, drawing ideas from their identity charts and journals.

- Time allowing or in the next advisory meeting, distribute white paper and markers so advisees can re-write and illustrate their bio-poems. If you have space, after your advisees share their work, hang the final versions of their poems on a bulletin board or wall of your advisory room.

3. Share Bio-Poems

There are many ways that advisees can share their bio-poems with the group. They can post them around the room for a **gallery walk** (visit facinghistory.org/advisory-media to learn about this teaching strategy) or read them in pairs or triads. Or you can try one of these sharing strategies:

- Advisees can read their bio-poems to the group. Each reader is assigned a "responder." After the bio-poem is read aloud, the responder comments about something he or she heard that was particularly interesting or surprising.

- Sit in a circle and ask advisees to pass their poems to their neighbor. Give time for a thorough reading. Have advisees silently write comments or questions in the margin. Every three to four minutes, have advisees pass the poems on to the next person. Repeat as time allows. At the end of the allotted time, advisees should have a poem filled with comments and questions. Be sure to remind advisees about their contract and expectations for appropriate comments.

HANDOUT

Bio-Poem Template

Directions: Use ideas from your journal to create your own bio-poem that reflects the things you value, your experiences, your interests, and your hopes and dreams. Feel free to add more categories or lines to your poem. You should make it your own!

(First name)
_____

(Adjectives that describe you)
_____
_____

Who loves
_____
_____

And who is scared
_____
_____

Who learned
_____
_____

Who hopes
_____
_____

Who lives
_____
_____

(Last name)
_____

ACTIVITY **23**

Who Is the Real You?

Purpose: Consider other aspects of individual identity and introduce the idea that an online identity might differ from a "real life" identity.

ADVISOR NOTES: None

APPROXIMATE TIME:
30 minutes

MATERIALS:
HANDOUT
Online-Search Identity Chart

VIDEO
Online vs. Offline Self:
Who Is the Real You?
(see y2u.be/SZAkZ4TzSEA)

PROCEDURE:

1. **Create a Mock Online Search Results Page**

   - Invite advisees to imagine what search results they would like to see if they did an online search for themselves.

   - Then pass out the handout **Online-Search Identity Chart** and ask advisees to complete it. You might create a model for yourself to share with your advisees before they start working on their own.

   - Then divide your advisees into groups of three and have them share their charts and discuss the following questions:

     - What does this chart reveal about your identity that your personal identity chart doesn't?

     - If you could add one more category to this online identity chart, what would you add and why?

2. **Explore Online versus Offline Identity**

   Next, play the video **Online vs. Offline Self: Who Is the Real You?** (03:10) at y2u.be/SZAkZ4TzSEA. Afterward, in small groups or as a whole group, discuss the following questions:

   - What are some of the ways that people create online identities for themselves?

   - How might an individual's online identity differ from their real identity? Why do you think these two identities might differ?

   - What do you think are some of the costs and benefits that come with our ability to "curate" online identities?

   - In the video, Chase argues that our tendency to curate our identities means we "become more brand than personality." What do you think he means by this statement? Do you agree or disagree with his observation? Why?

   - How can we continue to embrace social media while also maintaining our individual identities?

HANDOUT

Online-Search Identity Chart

Directions: Answer the questions below to brainstorm ideas for your mock online search.

What are **two websites** that might say something about who you are or connect to your identity? List and describe them below.

Sketch and label **two images** that represent you or say something about who you are.

What is **one product, object, or piece of clothing** that represents something about yourself?

What is **one place** that is important to you and connects to a part of who you are?

Is there **a video** that represents something about yourself or that you feel connected to? It could be a viral video that relates to your sense of humor, a music video, or a TV or movie clip.

What is **an important date** (besides your birthday) that is meaningful to you and that relates to who you are?

ACTIVITY **24**

Real Life vs. Online Identity

Purpose: Deepen the exploration of online versus "real life" identities by examining how the ways in which individuals present themselves on social media can emphasize some aspects of their identities while minimizing or hiding others.

> **APPROXIMATE TIME:**
> 45 minutes
>
> **MATERIALS:**
> READING
> Creating Ourselves Online and in "Real Life"
>
> Chart paper and markers

ADVISOR NOTES:

1. **Prepare for the Gallery Walk**

   Before the advisory meeting, familiarize yourself with the **Gallery Walk** and **Big Paper** strategies, which are available at facinghistory.org/advisory-media. Copy, cut out, and tape each excerpt from the reading **Creating Ourselves Online and in "Real Life"** on a separate piece of chart paper or butcher paper and post them around the room in preparation for the **Big Paper** gallery walk.

PROCEDURE:

1. **Reflect on Your Real Life versus Online Identity**

   - Explain to advisees that this activity includes excerpts from interviews with teens, conducted by the Pew Research Center, about how young people share their identities online.

   - Start by asking advisees to make a T-chart in their journals. Have them write the heading "In Real Life" in the left-hand column. Then ask them to make a list of all the labels and assumptions a total stranger might make about them based on how they look and act "in real life."

   - Next, have advisees write the heading "Social Media" in the right-hand column. Under that heading, they should list all the labels and assumptions a stranger might make about them based *only* on their social media persona.

   - Finally, give advisees two minutes to respond to the following prompt in their journals:

     > When I look at the two lists, I notice that my "real life" and "online" identities are _____.

   You might facilitate a brief discussion about this prompt or ask advisees to turn and talk with a partner.

Community Matters: A Facing History and Ourselves Approach to Advisory

2. **Explore How Advisees Represent Themselves Online**

    - If your advisees watched the video **Online vs. Offline Self: Who Is the Real You?** in Activity 23, remind them or ask them to explain how the profiles we create, the comments we make, and the posts of others that we "like" all contribute to an online identity that is often similar to—but sometimes very different from—our identity in "real life." If your advisees did not watch the short video, you might show it before the gallery walk.

    - Then invite advisees to respond in writing to the texts hanging around the room from the reading **Creating Ourselves Online and in "Real Life"** in a **gallery walk** (visit facinghistory.org/advisory-media to learn about this teaching strategy). You might have advisees respond in one or more of the following ways:

        - Read the excerpts and circle places where the speaker talks about choices he or she made about his or her online identity.

        - Draw an arrow that points to an idea that resonates, and write a brief explanation of why it does so.

        - Pose questions in reaction to the speaker's ideas.

3. **Discuss Online versus Real Identity**

    - As a group, take some time to read what everyone wrote in response to the teenagers' comments about how they represent themselves online.

    - Divide your advisees into groups of three to four and ask them to discuss the following questions:

        - What were some of the concerns that advisees raised about how their identity was expressed online?

        - How did other people's opinions of them affect what they chose to share or not share? Where would their choices fit on this one-to-ten scale?

            1 = choices based solely on personal desires and wishes

            10 = choices based entirely on what other people think

        - What advice would you give to someone who is creating their first social media profile?

        - How can the choices we make about our social media profiles and online personas influence how we see ourselves? How others see us?

READING

Creating Ourselves Online and in "Real Life"

In 2012, the Pew Research Center surveyed young people to learn about how they represented themselves online. The following are excerpts from interviews Pew conducted with teenagers.

1. **Female (age 14):** "OK, so I do post a good amount of pictures, I think. Sometimes it's a very stressful thing when it comes to your profile picture. Because one should be better than the last, but it's so hard. So . . . I will message [my friends] a ton of pictures. And be like which one should I make my profile? And then they'll help me out. And that kind of takes the pressure off me. And it's like a very big thing."

2. **Female (age 14):** "I think I wouldn't [become Facebook friends with my teachers]. Just because I'm such a different person online. I'm more free. And obviously, I care about certain things, but I'm going to post what I want. I wouldn't necessarily post anything bad that I wouldn't want them to see, but it would just be different. And I feel like in the classroom, I'm more professional [at] school. I'm not going to scream across the room oh my God, I want to dance! Or stuff like that. So I feel if they saw my Facebook they would think differently of me. And that would probably be kind of uncomfortable. So I probably would not be friends with them."

3. **Male (age 18):** "Yeah, I go to church and all, so I don't want to post certain things because I don't want the preacher looking at my Facebook. Because I go to church with her. So then if she sees me, yeah, baby, and yeah. I feel like it does affect the way you use social [media]. You have that respect for something or for a group that you're into or anything, like . . . yourself, because maybe that's who you are, but at the same time, you love that group and you never want to disrespect them. So at that point, I feel like it does affect you. Sometimes affecting you doesn't always mean negatively. It can sometime[s] be positively, you know?"

4. **Male (age 18):** "Yeah, I have some teachers who have connections that you might want to use in the future, so I feel like you always have an image to uphold. Whether I'm a person that likes to have fun and go crazy and go all out, but I don't let people see that side of me because maybe it changes the judgment on me. So you post what you want people to think of you, basically."

5. **Female (age 16):** "I deleted it [my Facebook account] when I was 15, because I think it [Facebook] was just too much for me with all the gossip and all the cliques and how it was so important to be—have so many friends—I was just like it's too stressful to have a Facebook, if that's what it has to take to stay in contact with just a little people. It was just too strong, so I just deleted it. And I've been great ever since."

6. **Female (age 16):** "And our SRO [School Resource Officer], he has information. He can see anything that we do, basically, because he's part of the police department. And so he's talked to my friends and I before. And he was like, anything you do, I can pull up. So if y'all tweet about a party, while you're there, just don't be surprised when it gets busted."[1]

---

1 Mary Madden and Amanda Lenhart, "What teens said about social media, privacy, and online identity," Pew Research Center, May 21, 2013, http://www.pewinternet.org/2013/05/21/what-teens-said-about-social-media-privacy-and-online-identity/.

ACTIVITY 25

Identity and Language

Purpose: Explore the relationship between identity and language and the decisions we make about how we choose to communicate with others.

ADVISOR NOTES: None

PROCEDURE:

1. **Reflect on the Different Languages We Use**

   - Ask advisees to respond to the following prompt in a journal reflection:

     What are the different "languages" you use when communicating with others? Consider speaking, reading, and writing for school, out of school, online, and with various audiences.

   - In pairs, small groups, or as an advisory, discuss responses to the journal prompt.

2. **Listen to a Student Spoken-Word Poem about Identity and Language**

   - Pass out the reading **Lost in Translation** and explain to the group that they will be hearing a spoken-word poem about identity and language that was written by Ruby Ibarra, a former Bay Area San Lorenzo High School and UC Davis student. She is a spoken-word poet featured in online blogs and articles from such media outlets as MTV, VH1, NPR, and BuzzFeed.

   - Play the audio **Lost in Translation** (02:53) at facinghistory.org/advisory-media. Tell advisees that as they listen, they should underline or star moments in the poem that resonate with them. Then have them choose one or two moments that they underlined or starred and write in their journals or on their handouts about why they chose them.

3. **Discuss "Lost in Translation"**

   - Have your advisees share their reflections in pairs or triads before moving into a circle for a discussion of the following questions:

     - What assumptions do people make about Ruby Ibarra based on language? What do those assumptions suggest about how they see her identity? How do these assumptions make her feel?

     - What lines or phrases resonated with you the most, and why?

     - Why do you think Ruby titled her poem "Lost in Translation"?

> **APPROXIMATE TIME:** 30 minutes
>
> **MATERIALS:**
>
> READING
> Lost in Translation
>
> AUDIO
> Lost in Translation
> (see facinghistory.org/advisory-media)

SECTION 2

4. **Create a Found Poem from "Lost in Translation"**

   - Explain the **Found Poems** strategy (visit facinghistory.org-advisory-media to learn about this teaching strategy), and then have advisees work in pairs to create a found poem from "Lost in Translation" that addresses the theme of identity and language.

   - Pairs should circle 10 to 15 words or short phrases in the poem and then arrange them in a new poem in their journals or on a piece of paper. Let them know that they can repeat their selected words and phrases, but they cannot add anything new (unless you want to allow them three "free words").

   - After pairs have drafted their poems, ask for volunteers to share with the class. Discuss any common ideas that emerge across the found poems that your group creates.

READING

Lost in Translation

Poet Ruby Ibarra is a rapper, spoken-word artist, and MPC beatmaker. Born in Tacloban, Philippines, she was introduced to rap at age five when she caught a glimpse of a Francis Magalona performance on television. At that young age, she quickly memorized his lyrics. She developed an affinity for poetry and hip-hop when her family migrated to Hayward, California, shortly thereafter. Ruby attended San Lorenzo High School and UC Davis. She released her first project, the *Lost in Translation* mixtape, in December 2012. She has been featured in such noted web-based publications as WorldStarHipHop, XXL Magazine, and MTV & VH1's blogs, as well as in several BuzzFeed and NPR pieces and in other media outlets. The following is a transcript of her spoken-word poem "Lost in Translation."

> I grew up like any other Filipino-American
>
> Immersed in frequent family gatherings with karaoke and an enormous banquet of food
>
> With titas and aunties that cover you with kisses, and the prize-winning question of . . .
>
> "Do you know how to speak Tagalog?"
>
> To which I reply with a phrase that has essentially become a verbal reflex of, "I can understand, but I can't speak it"
>
> I can understand . . .
>
> But I can't . . .
>
> Speak it.
>
> A sentence that I have longed to transform into a question to my mother
>
> Of why I was never taught of my country's native tongue
>
> So when I try to find the words to say, I'm forced to bite my tongue.
>
> Not feeling "Filipino enough" because I know I can't communicate a language that translates over a thousand years of history
>
> A language whose words have escaped the lips of battle-cry revolutions and propaganda movements
>
> A language birthed from colonization and screams of independence and political reform
>
> And though my mouth can't say it, my mouth can taste every flavor of the lumpia, lechon, and sinigang

But the aftertaste stings bittersweet as I'm left lost in translation

I can't blame my mother because I've seen her gentle face overshadowed with a crimson shade of red masked in humiliation

"Only speak English, you're in America now" she was told

If that person only knew that the English translation of her words was, "I'm glad that we're here"

And after that, she didn't have to speak a word, because right then I could understand

In this country, citizenship is obtained through assimilation

Acceptance is the American dream

And being foreign is either illegal, dangerous, or inferior

So I was taught to master English like it was a skill for survival

And so I spoke, but I couldn't understand why

Why I could speak it, yet my teachers spoke to me so slowly like I couldn't understand

Why every word that escaped my lips had to be carefully pronounced so as to mask any ethnic identity

Why playground children followed me mocking, "Ching chong, ching chong" while their parents stood at a distance with approval

Yet it was these same parents who tried to stop me from speaking a language just because they thought I was secretly mocking them

And as I grew older, language became the barrier between me and these two cultures

Separated by a wall of enunciations, grammatical rules, and accents

A wall built by past ancestors with hands drenched in brick layers of acculturation

My mouth had become far too American to grasp the Tagalog words correctly

So aunties, now when I say I can't speak it, maybe you will understand

But I'm not ashamed that I can understand, but I can't speak it

Because even some of the most powerful emotions and thoughts can't be expressed within the confines of frequencies and letters

Because after all, understanding is the essence, of communication

So though I've never learned to speak it I've always understood . . . WHY[1]

---

[1] Ruby Ibarra, "Lost in Translation (Spoken Word)," 2012. Reproduced by permission of Ruby Ibarra.

ACTIVITY **26**

Identity, Family, and Legacy

Purpose: Explore the relationship between legacy and identity by examining the extent to which we inherit or receive our identities and how the legacies of older generations can influence our identities.

APPROXIMATE TIME: 30 minutes

MATERIALS:

- **VIDEO** Condoleezza Rice's Family Matters (see facinghistory.org/advisory-media)
- **VIDEO** Deidre Prevett: American Dreams in Muskogee Nation (see facinghistory.org/advisory-media)
- **HANDOUT** Social Identity Map

ADVISOR NOTES:

Choose an *American Creed* Video Clip

There are two short video clips from the documentary film *American Creed* that you can choose from for this activity, or, time allowing, you might show both before having a circle discussion. While the activity is written for Condoleezza Rice's video clip, you can follow the same procedure and use the same questions if you choose to use Deidre Prevett's video clip instead. If you are interested in exploring American identity in greater depth using *American Creed*, visit facinghistory.org/advisory-media to access our collection of *American Creed* educator resources.

PROCEDURE:

1. **Make Connections between Components of Identity**

   - Before watching Condoleezza Rice's *American Creed* story, ask advisees to respond to the following prompt in their journals. Let them know that they will share their responses.

     - Make a list of five people and/or places that you think have helped shape who you are today.

     - Describe in detail one of these people and/or places, and explain how you think this person/place has impacted who you are today.

   - Ask advisees to share their responses in a **Think, Pair, Share** with a partner or in groups of three (visit facinghistory.org/advisory-media to learn about this teaching strategy).

2. **View and Discuss the Video**

   - Explain to the group that they will now hear from former Secretary of State Condoleezza Rice as she recalls some of her childhood memories and explains how her family legacy has influenced who she is today.

Community Matters: A Facing History and Ourselves Approach to Advisory

- Pass out the handout **Social Identity Map** and explain that advisees will be creating a social identity map for Condoleezza Rice as they watch the video. Consider pausing the video once to allow for note-taking.
- Play the video **Condoleezza Rice's Family Matters** (5:05) at facinghistory.org/advisory-media. Before asking advisees to discuss Rice's story, make sure that they understand the definition of *legacy:* something transmitted by or received from an ancestor or predecessor or from the past.
- As an advisory or in groups of three or four, share information from the handout, and then discuss Condoleezza Rice's story using the **3-2-1** strategy (visit facinghistory.org/advisory-media to learn about this teaching strategy).
    - What are three examples of how Rice's family legacy and history have influenced her identity?
    - What are two values that are important to Rice?
    - What is one idea from Rice's story that resonated with you?

3. **Make Personal Connections to Rice's Story**
    - Finally, write the following quotation on the board and move into a circle for a closing discussion of Condoleezza Rice's observation:

        "I think everyone has to come to terms at some point with your home and how it shaped you."

    - To unpack the quotation, first pass out blank copies of the **Social Identity Map** handout and have your advisees work individually to complete it. Encourage them to review their journals and other relevant materials, like their identity charts and bio-poems if they created them in an earlier advisory session. Then ask for volunteers to share one or more ideas from their maps.
    - Discuss the following questions as a group:
        - In your own words, what do you think Rice means in this quotation?
        - In what ways do you agree with, disagree with, or question Rice's ideas about coming to terms with your home?
        - How does Rice's family story and history impact how she understands herself and her world?
        - How does your own family's story and/or history impact how you understand yourself and the world?

Section 2: Exploring Identity: Who Am I?

HANDOUT

Social Identity Map

Directions: In each of the boxes, record your answers to the questions about identity. Depending on your teacher's instructions, you should answer from the perspective of yourself or the character or historical figure you are analyzing.

HOME	CULTURE & CUSTOMS
Where do you call home? What is something about yourself that you attribute to where you are from or where you call home?	What traditions or cultural practices are important to you?
What ideas and values are important to you? 	What 3–5 words best describe you? What makes you unique/different?
BELIEFS & VALUES	**ASPECTS OF IDENTITY**

ACTIVITY **27**

My Life Road Map

Purpose: Reflect on key choices that help shape one's identity and foster community through the sharing of personal stories.

APPROXIMATE TIME:
2 x 45 minutes

MATERIALS:
White paper, preferably legal size or larger

Colored markers, pens, and/or pencils

HANDOUT
Positive-Negative Line Graph (optional)

ADVISOR NOTES:

1. **Familiarize Yourself with the Life Road Maps Strategy**

   This activity is based on the **Life Road Maps** strategy, which you can learn about at facinghistory.org/advisory-media. As a variation or for advisees who need more structure, you can use the **Positive-Negative Line Graph** handout for this activity. After advisees reflect in their journals, have them choose eight to ten pivotal moments or decisions to chart on the line graph. They can determine what to plot on the y-axis. For example, they might plot the positive or negative impact the moment had on their emotions or how they rank the decision as a high or low point in their lives thus far.

2. **Pacing This Activity**

   You will probably need two advisory meetings for this activity. Advisees can brainstorm and create their maps in the first meeting and then share and discuss their maps in the second meeting. Some advisees, especially those who enjoy art and creative activities, might want to bring their maps home to finish after the first meeting. If they do so, make sure to remind them that they will need them for sharing in the next meeting. You might use the time while advisees are creating their maps for a round of mini-conferences.

PROCEDURE:

1. **Reflect on Your Life Journey**

   - Let advisees know that in this activity, they will be reflecting on significant events and choices that helped shape their identities.

   - Then either have them write a journal entry about pivotal moments or important decisions in their lives or create a timeline that represents the significant events and choices.

2. **Brainstorm "Life as Journey" Metaphors**

   Explain to the group that they will be drawing a "map" of their lives. Start by having them brainstorm things that people might encounter when they take a trip or journey, and record these ideas on the board. Items on this list might include stop signs, speed bumps, traffic lights, dead ends, detours, highways, tolls, and rest stops. Give advisees the opportunity to discuss what these items might represent when applied to the metaphor of "life as journey." For example, a dead end might represent a decision that did not yield the desired result. A green light might represent getting approval to move ahead. A rotary (roundabout) might represent a time when they had to make a choice or felt like they were going around in circles.

3. **Construct Life Road Maps**
    - Invite advisees to move into small groups, if they wish, to work on their road maps, and pass out white paper, markers, pens, and colored pencils. Remind them that the journey should represent important decisions and events that have shaped their lives. They can add details to their maps, including factors that may have influenced decisions, such as historical events, important relationships, goals, beliefs, and aspects of human behavior (fear, conformity, prejudice, etc.).
    - As they work, you might allow them to walk around the room to survey what their peers are doing. This can be a great way for advisees to generate new ideas about how to represent an individual's life as a journey.

4. **Share and Debrief**

    Share the "life road maps" in a circle discussion or as a **gallery walk** (visit facinghistory.org/advisory-media to learn about this teaching strategy). As advisees learn about their peers, ask them to pay attention to similarities and differences among these maps. Prompts you might use to guide advisees' reflections and a follow-up discussion include:
    - What factors influence the choices people make?
    - What factors help people move forward and make progress?
    - What factors set people back?
    - What is unique about this person's life, and what seems universal to the group?

HANDOUT

Positive-Negative Line Graph

Directions: Graph eight to ten high and low moments from your life. For each moment, draw a dot on the graph and write a short phrase to explain what happened. Then connect the dots with a line.[1]

1 Kelly Gallagher, *Deeper Reading: Comprehending Challenging Texts, 4–12* (Portland: Stenhouse Publishers, 2004), 98–100.

ACTIVITY **28**

Exploring Identity Final Reflection

Purpose: Review the overarching themes, questions, journal responses, and work from this section of *Community Matters* and reflect on new understanding and lingering questions.

APPROXIMATE TIME: 30 minutes

MATERIALS: NONE

ADVISOR NOTES:

1. **Create Time and Space for Reflection**

   Advisees will repeat this activity at the end of each section of *Community Matters*. Providing them with the time and space to reflect on their learning, growth, and lingering questions about the central themes from the section allows them to synthesize the material in meaningful ways before being introduced to new themes and concepts.

2. **Choose a Discussion Format**

   Before the advisory meeting, decide how you would like the group to engage in the final discussion. You might start with small groups and then move into a larger circle, or you might try the **Socratic Seminar** or **Fishbowl** teaching strategy. Visit facinghistory.org/advisory-media to learn about these teaching strategies.

PROCEDURE:

1. **Reflect on Individual Identity**

   - Tell advisees that for this reflection, they will need their journals and materials from this section. Advisees should first review their journals, handouts, and writing from this section of the advisory program and then do the following:

     - Place a star by two or three places where you arrived at a new insight or understanding of your identity, the factors that can influence identity, or another aspect of identity.

     - Place a question mark by one or two places that raise questions for you about identity or where you made note of something that you feel like you need to keep exploring in order to understand identity more fully.

   - Then ask advisees to spend some time writing a new journal entry in which they elaborate on a new understanding and/or a lingering question. If you feel like they would benefit from some structure, invite them to respond to one of the following questions:

- What new insights and understanding do you have about the theme of identity? What questions do you still have?
- I used to think _____ about identity, but now I think _____.

2. **Reflect on Advisees' Understanding of Identity in a Group Discussion**
   - In small groups and then in a circle or using the **Socratic Seminar** or **Fishbowl** teaching strategy, ask advisees to discuss their journal responses (visit facinghistory.org/advisory-media to learn about these teaching strategies).
   - You might record the questions that advisees still have on chart paper to refer to later in the year as they continue to explore identity through the lens of membership and belonging, ostracism and bullying, and civic participation.

SECTION 2

SECTION 3:
Understanding Community

ACTIVITIES

Revisiting Our Advisory Contract

What Is Community?

What Makes a Community Strong?

Crossing the Chocolate River

Human Knot

Transformers

Our Advisory Identity Chart

Advisory Jigsaw Puzzle

Understanding Community Final Reflection

SECTION 3

Purpose	Materials	Abridged Advisor Notes

29: Revisiting Our Advisory Contract — 30 min — page 120

Review, revise (as needed), and recommit to shared group norms and expectations. Draw connections between the factors that make a community strong and the norms that can help ensure it remains strong.	None	You will be prompted to revisit your advisory contract at the beginning of each section of *Community Matters* to reflect on the ways the group has been honoring its contract and where they feel they can do better. This activity also provides the opportunity to add to or revise any of the norms before moving forward with this section of the Facing History advisory program.

30: What Is Community? — 40 min — page 122

Explore the factors that make up a community and create a working definition of community.	HANDOUT: **What is Community? Anticipation Guide** Four Corners signs Index cards or slips of paper	This activity uses the Four Corners strategy (visit facinghistory.org/advisory-media to learn about this teaching strategy). Before the meeting, label the four corners of the room with signs reading "Strongly Agree," "Agree," "Disagree," and "Strongly Disagree."

31: What Makes a Community Strong? — 40 min — page 125

Reflect on the factors that make a community strong and consider the ways in which the advisory group might strengthen its sense of community.	Paper and markers	This activity opens with the exit cards from Activity 30: What Is Community?

32: Crossing the Chocolate River (Community-Building Activity) — 40 min — page 127

Foster teamwork, cooperation, problem-solving, and communication. Engage in thoughtful reflection about the decision-making process and group collaboration.	Two pieces of masking tape Paper plates, pieces of paper, or carpet squares (enough for ½ to ⅔ of the group) Empty space cleared of desks (about 20 feet)	Before the advisory meeting, clear a space for the "chocolate river" and lay down two long pieces of masking tape about 20 feet apart to designate the river banks.

33: Human Knot (Community-Building Activity) — 30 min — page 129

Foster teamwork, cooperation, problem-solving, and communication. Engage in thoughtful reflection about the decision-making process and group collaboration.	None	You can repeat this team-building activity in the middle and at the end of the year and reflect on any changes in the group's communication, strategy, or process.

34: Transformers (Community-Building Activity) — 20 min — page 131

Foster teamwork, cooperation, problem-solving, and communication. Engage in thoughtful reflection about the decision-making process and group collaboration.	None	To make the game more challenging, add a new rule that advisees must remain silent. After playing a few rounds of the game, or in a future meeting, invite your advisees to suggest ideas for shapes they can make.

Section 3: Understanding Community

Purpose	Materials	Abridged Advisor Notes
35: Our Advisory Identity Chart		40 min page 133
Connect the ideas of identity and community by considering the factors that members of the advisory community share.	**HANDOUT: Starburst Identity Chart** Chart paper and markers	If you have with extra time in this meeting or in a future meeting, you can have advisees work in groups to brainstorm a name, motto, and symbol that they feel represents their community identity.
36: Advisory Jigsaw Puzzle		45 min page 136
Discuss contributions each individual can make to the advisory community and how the advisory group can support each other.	Piece of chart paper cut into puzzle pieces (one per advisee) Pens, colored pencils, or markers, and clear tape	Before the advisory meeting, cut a piece of chart paper into pieces so there is one piece for each advisee in the group. Cut the pieces in such a way that they are unique shapes and will fit together like a puzzle when reassembled during the activity.
37: Understanding Community Final Reflection		30 min page 138
Review the overarching themes, journal responses, and discussions from this section of *Community Matters* and reflect on new understanding and lingering questions.	None	Providing advisees with the time and space to reflect on their learning, growth, and lingering questions allows them to synthesize the material in meaningful ways before being introduced to new themes and concepts.

Understanding Community

ACTIVITIES 29–37

OVERVIEW

We shape, and are shaped by, the communities to which we belong. Therefore, understanding ourselves as individuals requires thinking about the communities that influence our lives. After focusing on the factors that influence our individual identities, advisees now embark on the next stage of the Facing History scope and sequence, "We and They," by defining community and considering the factors that help make a community strong. They will see that while they are a collection of unique individuals, they are also members of a larger advisory community with shared characteristics and goals. Through journal reflections, activities, and discussions, advisees consider what unique qualities and attributes they bring to their community, what commonalities they share as a group, and how they might support one another over the course of the year. While this section focuses on the advisory community and how advisees will support each other this year, the next sections broaden the scope of the community from advisory to school and beyond.

NAVIGATING THE ACTIVITIES

All of the activities in this section focus on the theme of community.

- It is important to revisit the advisory contract periodically throughout the year in order to reassess and reaffirm group norms and expectations. Activity 29, and the first activity in each remaining section of *Community Matters*, offers ideas for how to reflect on and revise the contract.

- Activities 30–31 are important because they help advisees explore the many factors that help make a community strong, as well as those factors that can weaken a community.

- Activities 32–34 are community-building games. You can do all three, or you might pick one or two for now and do the third later in the year, maybe after a school break to reaffirm the group's commitment to each other and the advisory group.

- Activities 36–37 are important because they invite advisees to reflect on their roles in the advisory community and the contributions they can make to strengthen it.

ACTIVITY **29**

Revisiting Our Advisory Contract

Purpose: Review, revise (as needed), and recommit to shared group norms and expectations. Draw connections between the factors that make a community strong and the norms that can help ensure it remains strong.

APPROXIMATE TIME: 30 minutes

MATERIALS: NONE

ADVISOR NOTES:

Reaffirm Advisory Norms

You will be prompted to revisit your advisory contract at the beginning of each section of *Community Matters* to reflect on the ways the group has been honoring its contract and where they feel they can do better. This activity also provides the opportunity to add to or revise any of the norms before moving forward with this section of the Facing History advisory program.

PROCEDURE:

1. **Reflect Individually in Journals about Your Advisory Contract**
   - Start by reading aloud your advisory contract, perhaps using the **Wraparound** strategy (visit facinghistory.org/advisory-media to learn about this teaching strategy).
   - Then ask advisees to respond to the following questions in their journals, citing specific examples from past meetings to support their thinking. Tell advisees that they will be sharing their responses in small groups.
     - What are examples from past advisory meetings where we did a great job of honoring one or more norms from our contract? What helped us do a great job?
     - What are examples from past advisory meetings were we struggled to uphold one or more norms on our contract? Why do you think we struggled? What might we do differently in the future to honor that norm?
     - What do you think, if anything, needs to be revised (reworded, added, deleted), and why?

2. **Discuss and Revise the Advisory Contract**
   - Divide the advisees into small groups and have them discuss the three journal questions one at a time. Then ask them to share highlights from their discussion, making a list on the board in three columns of their main ideas.

- Depending on their input, decide as a group whether or not your advisory contract needs to be revised, and make the changes as needed. You might make changes to the original contract or create a new one.
- Then have everyone, including the advisor, sign the contract again.

3. **Commit to a Norm**
    - Finally, ask each advisee to complete the following sentence starter in their journals. Revise the sentence starter as needed to fit what you think your group needs at this time:

        For the next month, I am going to work on _____ (choose a norm from the advisory contract). One way that I will work on it is by . . .

    - Then have each advisee share their completed sentence starter in a **Wraparound**.

ACTIVITY **30**

What Is Community?

Purpose: Explore the factors that make up a community and create a working definition of community.

APPROXIMATE TIME: 45 minutes

MATERIALS:
- **HANDOUT** **What Is Community? Anticipation Guide**
- Index cards or slips of paper

ADVISOR NOTES:

1. **Prepare for Four Corners**

   This activity uses the **Four Corners** strategy, which you can learn about at facinghistory.org/advisory-media. Before the meeting, label the four corners of the room with signs reading "Strongly Agree," "Agree," "Disagree," and "Strongly Disagree."

2. **Revisit Exit Cards in Future Meetings**

   You will have the option to use this activity's final **exit cards** as an opening for Activity 31: What Makes a Community Strong? If you plan to do so, make sure to collect the exit cards at the end of this meeting. Visit facinghistory.org/advisory-media to learn about the Exit Cards teaching strategy.

PROCEDURE:

1. **Reflect in Journals on the Idea of Community**
   - Let advisees know that in this section of *Community Matters*, they will be exploring the topic of community.
   - In a quick journal response, ask advisees to respond to the following prompt:

     What is an example of a community that you belong to? What makes you feel a part of that community?
   - Ask advisees to share their ideas in pairs or triads.

2. **Discuss What a Community Is and Is Not**
   - Pass out the handout **What Is Community? Anticipation Guide** and ask advisees to work individually to respond to each statement.
   - Then explain the **Four Corners** strategy and choose a few of the prompts from the anticipation guide to discuss. You might begin by asking advisees which prompts they feel passionate about discussing together.

3. **Define *Community* on Exit Cards**

    - Pass out one index card (or slip of paper) to each advisee and ask them to finish two sentence starters as an **exit card**. Let them know that you will be sharing some of their ideas in the next meeting, but you will not be identifying the authors by name.

        - A strong community is . . .

        - One question that I have about *community* is . . .

    - Collect the exit cards as advisees leave the room.

HANDOUT

What Is Community? Anticipation Guide

Directions: Read the statement in the left column. Decide if you strongly agree (SA), agree (A), disagree (D), or strongly disagree (SD) with the statement. Circle your response.

Statement	Your opinion
1. Communities are a kind of group. But not all groups are communities.	SA A D SD
2. Communities are groups of people who come together for a common purpose—to achieve certain goals and/or to share similar interests.	SA A D SD
3. Communities are made up of people who are more or less the same.	SA A D SD
4. Communities have certain rules for membership; not just anyone can belong.	SA A D SD
5. It is unfair for a community to exclude someone from membership.	SA A D SD
6. People who occupy the same space, such as the same neighborhood or school, all belong to the same community.	SA A D SD
7. For a community to be strong, all members must like each other.	SA A D SD
8. For a community to be strong, all members must respect each other.	SA A D SD
9. All people want to belong to a community.	SA A D SD
10. Our advisory is a community.	SA A D SD

ACTIVITY **31**

What Makes a Community Strong?

Purpose: Reflect on the factors that make a community strong and consider the ways in which the advisory group might strengthen its sense of community.

APPROXIMATE TIME: 40 minutes

MATERIALS: Paper and markers

ADVISOR NOTES:

1. Revisit What Is Community? Exit Cards

This activity opens with the exit cards from Activity 30. If your group did not do Activity 30, you might pose the following question in your opening routine: What makes a community strong?

PROCEDURE:

1. Share Exit Card Responses from Activity 30: What Is Community?

Start the meeting in a circle by reading the exit card responses from the last meeting. Ask advisees to listen for commonalities as well as unique ideas. Do not include their names unless you asked them for permission before the advisory meeting.

2. Discuss the Qualities of a Strong Community in Small Groups

- Divide the advisory into groups of three or four and give each group a piece of paper and markers. Ask them to discuss the following questions and record their ideas on the paper in a T-chart:
    - Based on what you heard from the exit cards and your own ideas, what are the factors that make a community strong?
    - What are the factors that can weaken a community?
- Then ask each group to share their posters with the advisory group.

3. Discuss the Idea of Your Advisory as a Community

Rearrange the group into a circle and discuss the following two questions together. Try to include everyone's voice in the discussion.

- Looking at the lists you created and presented, what qualities of a strong community does our advisory currently have?
- What factors get in the way of our advisory being the strongest community it can be? How might we work together to overcome these factors?

4. **Commit to Improving the Advisory Community**
    - Ask each advisee to complete the following sentence starter in their journal.

        One small step I can take to help strengthen our advisory is . . .

    - Have everyone, including the advisor, share their sentences in a final **Wraparound** (visit facinghistory.org/advisory-media to learn about this teaching strategy).

ACTIVITY **32**

Crossing the Chocolate River
(Community-Building Activity)

Purpose: Foster teamwork, cooperation, problem-solving, and communication. Engage in thoughtful reflection about the decision-making process and group collaboration.

> **APPROXIMATE TIME:**
> 40 minutes
>
> **MATERIALS:**
> Two long pieces of masking tape
>
> Paper plates, legal-size pieces of paper, or carpet squares (enough for half the number of advisees in the group) to represent the marshmallows
>
> Large empty space clear of tables, desks, and chairs

ADVISOR NOTES:

1. Set Aside Time for Reflection

The amount of time this activity takes depends, in part, on the size of your advisory group and whether or not your advisees have played this game before. You might set a time limit, such as 15 minutes, at the outset of the activity or let the group work on the task for a longer period of time as needed. It is important that you set aside plenty of time for the group to reflect on their process and participation. This reflection is as important as the activity itself.

2. Know Your Advisees

If you have advisees with limited mobility who might struggle with the task, you can modify the game by using bigger "marshmallows" or distributing extra marshmallows to the group. Or you might allow part of the foot, such as the heel, to touch the river.

3. Prepare the Chocolate River

Before the advisory meeting, clear a space for the "chocolate river" and lay down two long pieces of masking tape about 20 feet apart to designate the river banks.

PROCEDURE:

1. Explain the Rules for "Crossing the Chocolate River"

- Tell your advisory group that they have spent a wonderful day at a chocolate factory. Unfortunately, prior to their departure, one of the chocolate vats sprung a leak and created a deep river of chocolate between the factory and their bus that they must cross together in order to get home. Luckily, the factory also produces big, fluffy, floating marshmallows and happens to have some extras on hand that the group can use to help cross the river.

- Have the group stand behind one of the "river banks" and give them their "marshmallows." You should distribute enough marshmallows for about half of the group (so if your advisory has 15 students, distribute 8 marshmallows).

- Explain the rules of the game:
  - The goal is to get everyone in the group across the chocolate river. They must cross using the marshmallows. They cannot swim or place a hand, foot, or body part in the river because the current is too strong and the chocolate has the same properties as quicksand.
  - Because the current is swift, each marshmallow touching the river must be anchored by at least one advisee's hand, foot, or body part at all times. Any marshmallows that are not anchored by a hand, foot, or body part will be swept away (taken by you) immediately. Multiple advisees can step on or place their hands on the same marshmallow at the same time.
  - If anyone touches or falls into the chocolate river, the whole group needs to start again. They will not get back any marshmallows that have been swept away by the current.
  - The group succeeds when it gets everyone to the bus on the other side of the river, which means that every advisee crosses the chocolate river successfully.
  - You might place a time cap on the activity, such as 15 minutes. It is important that you leave enough time for the group to reflect on their process in a circle discussion.

2. **Debrief the Activity**

   Sit in a circle to discuss a selection of the following questions about the activity. The final two questions are important because they provide the opportunity for advisees to reflect on their advisory contract and the theme of community.
   - How did you decide on a strategy get the group across the river? Was everyone involved in the decision-making process, or were decisions about strategy made by a few people? How did you feel during this time?
   - How did the group communicate during the challenge? In what ways was communication effective? What could you have done as a group and as individuals to make it more effective?
   - What observations did you make about how the group worked together? What are you proud of in terms of group collaboration and cooperation? What might you have done as individuals and as a group to improve collaboration and cooperation?
   - Did you achieve the goal of getting the whole group across the chocolate river? If so, what factors contributed to you attaining this goal? If not, what factors prevented you from attaining this goal?
   - Did the group honor our advisory contract? If so, what are examples of moments during the game when one or more norms was honored? If not, which norms were not honored, and what was the outcome? What could you have done differently to honor these norms?
   - What qualities of a strong community did you observe in the group during the activity? What factors that can weaken a community did you observe during the activity?

ACTIVITY **33**

Human Knot (Community-Building Activity)

Purpose: Foster teamwork, cooperation, problem-solving, and communication. Engage in thoughtful reflection about the decision-making process and group collaboration.

> **APPROXIMATE TIME:** 30 minutes
>
> **MATERIALS:** NONE

ADVISOR NOTES:

1. Set Aside Time for Reflection

The amount of time this activity takes depends, in part, on the size of your advisory group and whether or not your advisees have played this game before. You might set a time limit, such as 15 minutes, at the outset of the activity or let the group work on the task for a longer period of time as needed. It is important that you set aside plenty of time for the group to reflect on their process and participation. This reflection is as important as the activity itself.

2. Know Your Advisees

This activity may be difficult for advisees with limited mobility because it can involve crouching, stepping through tight spaces, and standing in awkward positions. If this is the case, you might need to choose one of the other community-building games in this section so everyone in the group can participate and feels comfortable and safe doing so.

3. Revisit the Human Knot

You can repeat this team-building activity in the middle and at the end of the year and reflect on any changes in the group's communication, strategy, or process.

PROCEDURE:

1. Set Up and Create the Human Knot

- After clearing a space in the center of the room, ask advisees to stand in a tight circle. Then have them place their right hand into the center of the circle and take the hand of one of their peers. They should not take the hand of the person next to them on either side. Then repeat with the left hand, making sure that they are grasping the hand of a different advisee.

- Then let the advisees know that they need to untangle the knot so they are standing in a big circle. They may not release and regrasp hands at any point during the activity.

- You might place a time cap on the activity, such as 15 minutes. It is important that you leave enough time for the group to reflect on their process in a circle discussion.

2. Debrief the Human Knot

Sit in a circle to discuss a selection of the following questions about the game. The final two questions are important because they provide the opportunity for advisees to reflect on their advisory contract and the theme of community.

- How did you decide on a strategy to untangle the knot? Was everyone involved in the decision-making process, or were decisions about strategy made by a few people? How did you feel during this time?

- How did the group communicate during the challenge? In what ways was communication effective? What could you have done as a group and as individuals to make it more effective?

- What observations did you make about how the group worked together? What are you proud of in terms of group collaboration and cooperation? What might you have done as individuals and as a group to improve collaboration and cooperation?

- Did you achieve the goal of untangling the knot and forming a circle? If so, what factors contributed to you attaining this goal? If not, what factors prevented you from attaining this goal?

- Did the group honor our advisory contract? If so, what are examples of moments during the human knot activity when one or more norms was honored? If not, which norms were not honored, and what was the outcome? What could you have done differently to honor these norms?

- What qualities of a strong community did you observe in the group during the activity? What factors that can weaken a community did you observe during the activity?

ACTIVITY **34**

Transformers (Community-Building Activity)

Purpose: Foster teamwork, cooperation, problem-solving, and communication. Engage in thoughtful reflection about the decision-making process and group collaboration.

APPROXIMATE TIME: 30 minutes

MATERIALS: NONE

ADVISOR NOTES:

1. **Up the Challenge**

   To make the game more challenging, add a new rule that advisees must remain silent.

2. **Make Space for Advisee Voice and Choice**

   In a future advisory meeting when you think the group would benefit from a kinesthetic community-building activity, invite your advisees to suggest ideas for shapes they can make. Pass out one or more index cards or slips of paper to each advisee, and have them write one idea on each card. Then pull them from a hat or box and play the game. Remember to save time to debrief the activity in a circle discussion.

PROCEDURE:

1. **Set Up, Explain, and Play Transformers**
   - After clearing a space in the center of the room, ask advisees to stand together there. Tell them that you will say the name of a shape or object, and they need to create the shape with their bodies. Every advisee must be part of the final shape, and they cannot use any outside props.
   - Form the shape of . . .
     - The letter H
     - An airplane
     - A whale
     - A zipper in motion that is zipping and unzipping
     - A cannonball shooting out of a cannon
     - A door opening and closing

2. Debrief Transformers

Sit in a circle to discuss a selection of the following questions about the game. The final two questions are important because they provide the opportunity for advisees to reflect on their advisory contract and the theme of community.

- How did you decide on a strategy to transform into the shape? Was everyone involved in the decision-making process, or were decisions about strategy made by a few people? How did you feel during this time?

- How did the group communicate during the challenge? In what ways was communication effective? What could you have done as a group and as individuals to make it more effective?

- What observations did you make about how the group worked together? What are you proud of in terms of group collaboration and cooperation? What might you have done as individuals and as a group to improve collaboration and cooperation?

- Did you achieve the goal of creating each shape? If so, what factors contributed to you attaining this goal? If not, what factors prevented you from attaining this goal?

- Did the group honor its advisory contract? If so, what are examples of moments during the transformation when one or more norms was honored? If not, which norms were not honored, and what was the outcome? What could you have done differently to honor these norms?

- What qualities of a strong community did you observe in the group during the activity? What factors that can weaken a community did you observe during the activity?

ACTIVITY **35**

Our Advisory Identity Chart

Purpose: Connect the ideas of identity and community by considering the factors that members of the advisory community share.

> **APPROXIMATE TIME:**
> 40 minutes
>
> **MATERIALS:**
> HANDOUT
> Starburst Identity Chart
>
> Chart paper and markers

ADVISOR NOTES:

1. **Create an Advisory Name, Motto, and Symbol**

   If you have extra time in this meeting or in a future meeting, you can have advisees work in groups to brainstorm a name, motto, and symbol that they feel represents their advisory group's identity. Each group can record its ideas on chart paper, and the advisory can vote or discuss which ones they think best represent them. You can then post the name, motto, and symbol alongside the advisory contract and community identity chart.

PROCEDURE:

1. **Introduce and Discuss the Idea of Community Identity**

   - Start by reminding the group that in an earlier advisory meeting, they created personal identity charts that reflected all of the factors that make up their identities—both those that they choose for themselves and those that are chosen for them. Then let them know that in this meeting, they will be considering the factors that make up a community's identity.

   - Ask advisees to move into small groups, and then ask them to discuss the following questions:
     - Where does a community's identity come from?
     - How can individuals with different identities come together to form a community identity? What might make this process challenging?

   - Ask each group to share their ideas with the larger advisory.

2. **Create an Advisory Identity Chart**

   - Explain to the groups that they will now think about the identity of their advisory community. They will first make an advisory identity chart using the Starburst Identity Chart template, and then the whole advisory will collaborate to create a big identity chart on a piece of chart paper to post in the room along with their advisory contract.

   - Pass out one **Starburst Identity Chart** handout to each group and instruct them to write "Our Advisory" in center. Then have them brainstorm words and phrases to add to the chart. If they seem to be struggling, you might prompt them with one or more of the following questions:

- What do members of the advisory have in common?
- What similarities have you noticed in our advisory discussions so far this year?
- To what communities do members of our advisory group belong?
- What interests do advisees in the group share?
- What labels or assumptions might other communities, like the school community or local community, make about the group?

- After groups have had time to work on their advisory identity charts, have each one present its ideas. Then, on a piece of chart paper, create an advisory identity chart together. You can invite one or more advisees to do the writing and help facilitate the discussion.
- Post the chart in the room to reference and possibly add to in future meetings.

HANDOUT

Starburst Identity Chart

Directions: Write "Our Advisory" in the circle. At the ends of the arrows pointing outward, write words or phrases that describe what you consider to be key aspects of your advisory's collective identity. At the ends of the arrows pointing inward, write labels others might use to describe your advisory. Add more arrows as needed.

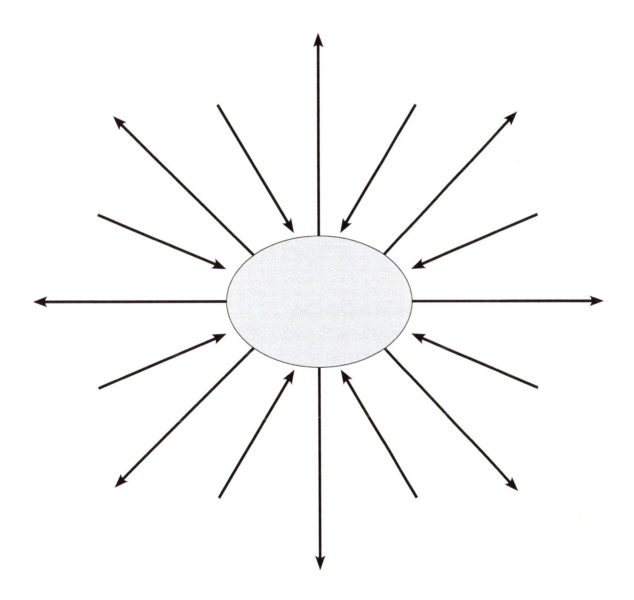

ACTIVITY **36**

Advisory Jigsaw Puzzle

Purpose: Discuss contributions each individual can make to the advisory community and how the advisory group can support each other.

> **APPROXIMATE TIME:** 45 minutes
>
> **MATERIALS:**
> Chart paper cut into jigsaw pieces
>
> Markers, pens, colored paper, and clear tape

ADVISOR NOTES:

1. **Prepare the Jigsaw Puzzle Pieces**

   Before the advisory meeting, cut a piece of chart paper into puzzle-shaped pieces so there is one piece for each advisee in the group. You should also cut a piece for yourself to model. Cut the pieces in such a way that they are unique shapes and will fit together like a puzzle when reassembled during the activity (i.e., don't make them all squares). *Because your advisees will reassemble the pieces during the meeting, it is important that after cutting, you reassemble the puzzle and mark the top side of each piece with a small X.* That way, when your advisees put the puzzle together, they all have their individual pieces oriented correctly.

2. **Adapt the Activity for a Large Advisory Group**

   For large advisory groups, you might need two pieces of chart paper.

PROCEDURE:

1. **Reflect on Your Contribution to the Advisory**

   Start by asking advisees to reflect on the following questions in their journals. Let them know that they will be sharing their responses with the group.

   - What do you share in common with one or more of your peers in our advisory?
   - What about you is unique?
   - What can you bring to our advisory that will help make it a strong community this year?
   - How can the group help you this year?

2. **Create Puzzle Pieces**

   - Then pass out one puzzle piece to each advisee, as well as the markers, pens, and colored pencils.
   - If you made your own puzzle piece, use it to help model the following instructions. Tell advisees that the side of their piece with the small *X* is the top. On it, they should write their name, what makes them unique, and what they can bring to

Community Matters: A Facing History and Ourselves Approach to Advisory

the advisory that will help make it strong. On the back, they should write how the group can help them this year. Advisees might want to get creative by outlining their pieces with marker or by including some artwork.

3. **Share by Assembling the Puzzle**
    - Sit in a circle around a table or on the floor. Have one advisee share what they wrote on both sides of their puzzle piece. Then have them place the piece on the table or floor. Others can ask questions to learn more about their peer. Then someone who thinks their piece might fit with the first one should volunteer to go next until the group has assembled the puzzle.
    - Tape the pieces together and, if you have space, hang it on the wall after the meeting alongside your advisory contract.
    - Reflect on the activity in a closing circle discussion:
        - What did you learn about each other today that you didn't already know?
        - In what ways does the puzzle represent our advisory community?

ACTIVITY **37**

Understanding Community Final Reflection

Purpose: Review the overarching themes, journal responses, and discussions from this section of *Community Matters* and reflect on new understanding and lingering questions.

APPROXIMATE TIME: 30 minutes

MATERIALS: NONE

ADVISOR NOTES:

1. **Set Aside Time and Space for Reflection**

   Advisees will repeat this activity at the end of each section of *Community Matters*. Providing them with the time and space to reflect on their learning, growth, and lingering questions about the central themes from the section allows them to synthesize the material in meaningful ways before being introduced to new themes and concepts.

2. **Choose a Discussion Format**

   Before the advisory meeting, decide—or invite your advisees to help you decide—how you would like the group to engage in the final discussion. You might start with small groups and then move into a larger circle, or you might try the **Socratic Seminar** or **Fishbowl** teaching strategy. Visit facinghistory.org/advisory-media to learn about these teaching strategies.

PROCEDURE

1. **Reflect on the Idea of Community**

   Tell advisees that for this reflection, they will need their journals and materials from the section. Advisees will first review their journals, handouts, and writing from this section of the advisory program and then respond to the following prompts.

   - Place a star by two or three places where you arrived at a new insight or understanding of community, the factors that can strengthen or weaken communities, or another idea about community.

   - Place a question mark by one or two places that raise questions for you about community or where you made note of something that you feel like you need to keep exploring in order to understand community more fully.

   - Then ask advisees to spend some time writing a new journal entry in which they elaborate on a new understanding or a lingering question. If you feel like they would benefit from some structure, invite them to respond to one of the following questions. Let them know that they will be discussing their ideas with the advisory group.

- What new insights and understanding do you have about the theme of community? What questions do you still have?
- I used to think _____ about community, but now I think _____.

2. **Reflect on Advisees' Understanding of Community in a Group Discussion**

   - In small groups and then in a circle or using the **Socratic Seminar** or **Fishbowl** teaching strategy, ask advisees to discuss their journal responses.
   - You might record the questions they still have on chart paper to refer to later in the year as they continue to explore community through the lens of membership and belonging, ostracism and bullying, and community participation.

SECTION 3

SECTION 4:

Membership and Belonging: Who Are "We"? Who Are "They"?

ACTIVITIES

Revisiting Our Advisory Contract

The Sneetches

What Is "Normal"?

Gaining Perspective on Perspectives

Analyzing Assumptions

I Am Not a Label

Defining Key Concepts

Encountering and Countering Stereotypes

What Is Your Perception?

The Bystander Effect

Responding to Injustice

"In" Groups and "Out" Groups

Choices and Consequences

Speaking Up against Injustice

Membership and Belonging Final Reflection

Purpose	Materials	Abridged Advisor Notes
38: Revisiting Our Advisory Contract — 30 min — page 147		
Remind the group of its shared expectations, revise expectations as needed, and set the tone for difficult conversations. Draw connections between the factors that make a strong community and the norms that can help ensure it remains strong.	Advisory contract	You will be prompted to revisit your advisory contract at the beginning of each section of *Community Matters* to reflect on the ways the group has been honoring its contract and where they feel they can do better. This activity also provides the opportunity to add to or revise any of the norms and expectations before moving forward with this section of the Facing History advisory program.
39: The Sneetches — 30 min — page 149		
Identify ways in which communities define membership, and consider how membership in a particular group can influence how people view those outside the group.	*The Sneetches* (borrow from library or have school purchase copies for library; you can also find print and animated versions of the story online) HANDOUT: *The Sneetches* Discussion Questions	If you do not have access to *The Sneetches*, Activity 40: What Is "Normal"? also introduces the theme of membership and belonging through an exploration of how people learn what is considered "normal" and "beautiful" in society.
40: What Is "Normal"? — 30 min — page 152		
Identify ways in which communities define membership, and consider how membership in a particular group can influence how people view those outside the group. Examine how people learn what is considered "normal" and "beautiful" in society.	READING: "Eye of the Beholder" Script Butcher paper (or long whiteboard) and markers	This activity can be used instead of *The Sneetches* or as a follow-up activity if you want to spend two days exploring the ways in which communities define membership and the benefits and privileges that can come with belonging. You may prefer to show students the *Twilight Zone* episode "Eye of the Beholder" rather than read the synopsis. This episode is available to borrow as a DVD from Facing History's library.
41: Gaining Perspective on Perspectives — 30 min — page 157		
Consider how membership in a particular group can influence how people view those outside of that group, and identify examples of "we" and "they" distinctions in our community, country, and world.	READING: "We and They" HANDOUT: Talking about "We and They"	This activity is designed to follow Activity 39: The Sneetches and/or Activity 40: What Is "Normal"? If you did not do either activity, adjust the final discussion questions.
42: Analyzing Assumptions — 30 min — page 162		
Examine how the assumptions we make about people and groups can impact how we choose to react to and interact with others.	IMAGE: Street Calculus HANDOUT: My Street Calculus	Activities 42–45 work well together, so, if possible, try to use them in consecutive advisory meetings.
43: I Am Not a Label — 40 min — page 166		
Explore the ways in which society and others can influence our identities and how accepting the labels that others impose on us can impact our perception and understanding of ourselves and others.	HANDOUT: I Am Not a Label Discussion Questions HANDOUT: Don't Misunderstand Me!	Activities 42–45 work well together, so, if possible, try to use them in consecutive advisory meetings.

Purpose	Materials	Abridged Advisor Notes

44: Defining Key Concepts — 40 min — page 170

Define and discuss the concepts of stereotyping, prejudice, and discrimination.	**HANDOUT:** Defining Stereotype, Prejudice, and Discrimination	Activities 42–45 work well together, so, if possible, try to use them in consecutive advisory meetings. Before the advisory meeting, take some time to read the Concept Maps teaching strategy at facinghistory.org/advisory-media.

45: Encountering and Countering Stereotypes — 40 min — page 174

Explore how assumptions and labels can lead to stereotyping and prejudice, and how they can impact how we think about ourselves.	**READING:** Still Me Inside **HANDOUT:** Still Me Inside Discussion Questions	Activities 42–45 work well together, so, if possible, try to use them in consecutive advisory meetings.

46: What Is Your Perception? — 30 min — page 179

Explore through a Facing History student's spoken-word poem how stereotyping and prejudice can influence our actions and lead to discrimination.	**VIDEO:** Jonathan Lykes Performs "Perception" (see facinghistory.org/advisory-media) **READING:** "Perception" Transcript	You can find additional resources for teaching and creating spoken-word poetry on the websites of Poetry Out Loud, Brave New Voices (an initiative of Youth Speaks), and The Poetry Society.

47: The Bystander Effect — 30 min — page 182

Discuss why people respond in different ways when they witness an injustice, something they know is wrong, or something that seems wrong.	**VIDEO:** The Bystander Effect (see y2u.be/OSsPfbup0ac)	This activity is designed to be paired with Activity 48 in the same advisory meeting or in consecutive meetings.

48: Responding to Injustice — 30 min — page 184

Develop vocabulary for discussing the range of responses in the face of unfairness, exclusion, discrimination, and injustice.	**HANDOUT:** The Range of Human Behavior Vocabulary Terms	This activity builds on the themes and vocabulary introduced in Activity 47. Advisees will revisit the terms *perpetrator*, *victim/target*, *bystander*, *rescuer*, and *upstander* in upcoming activities in *Community Matters*.

49: "In" Groups and "Out" Groups — 2 x 30 min — page 187

Discuss the desire to belong, the tendency for students to divide into "in" and "out" groups at school, and how this desire impacts the choices they make in the face of exclusion or injustice.	**READING:** The "In" Group **VIDEO:** The "In" Group (see facinghistory.org/advisory-media) **HANDOUT:** The "In" Group Discussion Questions Signs for Barometer Chart paper and markers	Before the start of the activity, hang two signs at opposite ends of the classroom that say "Strongly Agree" and "Strongly Disagree." The reading The "In" Group is divided into two parts. It is important that advisees do not read ahead to see what happens so they can participate in the paired discussion about Shalen's choices.

Purpose	Materials	Abridged Advisor Notes
50: Choices and Consequences		30 min — page 194
Reflect on the relationship between having the language to convey what you feel and the challenge of speaking out against injustice. Compare and contrast multiple texts to examine the bystander effect and the range of responses in the face of injustice.	HANDOUT: **The Silent Pact**	The reading is divided into two parts so advisees can discuss the first half of the story before learning the outcome. If you collect exit cards at the end of the meeting, you can check for understanding to see where advisees are making connections between the advisory content and their own lives and get a sense of their questions.
51: Speaking Up against Injustice		30 min — page 198
Analyze a spoken-word presentation about the consequences of silence in the face of unfairness and injustice and the power of choosing to speak up instead.	VIDEO: **The Danger of Silence** (see facinghistory.org/advisory-media) READING: **"The Danger of Silence" Transcript**	If your advisees submitted exit cards at the end of Activity 50, you can incorporate them into your opening routine. You might also use the journal response to Martin Luther King's quotation for a "quotation of the day" opening routine rather than the journal reflection.
52: Membership and Belonging Final Reflection		30 min — page 202
Review materials from this section of the advisory program and reflect on new understanding and questions.	Chart paper with Big Paper questions and markers Slips of paper with advisees' names	Providing advisees with the time and space to reflect on their learning, growth, and lingering questions from the section allows them to synthesize the material in meaningful ways before being introduced to new themes and concepts. Before the advisory meeting, write or print and tape the Big Paper questions on a piece of chart paper.

Membership and Belonging: Who Are "We"? Who Are "They"?

ACTIVITIES 38–52

OVERVIEW

In the first three sections of *Community Matters*, advisees examined the relationship between identity and community and learned that, like individuals, groups have identities that can impact how they perceive themselves and how others perceive them. As advisees delve deeper into their exploration of "We and They," they will now consider how the ways in which a group, even a group of strangers, defines itself can determine who belongs and who doesn't, and who is entitled to its benefits and who is not. While sometimes the consequences of being excluded feel small and insignificant, at other times they can feel and be substantial. Advisees also examine some of the ways we use labels to identify each other and how these labels affect how others think about us, the roles we play and the decisions we make when faced with an injustice, and, ultimately, how we come to view ourselves.

NAVIGATING THE ACTIVITIES

To prepare for this section's activities, it is important that advisees reaffirm their contract and commitment to fostering a safe and inclusive space that encourages sharing and risk-taking.

- Activities 39–40 invite advisees to question the idea of what is "normal." You might include one or both activities, depending on how deeply you want to explore this topic.

- Activities 42–44 and 47–48 are foundational to *Community Matters* and a Facing History approach and should not be skipped. They help advisees develop the vocabulary they need to engage in discussions about stereotyping, prejudice, inclusion and exclusion, and the roles people choose to play in the face of injustice.

- The texts in Activities 45–46 and 49–50 reinforce the themes listed in the previous bullet point and provide advisees with valuable opportunities to connect the content to their own lives. Choose between two or three activities if you don't have time for all four.

- Activity 51 ties together the ideas presented in this section of *Community Matters* with a compelling spoken-word presentation that considers the consequences of remaining silent and the power that comes with having the courage to speak up.

ACTIVITY **38**

Revisiting Our Advisory Contract

Purpose: Remind the group of its shared expectations, revise expectations as needed, and set the tone for difficult conversations. Draw connections between the factors that make a strong community and the norms that can help ensure it remains strong.

APPROXIMATE TIME: 30 minutes

MATERIALS: NONE

ADVISOR NOTES:

Reaffirm Advisory Norms

You will be prompted to revisit your advisory contract at the beginning of each section of *Community Matters* to reflect on the ways the group has been honoring its contract and where they feel they can do better. This activity also provides the opportunity to add to or revise any of the norms and expectations before moving forward with this section of the Facing History advisory program.

PROCEDURE:

1. **Reflect Individually in Journals about Your Advisory Contract**
   - Start by reading aloud your advisory contract, perhaps using the **Wraparound** strategy (visit facinghistory.org/advisory-media to learn about this teaching strategy).
   - Then ask advisees to respond to the following questions in their journals, citing specific examples from past meetings to support their thinking. Tell them that they will be sharing their responses in small groups.
     - What are examples from past advisory meetings where we did a great job of honoring one or more norms on our contract? What helped us do a great job?
     - What are examples from past advisory meetings were we struggled to uphold one or more norms on our contract? Why do you think we struggled? What might we do differently in the future to honor that norm?
     - What do you think, if anything, needs to be revised (reworded, added, deleted), and why?

2. **Discuss and Revise the Advisory Contract**
   - Divide the advisees into small groups and have them discuss the three journal questions one at a time. Then ask them to share highlights from their discussion, making a list on the board in three columns of their main ideas.

- Depending on their input, decide as a group whether or not your advisory contract needs to be revised, and make the changes as needed. You might make changes on the original contract or create a new one.
- Then have everyone, including the advisor, sign the contract again.

3. **Commit to a Norm as a Closing Activity**
    - Conclude the meeting by asking each advisee to complete the following sentence starter in their journals. Revise the sentence starter as needed to fit what you think your group needs at this time:

        For the next month, I am going to work on _____ (choose a norm from the advisory contract). One way that I will work on it is by . . .

    - Then have each advisee share their completed sentence starter in a **Wraparound**.

ACTIVITY **39**

The Sneetches

Purpose: Identify ways in which communities define membership, and consider how membership in a particular group can influence how people view those outside the group.

APPROXIMATE TIME:
30 minutes

MATERIALS:
The Sneetches by Dr. Seuss (see Advisor Notes)

 HANDOUT
The Sneetches Discussion Questions

ADVISOR NOTES:

1. **Borrow *The Sneetches***

   You can borrow *The Sneetches* by Dr. Seuss from your local library if your school does not have copies. You can also find print and animated versions of the story online.

2. **Prepare for the Barometer**

   Before advisory, familiarize yourself with the **Barometer** teaching strategy, which is available at facinghistory.org/advisory-media. Hang two signs at opposite ends of the room that say "Strongly Agree" and "Strongly Disagree."

3. **Substitute "Eye of the Beholder" for *The Sneetches***

   If you do not have access to *The Sneetches*, the reading "Eye of the Beholder" in Activity 40: What Is "Normal"? also introduces the theme of membership and belonging through an exploration of how people learn what is considered "normal" and "beautiful" in society.

PROCEDURE:

1. **Start with a Quick Barometer Warm-Up**

   - In a quick activity based on the Barometer teaching strategy, ask your advisees to think about the following statement and then take a stand along a continuum between "Strongly Agree" and "Strongly Disagree" signs: *It is natural for human beings to form groups that include some and exclude others.*

   - Provide an opportunity for advisees to explain their choices before returning to their seats.

2. **Read *The Sneetches***

   The story of the star-bellied Sneetches provides an opportunity for advisees to talk about how communities can break down when members are told they do not belong or when they are deemed inferior. You can read the book out loud or share the task of reading with your advisees. If you have access to a document camera, you can display the pictures while you are reading the story.

- Pass out the handout **The Sneetches Discussion Questions** and **read aloud** *The Sneetches*, stopping at page 8 before Sylvester McMonkey McBean enters the scene (visit facinghistory.org/advisory-media to learn about the Read Aloud teaching strategy).

- Ask your advisees to turn and talk with a partner to discuss questions 1–6 on their handouts.

- Then finish reading the story. Divide your advisory into small groups of three or four so they can discuss what the story can teach them about membership and belonging. You can have groups discuss questions 7–12 on their handouts or assign each group one or two questions to focus on and then share their ideas with the advisory, perhaps facilitating a short discussion with the whole group.

3. Draw Connections between *The Sneetches* and Your School Community

- Ask advisees to reflect on the story in a journal entry that responds to the following question. Let them know that they will be sharing their responses.

    What is an example of a lesson from *The Sneetches* that you think could help strengthen your school community? What makes you say that?

- Debrief the responses in small groups or a circle discussion. Challenge your advisees to consider *how* they might apply the lessons to their school community. Use the following question to prompt students' thinking:

    What small, concrete steps can you take as individuals and as a group to help strengthen your school community?

HANDOUT

The Sneetches Discussion Questions

Directions: Discuss the following questions about *The Sneetches* by Dr. Seuss. As you discuss the questions, think about what lessons Dr. Seuss might have wanted his readers to consider.

After reading pages 1–8:

1. How is membership in the "in" group defined by the Sneetches?
2. What benefits come with membership in the "in" group? What are the costs of being excluded from membership?
3. What are the different ways that Sneetches learn the rules of membership in the different groups in their community?
4. Why do you think the star-bellied Sneetches decide to remove their stars?
5. How do the rules of "in" and "out" group membership change? Why do they change?
6. What do you think will happen next?

After reading the whole story:

7. What are three ideas that this story reveals about group membership and belonging in a community?
8. How do the Sneetches get ideas about what is "normal" in their society?
9. How do their ideas about what is "normal" impact their identities, how they perceive themselves, and how they perceive others?
10. The media can depict teenagers as forming cliques. Compare the way the Sneetches treat each other to the way teenagers treat each other. What is the same? What is different?
11. Which do you respect more, the Sneetches at the beginning of the story or the Sneetches at the end? What makes you say that?
12. Often, stories are written to express a moral or teach a lesson. What is the moral of this story?

ACTIVITY **40**

What Is "Normal"?

Purpose: Identify ways in which communities define membership, and consider how membership in a particular group can influence how people view those outside the group. Examine how people learn what is considered "normal" and "beautiful" in society.

> **APPROXIMATE TIME:**
> 30 minutes
>
> **MATERIALS:**
> READING
> "Eye of the Beholder" Script
>
> Butcher paper (or long whiteboard) and markers

ADVISOR NOTES:

1. **Dig Deeper into Group Membership and Ideas about "Normal"**

   This activity can be used instead of *The Sneetches* or as a follow-up activity if you want to spend two days exploring the ways in which communities define membership and the benefits and privileges that can come with belonging.

2. **Watch "Eye of the Beholder"**

   You may prefer to show students the *Twilight Zone* episode "Eye of the Beholder" rather than read the synopsis. This episode is available to borrow as a DVD from Facing History's library.

3. **Use a Different Version of the Reading**

   If you don't want to use the script version of the reading for this activity, you can find the standard reading, **The Eye of the Beholder**, at facinghistory.org/advisory-media.

PROCEDURE:

1. **Reflect on Notions of "Normal"**

   - On a whiteboard or large piece of paper that the whole group can write on at the same time, write or paste the following questions in the center, and then explain the **Graffiti Boards** strategy (visit facinghistory.org/advisory-media to learn about this teaching strategy).
   - Have advisees respond to the first question on the graffiti board. After they have had time to write, have them move on to the second question.
     - Where do we get our ideas about what is "normal" in our society?
     - How do we learn what is "normal" in our society?
   - Then discuss as a group what you notice about their responses. Where are there places of agreement and disagreement?

2. **Read and Discuss a Synopsis of a *Twilight Zone* Episode**

    - Sit in a circle and explain to the group that today they will be exploring the idea of "normal" in society, specifically in relation to the idea of beauty.

    - Pass out copies of the reading **"Eye of the Beholder" Script** and explain that advisees will be taking roles to read it out loud. Ask for five volunteers and assign the following roles: Narrator, Janet, Nurse, Doctor, and Walter Smith. You might change readers halfway through for the Narrator, Janet, and the Doctor to give more advisees a chance to participate.

    - Then divide the advisory into small groups and discuss the questions at the end of the reading.

    - Move back into a circle and have each group report on their ideas.

3. **Reflect on Ideas about "Normal" in your School Community**

    To help advisees connect the text to their own experiences, choose one or more of the following questions to discuss as a group:

    - What does *Twilight Zone* producer and writer Rod Serling challenge his audience to think about as a result of watching this episode of the program?

    - What is a lesson from this text that you could apply to your school in order to strengthen the community? What ideas do you have about how you could apply the lesson, both as an individual and as an advisory group?

READING

"Eye of the Beholder" Script

Directions: "Eye of the Beholder" is an episode of a popular television show called *The Twilight Zone* that ran from 1959 to 1965. For this reading, a synopsis of the episode, you will take roles and deliver the characters' lines. While you don't need to read phrases like "Janet asks urgently," the person playing Janet can try to deliver the line in an urgent way.

Narrator: Meet the patient in room 307, Janet Tyler. A rigid mask of gauze bandages covers her face. Only her voice and her hands seem alive as she pleads with a nurse to describe the weather, the sky, the daylight, clouds—none of which she can see. The nurse, visible only by her hands, answers kindly but briefly.

Janet: "When will they take the bandages off?" Janet asks urgently. "How much longer?"

Nurse: "When they decide they can fix your face," the nurse replies.

Janet: "It's pretty bad, isn't it? Ever since I was little, people have turned away when they looked at me.... The very first thing I can remember is another little child screaming when she saw me. I never wanted to be beautiful, to look like a painting. I just wanted people not to turn away."

Narrator: With a consoling pat, the nurse moves away. A doctor enters Janet Tyler's room. We see only his hands, his shadow, his back as he looks out a window. Janet questions him with a mixture of fear and hope. When will he remove the bandages? Will her face be normal? The doctor tries to comfort her. His voice is gentle. Perhaps this time the treatment will be successful. But he also issues a warning. He reminds her that she has had treatment after treatment—eleven in all. That is the limit. If this effort fails, she can have no more.

Doctor: "Each of us is afforded as much opportunity as possible to fit in with society," he says. "In your case, think of the time and effort the state has expended, to make you look—"

Janet: "To look like what, doctor?"

Doctor: "Well, to look normal, the way you'd like to look.... You know, there are many others who share your misfortune, who look much as you do. One of the alternatives, just in case the treatment is not successful, is to allow you to move into a special area in which people of your kind have congregated."

Narrator: Janet twists away from the doctor.

Janet: "People of my kind? Congregated? You mean segregated! You mean imprisoned! You are talking about a ghetto—a ghetto for freaks!"

Narrator: Her voice rises in a crescendo of anger.

Doctor: "Miss Tyler!" the doctor remonstrates sharply. "You're not being rational. You know you couldn't live any kind of life among normal people." His words are harsh, but his voice is sad and patient.

Narrator: Janet refuses to be mollified.

Janet: "Who are these normal people?" she asks accusingly. "Who decides what is normal? Who is this state that makes these rules? The state is not God! The state does not have the right to make ugliness a crime. . . . Please," she begs. "Please take off the bandages. Please take them off! Please help me."

Narrator: Reluctantly the doctor agrees, and the staff prepares for the removal. Bit by bit, he peels the gauze away. She sees at first only the light, then the shadowy forms of the doctor and nurses. As the last strip of gauze comes off, the doctor and nurses draw back in dismay.

Doctor: "No change!" the doctor exclaims. "No change at all!"

Narrator: Janet Tyler gasps and raises her face. She has wide-set eyes, delicate brows, fine skin, and regular features, framed by wavy blonde hair. She begins to sob and struggle away from the nurses.

Doctor: "Turn on the lights," the doctor orders. "Needle, please!"

Narrator: As the lights come on, the doctor and nurses are clearly visible for the first time. Piglike snouts dominate their lopsided, misshapen features. Their mouths are twisted, their jowls sag. Janet runs through the hospital in a panic, pursued by nurses and orderlies. She passes other staff and patients. Each face is a little different but all share the same basic pattern—snouts, jowls, and all. She flings open a door and freezes in sudden shock. The doctor and another man are in this room. She sinks down by a chair and hides her face in fear.

Doctor: "Miss Tyler, Miss Tyler, don't be afraid," the doctor urges. "He's only a representative of the group you are going to live with. He won't hurt you. . . . Miss Tyler, this is Walter Smith."

Narrator: Walter Smith steps forward, and Janet Tyler cringes away. He too has regular features, lit by a friendly smile. A stray lock of dark hair curls falls over his forehead.

Walter Smith: "We have a lovely village and wonderful people," he tells Janet. "In a little while, a very little while, you'll feel a sense of great belonging."

Janet: She looks at his face. "Why do we have to look like this?" she murmurs.

Walter Smith: "I don't know, I really don't," he replies with sadness. "But there is a very old saying—beauty is in the eye of the beholder. Try to think of that, Miss Tyler. Say it over and over to yourself. Beauty is in the eye of the beholder."

Narrator: He holds out his hand to her. Slowly, hesitantly, she takes it, and they walk away together, through a corridor lined with pig-faced spectators.[1]

---

1 Marc Scott Zicree, *The Twilight Zone Companion*, 2nd ed. (New York: Bantam Books, 1989), 144–45.

Discussion Questions:

1. What is the "twist" in this episode of *The Twilight Zone*? What might creator Rod Serling be trying to communicate with this unexpected twist in the story?

2. Where do we get our ideas about beauty? How do we learn what is normal?

3. How would you adapt "Eye of the Beholder" to today's world? What changes would you make in the story?

4. What is a lesson from this text that you could apply to your school in order to strengthen the community? What ideas do you have about how you could apply the lesson, both as an individual and as an advisory group?

ACTIVITY **41**

Gaining Perspective on Perspectives

Purpose: Consider how membership in a particular group can influence how people view those outside of that group, and identify examples of "we" and "they" distinctions in our community, country, and world.

> **APPROXIMATE TIME:**
> 40 minutes
>
> **MATERIALS:**
> READING
> "We and They"
>
> HANDOUT
> Talking about
> "We and They"

ADVISOR NOTES:

1. **Edit the Final Discussion Questions**

   This activity is designed to follow Activity 39: The Sneetches and/or Activity 40: What Is "Normal"? If you did not do either activity, adjust the final discussion questions.

PROCEDURE:

1. **Reflect on "Perspective"**
   - Ask your advisees to respond to the following prompt in their journals. Let them know that they will be sharing their responses with their peers.
     - How do you get ideas and form impressions about people who live in your community or people who you interact with on a regular basis?
     - How do you get ideas and form impressions about people who live in places far away from you?
   - Sitting in a circle and using the **Wraparound** or "popcorn" strategy (visit facinghistory.org/advisory-media to learn about this teaching strategy), have advisees share their responses to the first question. Then discuss the following question as a group:
     - How do we form opinions about people and the world around us?

2. **Apply the Concept of Perspective to a Poem**
   - Either ask for volunteers to define "perspective" or provide this definition: *Perspective is your point of view. Perspective is how you see and understand the world and the people around you.*
   - If their journal discussion about the factors that shape how we see people and the world around us didn't touch on this point, remind advisees that we each have a perspective that is influenced by our unique identity as well as the communities to which we belong.

Section 4: Membership and Belonging: Who Are "We"? Who Are "They"? 157

- Next, pass out the reading **"We and They"** and ask for volunteers to read it out loud. Or you might choose a **read aloud** strategy like "popcorn style" (visit facinghistory.org/advisory-media to learn about this teaching strategy).
- Pass out the handout **Talking about "We and They"** and divide your advisory into pairs or small groups of three to discuss the poem together.
- Then form a circle for an advisory discussion that touches on some or all of the following questions:
    - What factors shape the idea of "We" and "They" in the poem?
    - What sorts of things does the "We" group focus on when describing the "They" group?
    - Kipling, who lived from 1865 to 1936, was a British journalist, writer, and poet who was born in Bombay (now Mumbai), India. At age five, he was sent to England for school, and he returned to India when he was 17 years old to start his career as a journalist before moving back to England when he was in his 20s. How might Kipling's childhood experiences have impacted his sense of identity? How might they have impacted his perspective on the world?
    - How do we make distinctions between "we" and "they" in our own lives, in the media, and online? When, if ever, are these distinctions beneficial? When, if ever, are they harmful?

READING

"We and They"

By Rudyard Kipling

Father and Mother, and Me,
  Sister and Auntie say
All the people like us are We,
  And every one else is They.
And They live over the sea,
  While We live over the way,
But—would you believe it—They look upon We
  As only a sort of They!

We eat pork and beef
  With cow-horn-handled knives.
They who gobble Their rice off a leaf,
  Are horrified out of Their lives;
While they who live up a tree,
  And feast on grubs and clay,
(Isn't it scandalous?) look upon We
  As a simply disgusting They!

We shoot birds with a gun.
  They stick lions with spears.
Their full-dress is un-.
  We dress up to Our ears.
They like Their friends for tea.
  We like Our friends to stay;
And, after all that, They look upon We
  As an utterly ignorant They!

We eat kitcheny food.
> We have doors that latch.

They drink milk or blood,
> Under an open thatch.

We have Doctors to fee.
> They have Wizards to pay.

And (impudent heathen!) They look upon We
> As a quite impossible They!

All good people agree,
> And all good people say,

All nice people, like Us, are We
> And every one else is They:

But if you cross over the sea,
> Instead of over the way,

You may end by (think of it!) looking on We
> As only a sort of They![1]

---

1 "We and They," Rudyard Kipling, "Debits and Credits" (1919–1923), Kipling Society website, http://www.kiplingsociety.co.uk/poems_wethey.htm.

HANDOUT

Talking about "We and They"

Directions: Use Rudyard Kipling's poem "We and They" to help answer the following questions.

1. In the first stanza, who is "We"? Who is "They"? How are the two groups different? How are they similar?

2. What words and phrases does the poet use to describe "We" and "They" in stanzas 2–4?

"We"	"They"

3. What does the poet realize in the final stanza of the poem?

4. How do we make distinctions about "we" and "they" in our own lives? How do we make them online? How do we see them made in the media?

5. When can distinctions between "we" and "they" be beneficial (positive)? When can they be harmful?

ACTIVITY **42**

Analyzing Assumptions

Purpose: Examine how the assumptions we make about people and groups can impact how we choose to react to and interact with others.

APPROXIMATE TIME:
30 minutes

MATERIALS:
IMAGE
Street Calculus

HANDOUT
My Street Calculus

ADVISOR NOTES:

1. **Important Facing History Activities**

   Activities 42–45 work well together, so, if possible, try to use them in consecutive advisory meetings to help your advisees consider how assumptions can lead to stereotyping, prejudice, and discrimination.

PROCEDURE:

1. **Reflect in a Journal Response on Assumptions People Can Make**

   Begin the activity by giving advisees a few minutes to write in their journals in response to the following questions. Let them know that they will not be sharing their responses with their peers.

   - Has someone ever made an assumption about you because of some aspect of your identity or because of a group that you belong to?
   - Was it a positive assumption or a negative one?
   - How did you find out about the assumption? How did you respond?

2. **Analyze a Garry Trudeau Cartoon**

   - Project or pass out the image **Street Calculus** and discuss first impressions of the cartoon using the following questions:
     - What's happening in this image?
     - What do you notice about what each person is thinking in his thought bubble?
     - How are each of their thoughts similar? How are they different?
   - Next, analyze the cartoon more deeply by having advisees discuss the following questions in small groups:
     - Do you think the situation depicted here is realistic?
     - Do people use similar "lists" to make judgments about each other?
     - How aware do you think people are of the lists they make?

- When someone sees you walking down the hallway at school or down the street, what lists might they make about you?
- What lists do you sometimes make about others?
- How might these lists shape the choices people make (beyond greeting each other)?
- What would it take to change the lists people make about each other?

3. **Create Your Own "Street Calculus"**

- Pass out the handout **My Street Calculus**. Working individually or in pairs, invite advisees to create their own "Street Calculus" cartoons that reflect an encounter that could happen in their school or local community. They should create two characters and discuss their physical appearances, mitigating factors, risk factors, and the final "street calculus."
- After they have created their cartoons, invite advisees to share with the class, using a document camera to project their images if you have one available.

Street Calculus

Garry Trudeau's cartoon from the *Doonesbury* comic strip comments on the calculations we make about one another.

HANDOUT

My Street Calculus

Directions: Make your own "Street Calculus" cartoon that reflects an encounter that could happen at your school or in your community. Envision your characters, discuss their physical appearance, and decide on a setting. You can sketch these details in the cartoon frame. Then list the possible risk and mitigating factors and calculate how each character assesses the risk of their encounter with the other.

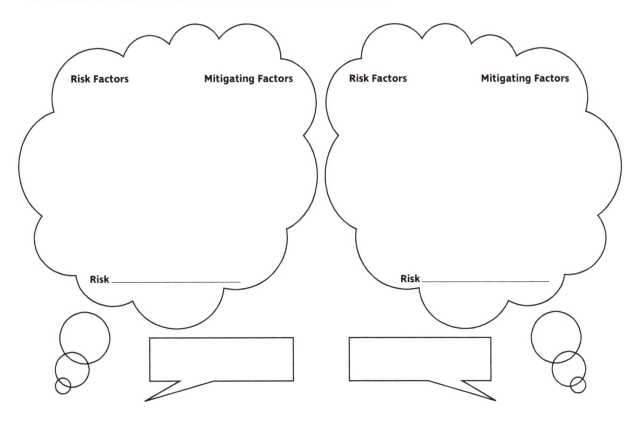

1. Who are the characters and what do they look like?

2. What is the setting?

3. List two or three significant factors that affect the way the characters react to one another, and explain why they are important.

ACTIVITY **43**

I Am Not a Label

Purpose: Explore the ways in which society and others can influence our identities and how accepting the labels that others impose on us can impact our perception and understanding of ourselves and others.

> **APPROXIMATE TIME:** 40 minutes
>
> **MATERIALS:**
> - **HANDOUT** I Am Not a Label Discussion Questions
> - **HANDOUT** Don't Misunderstand Me!

ADVISOR NOTES:

1. **Examining Stereotyping in Activities 42–45**

   Activities 42–45 work well together, so, if possible, try to use them in consecutive advisory meetings to help your advisees consider how assumptions can lead to stereotyping, prejudice, and discrimination.

PROCEDURE:

1. **Reflect on the Labels that Are Placed on You by Others and Society**
   - Start by asking your advisees to review their Starburst Identity Chart from Activity 20, and invite them to add new ideas that come to them. Model this process by projecting or recreating your identity chart on the board and doing a "think aloud" where you explore how the recent advisory discussions about identity, assumptions, and perception help generate new ideas about your identity.
   - Next, ask advisees to respond to the following questions in their journals. Tell them that they will not have to share if they don't feel comfortable doing so.
     - Look at your arrows pointing inward, which represent how others and society perceive you. Choose one that you feel does not represent you. What is it, and why does it misrepresent your identity?
     - How does it feel to have others or society label you in this way?
     - If you could share how you feel with someone who has this belief about your identity, what would you tell them?
   - Invite volunteers to share an idea from their response and then move to the next activity.

2. **Have a Discussion about Labels and Identity**
   - Pass out the handout **I Am Not a Label Discussion Questions** and give your advisees a few minutes to jot down some ideas for each question.

- Explain that the group will use the **Fishbowl** discussion strategy to explore the questions (visit facinghistory.org/advisory-media to learn about this teaching strategy). You can invite advisees to "tap" each other out when they would like to enter the conversation.

3. **Don't Misunderstand Me**

    - End the meeting with the handout **Don't Misunderstand Me!** Explain that everyone should complete the two sentence starters. Let them know that they will be sharing what they write with the group.

    - Sit in a circle and use the **Wraparound** strategy to share misunderstandings and truths about group members' identities (visit facinghistory.org/advisory-media to learn about this teaching strategy).

HANDOUT

I Am Not a Label Discussion Questions

Directions: Record your responses to the following questions in the space provided.

1. Where do we get ideas about the labels we use to describe other individuals and groups of people?

2. When, if ever, are labels useful?

3. When, if ever, are labels dangerous?

4. How do you feel when society, a group, or another individual labels you in a positive or negative way?

5. How can you challenge and remove the labels that others impose on you?

6. How can you become more aware of the labels you place on others and the consequences that those labels may have?

HANDOUT

Don't Misunderstand Me!

Don't Misunderstand Me!

Name: _____

One misunderstanding someone might have about me is . . .

But in reality, the truth about me is . . .

Don't Misunderstand Me!

Name: _____

One misunderstanding someone might have about me is . . .

But in reality, the truth about me is . . .

Adapted from Kristina J. Doubet and Jessica A. Hockett, *Differentiation in Middle and High School: Strategies to Engage All Learners* (Alexandria: ASCD, 2015), 165.

ACTIVITY **44**

Defining Key Concepts

Purpose: Define and discuss the concepts of stereotyping, prejudice, and discrimination.

APPROXIMATE TIME: 40 minutes

MATERIALS:
- **HANDOUT** Defining Stereotype, Prejudice, and Discrimination

ADVISOR NOTES:

1. **Examining Stereotyping in Activities 42–45**

    Activities 42–45 work well together, so, if possible, try to use them in consecutive advisory meetings to help your advisees consider how assumptions can lead to stereotyping, prejudice, and discrimination.

2. **Familiarize Yourself with the Concept Maps Teaching Strategy**

    Before the advisory meeting, take some time to read the **Concept Maps** teaching strategy, which you can find at facinghistory.org/advisory-media. While this activity calls for pairs or groups of three to create their maps together, you can also make it an individual activity. After advisees have generated their ideas in their journals, consider having them sort, connect, and elaborate on white paper, using markers or colored pens (if available) to help show relationships between ideas and label their maps.

PROCEDURE:

1. **Create a Stereotype Concept Map**

    - Start by asking advisees to recall what they discussed about assumptions and labeling in the last meeting when they analyzed the "Street Calculus" cartoon. Then tell them that today they will be expanding on their discussion to include the idea of stereotyping.

    - Explain the **Concept Maps** strategy to the group, and then have advisees work in pairs or triads to create concept maps for "stereotype." Alternatively, you might make a "stereotype" **graffiti board** if you think it will work better for your group. Visit facinghistory.org/advisory-media to learn about these two teaching strategies.

    - Have the pairs and triads combine into small groups of four to six to share their concept maps, and then ask the groups to discuss what they think the difference is between the concepts of stereotype, prejudice, and discrimination. Debrief as a whole group, recording their ideas on the board.

2. **Learn the Definitions of Stereotype, Prejudice, and Discrimination**

    - Come back together in a circle. Then pass out the handout **Defining Stereotype, Prejudice, and Discrimination** and read it aloud as a whole group.

    - After answering any clarifying questions, divide the advisory into small groups to examine the ways in which the three concepts are similar and different. Have them record their ideas on the modified Venn diagram on the back side of the handout and then discuss the questions under the diagram.

3. **Reflect on New Understanding**

    - Bring the group together and debrief the reading by creating a large Venn diagram on the board. Have advisees share their ideas and then discuss the following questions as a group:

        - What is one idea from this reading that you think is most important for people to understand? What makes you say that?

        - What questions do you have about the definitions or relationship between stereotyping, prejudice, and discrimination?

    - Time allowing, invite your advisees to revisit their stereotype concept maps, adding any new ideas, connections, or questions.

    - Use the "fist to five" routine to check the group's understanding of the distinction between stereotype, prejudice, and discrimination (see **Opening Routines for Advisory Meetings** on page 12).

HANDOUT

Defining Stereotype, Prejudice, and Discrimination

Directions: Read the following two paragraphs and then use information from this reading, other advisory readings, videos, images, discussions, and your own experiences to complete the Venn diagram on the second page of the handout.

Psychologist Deborah Tannen writes:

> We all know we are unique individuals, but we tend to see others as representatives of groups. It's a natural tendency, since we must see the world in patterns in order to make sense of it; we wouldn't be able to deal with the daily onslaught of people and objects if we couldn't predict a lot about them and feel that we know who and what they are. But this natural and useful ability to see patterns of similarity has unfortunate consequences. It is offensive to reduce an individual to a category, and it is also misleading.[1]

A *stereotype* is a belief about an individual based on the real or imagined characteristics of a group to which that individual belongs. Stereotypes can lead us to judge an individual or group negatively. Even stereotypes that seem to portray a group positively reduce individuals to categories and tell an inaccurate "single story." *Prejudice* occurs when we form an opinion about an individual or a group based on a negative stereotype; the word *prejudice* comes from the word *pre-judge*. When a prejudice leads us to treat an individual or group negatively, *discrimination* occurs.

---

1   Deborah Tannen, You Just Don't Understand: Men and Women in Conversation (New York: Morrow, 1990), 16.

Discuss the questions and record your ideas in the Venn diagram.

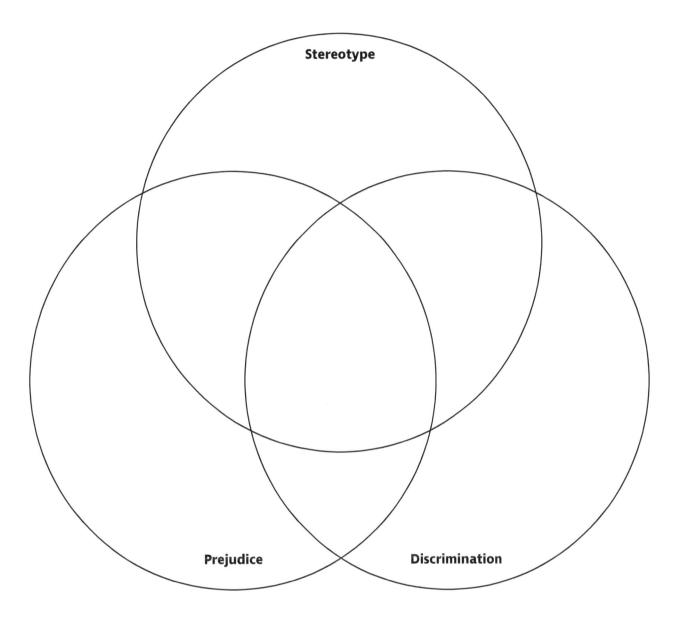

1. What are the key differences between stereotypes, prejudice, and discrimination?
2. In what ways are the three concepts similar?
3. What is one idea from this reading that you think is most important for people to understand? What makes you say that?
4. What questions do you have about the definitions or relationship between stereotyping, prejudice, and discrimination?

ACTIVITY **45**

Encountering and Countering Stereotypes

Purpose: Explore how assumptions and labels can lead to stereotyping and prejudice and how they can impact how we think about ourselves.

APPROXIMATE TIME:
40 minutes

MATERIALS:

- **READING**
  Still Me Inside
- **HANDOUT**
  Still Me Inside Discussion Questions

ADVISOR NOTES:

1. **Examining Stereotyping in Activities 42–45**

   Activities 42–45 work well together, so, if possible, try to use them in consecutive advisory meetings to help your advisees consider how assumptions and labels can lead to stereotyping, prejudice, and discrimination.

PROCEDURE:

1. **Consider Assumptions Others Make about You**

   - Ask advisees to complete the following sentence starter in their journals. Let them know that they will not have to share if they prefer to keep their ideas private. *Based only on my appearance, people would never expect that I _____.*

   - Ask if any volunteers would like to read their completed sentence. You can follow up by having the group consider why people might make assumptions about them based on their appearance.

2. **Read One Student's Story about Being Stereotyped**

   - Pass out and **read aloud** the reading **Still Me Inside** (visit facinghistory.org/advisory-media to learn about the Read Aloud teaching strategy). You can ask advisees to put a star in the margin alongside ideas that resonate with them or reflect their personal experiences. They can also circle unfamiliar vocabulary terms.

   - After giving advisees a chance to share what they starred and to clear up any vocabulary questions, pass out the handout **Still Me Inside Discussion Questions** and divide your advisory into small groups. Alternatively, you can discuss Mai Goda's story and work though the handout together.

3. **Discuss the Relationship between Labels, Assumptions, and Stereotypes**

   Close the activity with a full-group discussion based on the following questions:

   - What do you think Goda means when she says she now enjoys proving the people who make assumptions about her wrong? How does she do this?
   - Have you ever proved someone wrong who made an assumption about you? What did you do?
   - Did Goda's identity ever really change? What did change about her?
   - How do labels, assumptions, and stereotypes affect how other people identify each of us?
   - How might labels, assumptions, and stereotypes affect how we think about ourselves?

READING

Still Me Inside

Mai Goda describes how changing her appearance affected the way that others perceived her identity and how she thought about herself:

> "I need a change!"
>
> And so on that single whim, I cut my long black hair, streaked it bright red, and, to top it off, pierced my eyebrow. I had gone from dork to punk in a week, and as trivial as it seems, this transformation has had a great effect on my life.
>
> As long as I can remember, I had always been a good girl. In school, I got decent grades and never was in trouble. At home, I tried not to give my parents too much grief. But more than that, I had the "look" of a good girl. People always stereotyped me as a quiet, studious, Asian girl. Friends' parents often asked if I played the violin or the piano. "No, the flute," I'd say, and they would nod, not surprised. Walking around with my long black hair over my face, I hid behind my stereotype. I felt somewhat obliged to appease the stereotype imposed on me.
>
> Needless to say, heads turned the day I walked into school sporting a new, short, bright red hairdo. I enjoyed the reaction and attention I received from my friends and teachers. I didn't listen to my friends' warnings about people seeing me differently, people who frowned on a "rebellious punkster." After all, I was still the same person inside, so why should this change matter? I soon found out how naive I was.
>
> One day, I was late for school and needed a pass from my vice principal. I was met by a surprisingly stern look. Writing one, his voice and stare were cold and condescending. Mistaking me for "one of those punk delinquents," he left me with a warning: "Don't make a habit of it." Had I come to school late a week before, my vice principal would have said nothing. I was not used to this discriminating treatment, and I felt angry, embarrassed, and somewhat defeated. Now every time I go to the mall, suspicious eyes follow me. Store clerks keep a cautious watch. But the worst was yet to come.
>
> It was the night of our music recital for advanced students. For weeks, I had prepared my piece, and I was excited. The room was packed with parents waiting to hear their children. But, as soon as I walked into the room, all attention was focused on my head. As I sat waiting my turn, I felt the critical eyes of the parents.
>
> I performed well but felt awful. Afterward, I still saw those disapproving looks as they walked out with their children. I even overheard a friend being lectured on how she shouldn't color her hair or pierce her face to become a "punk like

Mai." Once again, I was ready to go home feeling angry when my friend's father stopped me.

"You were very good tonight. At first I didn't recognize you," he said, looking at my head.

"Oh yes, I look very different from last time, don't I?"

"Well, you played even better than last year. Look forward to hearing you again."

I went home feeling good, as if I had finally won a battle. Now the stern look of the vice principal, the suspicious stares of the store clerks, and the disapproving eyes of my friends' mothers didn't bother me. I was still the same person inside, punk or not. There was nothing wrong with me; it was the other judgmental people who had the problem. I regained my confidence.

I still get looks and the stares, but it doesn't upset me. In a way, I traded in one stereotype for another, but this time I enjoy proving them wrong. People are surprised to see me getting good grades and applying to good colleges. They're surprised to hear me play the flute so well. And they are absolutely shocked to see me standing in front of the football field, red hair shining in the sun, conducting the marching band.

As for my red hair, I re-dye it occasionally to keep it bright, burning red. It seems to give me the power to fight against stereotypes forced on me and gives me the confidence that I never had before.[1]

---

[1] Mai Goda, "Still Me Inside," in *Chicken Soup for the Teen Soul: Real-Life Stories by Real Teens*, ed. Jack Canfield, Mark Victor Hansen, Stephanie H. Meyer, and John Myer (Backlist, LLC, 2012), 261–263. Reproduced by permission of Backlist, LLC.

HANDOUT

Still Me Inside Discussion Questions

Directions: Discuss the following questions about Mai Goda's story and record your ideas in the space provided.

1. What factors do you think impacted the assumptions people made about Goda after she changed her appearance? First list the factors and then rank them from what you think are most influential to least influential.

2. A *stereotype* is a belief—positive or negative—about an individual based on the real or imagined characteristics of a group to which that individual belongs.

    a. What stereotypes do people form about Goda based on her "old look"?

    b. What stereotypes do people form about Goda after she changes her look by dyeing her hair and piercing her eyebrow?

3. *Prejudice* occurs when we form an opinion about an individual or a group based on a negative stereotype; the word *prejudice* comes from the word *pre-judge*. While stereotypes are thoughts, prejudice is rooted in feelings and attitudes about an individual or group of people.

    a. Where does Goda encounter prejudice in the story? What evidence does she give about others' opinions of her?

4. When a prejudice leads us to treat an individual or group negatively, *discrimination* occurs.

    a. What is a moment in the story where someone discriminated against Goda? What happened? In this case, how did stereotyping and prejudice lead to the act of discrimination?

ACTIVITY **46**

What Is Your Perception?

Purpose: Explore through a Facing History student's spoken-word poem how stereotyping and prejudice can influence our actions and lead to discrimination.

> **APPROXIMATE TIME:** 30 minutes
>
> **MATERIALS:**
>
> ▶ VIDEO
> **Jonathan Lykes Performs "Perception"**
> (see facinghistory.org/advisory-media)
>
> 💬 READING
> **"Perception" Transcript**

ADVISOR NOTES:

1. **Creating and Performing Spoken-Word Poems**

   If one or more of your advisees is inspired by Jonathan Lykes's spoken-word performance, you can encourage them to create their own spoken-word poems (or haiku, raps, short stories, essays, illustrations, or cartoons) that explore themes of identity, assumptions, perception, and stereotyping. You can find additional resources for teaching and creating spoken-word poetry on the websites of Poetry Out Loud, Brave New Voices (an initiative of Youth Speaks), and The Poetry Society.

PROCEDURE:

1. **Hear a Student's Perspective on Perception**

   - Explain that today, advisees will hear a Facing History student's spoken-word performance in which he explores the idea of perception and how the labels imposed on him by society and the ways individuals act on those labels impact him in his daily life.

   - Play the video **Jonathan Lykes Performs "Perception"** (04:08) at facinghistory.org/advisory-media.

   - Then pass out the **"Perception" Transcript** and have advisees read it and underline or star one or two short sections that resonate with them, perhaps because they identify with Lykes in that moment, they have a new, different, or deeper understanding of identity, labels, stereotypes, prejudice, and/or discrimination, or the section raises a question for them.

   - Ask advisees to reflect in their journals on one or both sections that they identified by explaining its significance to them.

2. **Discuss Responses to "Perception"**

   - Divide the advisory into groups of four and explain the **Learn to Listen, Listen to Learn** strategy (visit facinghistory.org/advisory-media to learn about this teaching strategy).

   - Guide the groups through the steps of the strategy as needed.

   - Then move into a circle so groups can share highlights from their discussion and any new understanding or questions that arose about the poem or related themes.

READING

"Perception" Transcript

The following is the transcript of a spoken-word performance by Jonathan Lykes, a Facing History student, in which he explores the idea of perception.

Good afternoon again, everyone. Or good night, or whatever you want to call it. Back when I was in the Facing History class in my ninth-grade year, I actually wrote a poem inspired by what I was learning in the class. And I actually got an opportunity to perform it at the National Poetry Competition in New York last year. So this is the poem that I wrote.

How do they see me? How do I see them? For I notice that there's this thing called perception that gives people the opportunity for exceptions. Or on the flip side, to be in the circle of rejection. All different types of sections and groups of cliques, making fun of this person and talking bad about that person. So I ask, what is your outlook on things? All these different stereotypes and all types of legal rights being violated because you look this way and you act that way. And you're telling me it's okay to give a blind eye to the less fortunate simply because they're beneath you?

Test. You, in a dark suburban alley alone, see a black man. Looks like he's far away from home. Fear runs down your spine and your thoughts roam as you say in your mind, this little black boy's up to no good and should be picked up by the police. But would you believe that that boy was me and what you didn't see was I was coming home from youth group?

So tell me why the mode of predetermined thought towards me? I'm not in that percentile. I'm trying to be all that I can be and they still stone me with their misconceptions about black men. They tend to understand that I'm into mis-conjugated verbs, oversized pants, and hip-hop. And when I say I'm not, it's said that I'm not a real black man. Perception, many times, leads to this open door of deception. Stop. Rewind. I'm here to make a correction, because everything that seems true might not be true.

Perception. For one second, make an exception and listen to a person younger than you, not really wiser than you. Give me a minute and I just might surprise you. Let's go back to the day of 1933, for this is the day that Hitler came to be the ruler of a country called Germany. Let's look back and see the repercussions that someone could have stopped, yet no one dropped their personal business to help the bigger picture. Now 12 years later, 12 million people dead. The year is 1945 as we attempt to look ahead. Why do you think no one said, stop all these horrible actions? No reactions until it was too late.

Yet, the fate of the Holocaust we all regret and we even made a bet never to let it happen again. Yet, in the mid '90s, genocide appears to us again? And when this happens, no one still stops to step in. Location: country of Rwanda. No one chose to send in their hospitality, so they had to fend for themselves. Perception. Now I see people plagued with this lasting infection of carelessness. Once we face history and look it in the eye, it's an embarrassment. Yes, yes, good intentions meant. But we still went wrong on our encouragement to have the right perception.

For now, I see people killing people in Darfur, Sudan. And you say to me, friend, how can we help them over in Africa when the woman down the street's still recovering from Katrina? We see how the government put them in the political back seat. The very same woman is crippled and weak and they're trying to cut off her welfare. Question. Is it fair or not fair? For it's my understanding that none of you have ever been stripped bare for the whole world to see. But what I want us to be is a society free from all these detrimental mentalities. What is your perception?

[APPLAUSE][1]

---

[1] "Jonathan Lykes Performs Perception," Facing History and Ourselves, accessed May 14, 2019, https://www.facinghistory.org/resource-library/video/jonathan-lykes-performs-perception.

ACTIVITY 47

The Bystander Effect

Purpose: Discuss why people respond in different ways when they witness an injustice, something that they know is wrong, or something that seems wrong.

ADVISOR NOTES: None

APPROXIMATE TIME: 30 minutes

MATERIALS:
▶ VIDEO
The Bystander Effect
(see y2u.be/OSsPfbup0ac)

PROCEDURE:

1. **Reflect on Taking a Stand in the Face of Injustice**

   - Ask advisees to reflect on the following questions in a journal response. Let them know that they will be sharing their responses. Give them at least three minutes to answer the first question before giving them the second one.

     - What factors motivate a person to help someone? Make a list of as many ideas as you can think of.

     - What factors hold a person back from helping someone? Again, make a big list.

   - Make a T-chart on chart paper (so you can refer back to it in upcoming meetings) and ask advisees to contribute their ideas.

     - Factors that Motivate Us: Share answers to the first question in a **Wraparound** (visit facinghistory.org/advisory-media to learn about this teaching strategy). Each advisee should add at least one idea to the list before soliciting additional responses.

     - Factors that Hold Us Back: Share answers to the second question in the same way.

   - Time allowing, have advisees work in pairs or triads to rank each list of factors from 1 to 5, from most to least likely to motivate someone to take action and hold them back from taking action. Alternatively, you might have half of the pairs work with one list and half with the other list. Then ask them to share their ideas and discuss points of agreement and difference as a whole group.

2. **Learn about the Bystander Effect**

   - Play the video **The Bystander Effect** (03:35) at y2u.be/OSsPfbup0ac. Have advisees jot down notes in their journals about points they find interesting. Time allowing, show the video twice, once just watching and once with note-taking.

- Have advisees use the **S-I-T** strategy to respond to the video in their journals (visit facinghistory.org/advisory-media to learn about this teaching strategy), noting:
    - One surprising idea
    - One interesting idea
    - One troubling idea
- Debrief the S-I-T reflection in pairs, small groups, or as a whole advisory.

3. **Discuss the Bystander Effect**

   Move into a circle (or small groups) to discuss the video. You might select from the following questions:
   - Why is it easier to ignore someone who needs help when you are in a group than when you are alone (what scientists call the "diffusion of responsibility")?
   - How can a crowd of strangers become a group with an identity? How do people learn the rules of the group? How does being a member of the group impact people's decision-making process?
   - What new, different, or deeper understanding do you have about the factors that motivate people to help and the factors that hold people back from helping someone?
   - Is it ever okay to be a bystander? How might learning about the bystander effect impact the choices you make if you see someone who needs help?

ACTIVITY **48**

Responding to Injustice

Purpose: Develop vocabulary for discussing the range of responses in the face of unfairness, exclusion, discrimination, and injustice.

> **APPROXIMATE TIME:**
> 30 minutes
>
> **MATERIALS:**
> HANDOUT
> The Range of Human Behavior Vocabulary Terms

ADVISOR NOTES:

1. **Understanding the Importance of This Activity in a Facing History Advisory**

    This activity builds on the themes and vocabulary introduced in Activity 47: The Bystander Effect. Advisees will revisit the terms *perpetrator, victim/target, bystander, rescuer,* and *upstander* in upcoming *Community Matters* activities.

2. **The Range of Human Behavior: Understanding the Nuances**

    - Often when students think about acts of injustice, they divide the people involved into two groups: the *victims* (or targets) and the *perpetrators.* But other individuals and groups contribute to the prevention or the perpetuation of injustice. For example, a *bystander* is someone who witnesses or knows about an act of injustice but chooses not to do anything about it. On the other hand, when confronted with information about an unjust act, an *upstander* takes steps to prevent or stop this act from continuing.

    - The term *bystander* can be complicated. In most dictionaries, it means a person who is simply "standing by" or who is present without taking part in what is going on—a passive spectator. But some scholars, like psychologist Ervin Staub, believe that even passive spectators play a crucial role in defining the meaning of events by implicitly approving the actions of perpetrators. As seen in Activity 47's video, "The Bystander Effect," the choice not to act or speak up is still a choice.

PROCEDURE:

1. **Define Terms to Describe the Range of Responses to Injustice**

    - The video **The Bystander Effect** from Activity 47 provided an opportunity to introduce advisees to some of the terms that describe a range of responses that people might have to an act of exclusion, discrimination, or injustice. For the first part of this activity, advisees will now use context clues to help establish the definitions of four concepts that can be used to describe this range of behavior.[1]

---

1 Kelly Gallagher, *Deeper Reading: Comprehending Challenging Texts, 4–12* (Portland, ME: Stenhouse Publishers, 2004), 77–78.

- Pass out the handout **The Range of Human Behavior Vocabulary Terms** and instruct advisees to work in pairs to use the context clues in the sentences of the first column to predict the definitions of the underlined words.

- After asking a few pairs to share their predicted meanings of each word and how they came to that conclusion, you can share the dictionary definition and have them record the information in the third column of the chart.

    - **Perpetrator:** A person carrying out a harmful, illegal, or immoral act.
    - **Victim:** A person being targeted by the harmful, illegal, or immoral acts of a perpetrator.
    - **Bystander:** A person who is present but not actively taking part in a situation or event.
    - **Upstander:** A person speaking or acting in support of an individual or cause, particularly someone who intervenes on behalf of a person being attacked or bullied.

- Invite advisees to critique the dictionary definitions. Do they have any questions about these definitions? How are they similar to or different from their own definitions? Are the dictionary definitions adequate, or do they need to be further revised?

- You might point out that these dictionary definitions are written in the present tense ("carrying out" and "being targeted") and ask advisees to give examples of how a person may act as a perpetrator or bystander at one moment in time and be targeted as a victim at another moment in time. Therefore, these are *roles* that people play and not permanent identities.

2. Apply Vocabulary to Your Own Experience

- Have advisees take out their journals, and tell them that they will not have to share what they write if they don't feel comfortable doing so. Then ask them to respond to the following two prompts. Don't reveal the second prompt until they have had time to respond to the first one.

    - Write about a time when you were a perpetrator, victim of an injustice, bystander, or upstander. What happened? What choices did you have? What factors motivated your choices? How did you feel in the moment?

    - Next, write about a time when you chose a different role. If you wrote about being an upstander, now write about another time when you were a perpetrator, victim of injustice, or bystander. What happened? What choices did you have? What factors motivated your choices? How did you feel in the moment?

- After they have had time to write, you might ask if there are any volunteers who want to share the factors that motivated their choices and how they felt in the moment. You can also revisit the T-charts from Activity 47 to see if the group wants to add any new factors.

HANDOUT

The Range of Human Behavior Vocabulary Terms

Directions: Use the context clues in the sentence in the first column to predict the meaning of the each underlined term, and write your definition the center column. Leave the third column blank.[1]

Sentence	Predicted Meaning	Actual Meaning
The **perpetrator** of the crime was caught not long after robbing the convenience store and fleeing on foot down the crowded street.		
The **victim** of bullying didn't want to go to school and instead crawled back into bed and pretended to be sick.		
Despite feeling a knot in her stomach while reading the hateful comments on her childhood friend's social media feed, the **bystander** put away her phone and headed to the gym for volleyball practice.		
After three days of reading the increasing number of homophobic comments and threats on his friend's blog, the **upstander** picked up his phone and texted: "You don't deserve this treatment."		

1 Kelly Gallagher, *Deeper Reading: Comprehending Challenging Texts, 4–12* (Portland, ME: Stenhouse Publishers, 2004), 77–78.

ACTIVITY **49**

"In" Groups and "Out" Groups

Purpose: Discuss the desire to belong, the tendency for students to divide into "in" and "out" groups at school, and how this desire impacts the choices they make in the face of exclusion or injustice.

ADVISOR NOTES:

1. **Preparing for the Barometer Warm-Up Activity**

   Before the start of the activity, hang two signs at opposite ends of the classroom that say "Strongly Agree" and "Strongly Disagree." You might use the barometer as the opening routine for this meeting.

2. **Present the "In" Group Reading in Two Parts**

   The reading **The "In" Group** is divided into two parts. It is important that advisees do not read ahead to see what happens so they can participate in the paired discussion about Shalen's choices. For this reason, we recommend that you read this story aloud as an advisory rather than in small groups. If you choose to show the video version of **The "In" Group** (available at facinghistory.org/avisory-media) rather than using the reading, pause at minute 02:10 for the discussion of Eve's choices.

3. **Mini-Project: Creating Inclusive Spaces in Your School**

   The closing circle discussion invites your advisees to consider how they might collaborate to create more inclusive spaces in your school. If they are excited and motivated by the conversation, you can encourage them to choose a space that they would like to help make more inclusive, develop an action plan in upcoming advisory meetings, implement the plan, and reflect on how it went and how they worked as a group. Activity 65: The Bully Zones Project includes a video about a student-led project in which students in the school mapped areas where they witnessed or experienced disrespect or bullying. Your advisees could implement a similar type of mapping project in which they identify spaces in their school that feel unsafe or exclusive and then raise awareness through presentations, posters, social media, or announcements to start the process of making them more welcoming and inclusive. Additionally, the Advisory Community-Building Project portion of Section 6 has brainstorming strategies and a framework to support an advisory project.

APPROXIMATE TIME:
2 x 30 minutes

MATERIALS:

- READING
  The "In" Group
- VIDEO
  The "In" Group
  (see facinghistory.org/advisory-media)
- HANDOUT
  The "In" Group Discussion Questions

Chart paper and markers

Section 4: Membership and Belonging: Who Are "We"? Who Are "They"?

PROCEDURE:

First Advisory Meeting

1. **Warm Up by Taking a Stand**

    - In a quick activity based on the **Barometer** strategy, ask advisees to think about the following statement (visit facinghistory.org/advisory-media to learn about this teaching strategy):

        It is natural for human beings to form groups that include some and exclude others.

    - Then have them take a stand along the continuum between the "Strongly Agree" and "Strongly Disagree" signs. Provide an opportunity for advisees to explain their choices before they return to their seats.

2. **Read Eve Shalen's Story about Wanting to Belong**

    - Choose a **Read Aloud** strategy (visit facinghistory.org/advisory-media to learn about this teaching strategy), and pass out the first part of the reading **The "In" Group** (see Advisor Notes). Alternatively, prepare to show the video **The "In" Group**, which is available at facinghistory.org/advisory-media. Let your advisees know that in this story, Eve Shalen is a high school student reflecting on an incident that occurred when she was in eighth grade.

    - Read aloud, stopping at "One of them read aloud from a small book, which I was told was the girl's diary." This moment occurs at minute 02:10 in the video version of the text.

    - Use the **Think, Pair, Share** strategy to have advisees make a list of Shalen's options in this moment and the possible outcomes for each one (visit facinghistory.org/advisory-media to learn about this teaching strategy). You may want to model one response with the group, or have them dive straight into their discussions.

    - To debrief, record advisees' ideas for options and outcomes, and then read aloud or show the ending of Eve Shalen's story.

3. **Discuss the "In" Group Reading in Small Groups**

    - Next, divide advisees into four groups and let them know that each group will be discussing its own set of questions about the reading (or video).

    - Pass out the handout **The "In" Group Discussion Questions** and a piece of chart paper and markers to each group. Assign each group one set of questions, and tell advisees that they should record their answers on chart paper. They will share their posters with the advisory group in the next meeting.

Second Advisory Meeting

1. Share Responses to Reading Discussion Questions

- Start in the groups from the last meeting so advisees can review their posters and Eve Shalen's story as needed.
- Then invite each group to present its questions and the main ideas from its discussion. Invite advisees to respond with positive feedback, connections, or questions.

2. Draw Connections between Shalen's Story and Your School Community

Move into a circle discussion that draws from the following questions. See the Advisory Notes section for ideas about how your group might create a mini-project based on their discussion.

- Where in your school do you see evidence of isolation and separation between different individuals or groups of people?
- Where in your school do you see evidence of cooperation between different individuals or groups of people?
- Where in your school do you see evidence of individuals or groups trying to create a sense of belonging and inclusion in places where there is isolation and tension?
- What are some ways that you can work together as an advisory group to create more inclusive spaces in your school?

READING

The "In" Group

Part One:

My eighth grade consisted of 28 students, most of whom knew each other from the age of five or six. The class was close-knit and we knew each other so well that most of us could distinguish each other's handwriting at a glance. Although we grew up together, we still had class outcasts. From second grade on, a small elite group spent a large portion of their time harassing two or three of the others. I was one of those two or three, though I don't know why. In most cases when children get picked on, they aren't good at sports or they read too much or they wear the wrong clothes or they are of a different race. But in my class, we all read too much and didn't know how to play sports. We had also been brought up to carefully respect each other's races. This is what was so strange about my situation. Usually, people are made outcasts because they are in some way different from the larger group. But in my class, large differences did not exist. It was as if the outcasts were invented by the group out of a need for them. Differences between us did not cause hatred; hatred caused differences between us.

The harassment was subtle. It came in the form of muffled giggles when I talked, and rolled eyes when I turned around. If I was out in the playground and approached a group of people, they often fell silent. Sometimes someone would not see me coming and I would catch the tail end of a joke at my expense.

I also have a memory of a different kind. There was another girl in our class who was perhaps even more rejected than I. She also tried harder than I did for acceptance, providing the group with ample material for jokes. One day during lunch I was sitting outside watching a basketball game. One of the popular girls in the class came up to me to show me something she said I wouldn't want to miss. We walked to a corner of the playground where a group of three or four sat. One of them read aloud from a small book, which I was told was the girl's diary.[1]

---

[1] Eve Shalen, in *A Discussion with Elie Wiesel: Facing History Students Confront Hatred and Violence* (Brookline: Facing History and Ourselves, 1993).

Part Two:

I sat down and, laughing till my sides hurt, heard my voice finally blend with the others. Looking back, I wonder how I could have participated in mocking this girl when I knew perfectly well what it felt like to be mocked myself. I would like to say that if I were in that situation today I would react differently, but I can't honestly be sure. Often being accepted by others is more satisfying than being accepted by oneself, even though the satisfaction does not last. Too often our actions are determined by the moment.[2]

---

[2] Eve Shalen, in *A Discussion with Elie Wiesel: Facing History Students Confront Hatred and Violence* (Brookline: Facing History and Ourselves, 1993).

HANDOUT

The "In" Group Discussion Questions

Group 1: Make a list of individuals who chose the following roles in the story. Remember that these are roles and not permanent identities, so an individual might take on more than one role. If there is a role that you don't think anyone chose, discuss what it might have looked like had someone chosen it.

1. Perpetrator(s):
2. Target(s):
3. Bystander(s):
4. Upstander(s):

Group 2: How do you understand Shalen's statement at the end of the first paragraph of her story: "It was as if the outcasts were invented by the group out of a need for them. Differences between us did not cause hatred; hatred caused differences between us"?

1. What is the difference between *difference causing hatred* and *hatred causing difference*?
2. Why might a group feel the need to invent outcasts?
3. Why do humans so often divide themselves into "we" and "they," or "in" groups and "out" groups? Is this division always negative? When does it become a problem?
4. What are strategies for confronting the problem of "in" and "out" groups?

Group 3:

1. What factors contribute to Eve Shalen's choice in the story?
2. How does our need to be part of a group impact the choices we make? Why is it so difficult for a person to go against a group?
   a. How can Eve Shalen help you answer these questions?
   b. How can your own experiences help you answer these questions?
3. How is the situation in this story similar to or different from the one in "The Bystander Effect," the video that you discussed in a previous advisory meeting?

Group 4:

1. Where do you think our desire to belong to a group or a community comes from?
2. When can it be useful to conform in order to belong to a group? When can conformity be harmful?
3. Why do you think people do nothing even when they know something happening around them is wrong?
4. How can Eve Shalen's story help you answer these questions?
5. How can the video "The Bystander Effect" help you answer these questions?

ACTIVITY **50**

Choices and Consequences

Purpose: Reflect on the relationship between having the language to convey what you feel and the challenge of speaking out against injustice. Compare and contrast multiple texts to examine the bystander effect and the range of responses in the face of injustice.

APPROXIMATE TIME: 30 minutes

MATERIALS:
HANDOUT
The Silent Pact

ADVISOR NOTES:

1. **Tips for Reading "The Silent Pact"**

   The handout **The Silent Pact** is divided into two parts. It is important that advisees do not read ahead to see what happens so they can participate in the paired discussion about Patel's motivations and choices. For this reason, we recommend that you read this story aloud as an advisory rather than in small groups.

2. **Revisiting the Exit Cards**

   If you collect **exit cards** at the end of the meeting, you can check for understanding to see where advisees are making connections between the advisory content and their own lives and get a sense of their questions. You might save their questions for mini-conferences or, if you notice recurring questions, use them as the opening routine in a future meeting (keeping the names of the writers private). Visit facinghistory.org/advisory-media to learn more about the Exit Cards teaching strategy.

PROCEDURE:

1. **Read and Discuss Eboo Patel's Response to an Injustice He Witnessed**

   - Pass out **The Silent Pact** and read the first part of Patel's story out loud to the group. Then have advisees "turn and talk" with a partner to discuss the four questions on the front side of the handout.

   - Then read the second part of the story out loud as a group. Have advisees "turn and talk" with a partner to discuss the three questions about that part of the story.

   - Choose from the following questions to discuss in pairs, small groups, or as an advisory.

     - In the second paragraph of his story, Eboo Patel discusses the roles that language and silence played in his decision-making process. Reread the paragraph and then discuss the following questions:

       – What do you think Patel means by the statement, "We were not equipped with a language that allowed us to explain our faith to others or to ask about anyone else's"?

       – Why do you think they didn't have the language to talk about religion?

- Why do we so often remain silent in the face of an injustice? How can the video **The Bystander Effect** (Activity 47) and Eve Shalen' story in **The "In" Group** (Activity 49) also help you answer this question? How does it feel to remain silent when you witness something wrong or an injustice? How does it feel to try to speak up in those situations?
- What role does silence play in your school community?

2. **Reflect on Recent Advisory Themes and Content with Exit Cards**

   Ask advisees to respond to the following questions on a **3-2-1 exit card** (visit facing-history.org/advisory-media to learn about this teaching strategy). Let them know that you will be collecting their exit cards at the end of the meeting and that you might share their ideas in a future opening routine, but you will not include their names. They can indicate on their exit cards if they do not wish to have one or more of their responses shared anonymously with the group.

   - Consider "The Bystander Effect" and the stories of Eve Shalen and Eboo Patel when responding to these questions on your exit card:
     - What are **3** new, different, or deeper understandings that you have about the roles people play and the choices they make in the face of injustice or unfairness?
     - What are **2** connections that you can make between one or more of the texts and your own experiences?
     - What is **1** question that you have about the bystander effect, the roles people play in the face of injustice, or one of the texts?

HANDOUT

The Silent Pact

Eboo Patel is the founder and executive director of the Interfaith Youth Core. The goal of the program is to create a community of young people who are working to foster understanding between people of different religious backgrounds. In his memoir, *Acts of Faith*, Patel describes the roots of his own activism.

Part One

> . . . In high school, the group I ate lunch with included a Cuban Jew, a Nigerian Evangelical, and an Indian Hindu. We were all devout to a degree, but we almost never talked about our religions with one another. Often somebody would announce at the table that he couldn't eat a certain kind of food, or any food at all, for a period of time. We all knew religion hovered behind this, but nobody ever offered any explanation deeper than "my mom said," and nobody ever asked for one.
>
> This silent pact relieved all of us. We were not equipped with a language that allowed us to explain our faith to others or to ask about anyone else's. Back then, I thought little about the dangers lurking within this absence.
>
> A few years after we graduated, my Jewish friend reminded me of a dark time during our adolescence. There were a group of kids in our high school who, for several weeks, took up scrawling anti-Semitic[1] slurs on classroom desks and making obscene statements about Jews in the hallways.[2]

Turn and Talk

1. What choices does Eboo Patel have in this moment?

2. What are the possible consequences of each choice?

3. What are the factors that might motivate him to take action?

4. What are the factors that might motivate him not to take action?

---

[1] Antisemitism is prejudice toward or hatred of Jewish people.
[2] Eboo Patel, *Acts of Faith: The Story of an American Muslim, the Struggle for the Soul of a Generation* (Boston: Beacon Press, 2019), XVII–XIX.

Part Two

> I did not confront them. I did not comfort my Jewish friend. I knew little about what Judaism meant to him, less about the emotional effects of anti-Semitism, and next to nothing about how to stop religious bigotry. So I averted my eyes and avoided my friend, because I couldn't stand to face him.
>
> A few years later, he described to me the fear he had experienced coming to school those days, and his utter loneliness as he had watched his close friends simply stand by.
>
> Hearing him recount his suffering and my complicity is the single most humiliating experience of my life. I did not know it in high school, but my silence was betrayal: betrayal of Islam, which calls upon Muslims to be courageous and compassionate in the face of injustice; betrayal of America, a nation that relies on its citizens to hold up the bridges of pluralism when others try to destroy them; betrayal of India, a country that has too often seen blood flow in its cities and villages when extremists target minorities and others fail to protect them.[3]

Turn and Talk

1. What factors motivated Eboo Patel to take or not take action in the face of injustice?

2. How did he feel about his decision while he was in high school?

3. How does he feel about his decision as an adult?

Discussion Questions

1. The following questions are about paragraph two in the first part of the story, where Eboo Patel discusses the roles that language and silence played in his decision-making process.

    a. What do you think Patel means when he writes, "We were not equipped with a language that allowed us to explain our faith to others or to ask about anyone else's"?

    b. Why do you think they didn't have the language to talk about religion?

2. Why do people so often remain silent in the face of an injustice? How can the video "The Bystander Effect" and Eve Shalen's story also help you answer this question?

3. How does it feel to remain silent when you witness something wrong or an injustice? How does it feel to try to speak up in those situations?

4. What role does silence play in your school community?

---

3 Patel, *Acts of Faith: The Story of an American Muslim, the Struggle for the Soul of a Generation.*

ACTIVITY **51**

Speaking Up against Injustice

Purpose: Analyze a spoken-word presentation about the consequences of silence in the face of unfairness and injustice and the power of choosing to speak up instead.

APPROXIMATE TIME:
30 minutes

MATERIALS:

VIDEO
The Danger of Silence
(see facinghistory.org/advisory-media)

READING
"The Danger of Silence" Transcript

ADVISOR NOTES:

1. **Re-crafting Exit Cards into an Opening Routine**

   If you had your advisees submit exit cards in Activity 50, you can incorporate them into your opening routine. For example, type up some of the recurring or thought-provoking comments and questions and then cut them into strips so each strip has one comment or question. Then give one strip to each advisee and have them read them aloud in a **Wraparound** before discussing what they noticed. Visit facinghistory.org/advisory-media to learn about this teaching strategy. Alternatively, you could use this activity's first journal prompt for a "quote of the day" opening routine rather than the suggested journal reflection.

2. **References to Activities 48–49**

   If you did not do Activity 48 or Activity 49, skip the second part of the journal prompt. Your advisees can respond to the first and third questions instead.

PROCEDURE:

1. **Reflect on the Nature of Silence in the Decision-Making Process**

   - Ask advisees to respond in their journals to the following quotation from Martin Luther King Jr. Let them know that they will be sharing their responses with their peers. If your group would like some guidance, you can give them some questions like the ones suggested below to prompt their thinking:

     "In the end, we will remember not the words of our enemies but the silence of our friends." —Dr. Martin Luther King Jr.

     - What does King want people to consider about the power of language and silence?
     - Which do you think is more powerful, the "words of enemies" or the "silence of friends"? What makes you say that?

   - Invite advisees to share their ideas with a partner or in triads.

Community Matters: A Facing History and Ourselves Approach to Advisory

2. Watch and Discuss a Short Video about the Consequences of Silence

- Play the video **The Danger of Silence** (04:18) at facinghistory.org/advisory-media. This video features a TED@NYC presentation delivered by teacher, author, and activist Clint Smith. Then pass out the reading **"The Danger of Silence" Transcript**, which is available in 40 languages on TED's website if you have advisees who are English Language Learners. If you have time, show the video again while your advisees have the transcript in front of them.

- Ask advisees to underline one to three moments in the text that resonate with them. Perhaps the moment raises a question, sparks debate, connects to them personally, or helps shed light on a new understanding.

- Divide the advisory into small groups and use the **Learn to Listen, Listen to Learn** strategy to discuss Smith's presentation (visit facinghistory.org/advisory-media to learn about this teaching strategy).

- Then form a circle and ask advisees to think about how they would complete one of the following sentence starters, which they will share in a **Wraparound** and use to discuss Smith's TED Talk together (visit facinghistory.org/advisory-media to learn about this teaching strategy).

    - After watching and discussing "The Danger of Silence," I am thinking about . . .
    - After watching and discussing "The Danger of Silence," I wonder . . .
    - I used to think _____, but after watching and discussing "The Danger of Silence," now I think . . .

READING

"The Danger of Silence" Transcript

Directions: As you listen to Clint Smith's TED Talk, underline two or three moments in the text that resonate with you for some reason. Perhaps the moments raise a question, spark debate, connect to you personally, or shed light on a new understanding about the ways we choose to respond when we witness an injustice.

Dr. Martin Luther King Jr., in a 1968 speech where he reflects upon the civil rights movement, states, "In the end, we will remember not the words of our enemies but the silence of our friends."

As a teacher, I've internalized this message. Every day, all around us, we see the consequences of silence manifest themselves in the form of discrimination, violence, genocide, and war. In the classroom, I challenge my students to explore the silences in their own lives through poetry. We work together to fill those spaces, to recognize them, to name them, to understand that they don't have to be sources of shame. In an effort to create a culture within my classroom where students feel safe sharing the intimacies of their own silences, I have four core principles posted on the board that sits in the front of my class, which every student signs at the beginning of the year: read critically, write consciously, speak clearly, tell your truth.

And I find myself thinking a lot about that last point, tell your truth. And I realized that if I was going to ask my students to speak up, I was going to have to tell my truth and be honest with them about the times where I failed to do so.

So I tell them that growing up, as a kid in a Catholic family in New Orleans, during Lent I was always taught that the most meaningful thing one could do was to give something up, sacrifice something you typically indulge in to prove to God you understand his sanctity. I've given up soda, McDonald's, french fries, french kisses, and everything in between. But one year, I gave up speaking. I figured the most valuable thing I could sacrifice was my own voice, but it was like I hadn't realized that I had given that up a long time ago. I spent so much of my life telling people the things they wanted to hear instead of the things they needed to, told myself I wasn't meant to be anyone's conscience because I still had to figure out being my own, so sometimes I just wouldn't say anything, appeasing ignorance with my silence, unaware that validation doesn't need words to endorse its existence. When Christian [a peer] was beat up for being gay, I put my hands in my pocket and walked with my head down as if I didn't even notice. I couldn't use my locker for weeks because the bolt on the lock reminded me of the one I had put on my lips when the homeless man on the corner looked at me with eyes up merely searching for an affirmation that he was worth seeing. I was more concerned with touching the screen on my Apple than actually feeding him one. When the woman at the fundraising gala said, "I'm so proud of you. It must be so hard teaching those poor, unintelligent kids," I bit my lip, because apparently we needed her money more than my students needed their dignity.

We spend so much time listening to the things people are saying that we rarely pay attention to the things they don't. Silence is the residue of fear. It is feeling your flaws gut-wrench guillotine your tongue. It is the air retreating from your chest because it doesn't feel safe in your lungs. Silence is Rwandan genocide. Silence is Katrina. It is what you hear when there aren't enough body bags left. It is the sound after the noose is already tied. It is charring. It is chains. It is privilege. It is pain. There is no time to pick your battles when your battles have already picked you.

I will not let silence wrap itself around my indecision. I will tell Christian that he is a lion, a sanctuary of bravery and brilliance. I will ask that homeless man what his name is and how his day was, because sometimes all people want to be is human. I will tell that woman that my students can talk about transcendentalism like their last name was Thoreau, and just because you watched one episode of *The Wire* doesn't mean you know anything about my kids. So this year, instead of giving something up, I will live every day as if there were a microphone tucked under my tongue, a stage on the underside of my inhibition. Because who has to have a soapbox when all you've ever needed is your voice?[1]

---

1 Clint Smith, "The Danger of Silence," TED@NYC Talk, July 2014, accessed June 27, 2018, https://www.ted.com/talks/clint_smith_the_danger_of_silence.

ACTIVITY 52

Membership and Belonging Final Reflection

Purpose: Review materials from this section of the advisory program and reflect on new understanding and questions.

APPROXIMATE TIME: 30 minutes

MATERIALS:
Chart paper with the Big Paper questions and markers for each advisee

Slips of paper with advisees' names

ADVISOR NOTES:

1. **The Importance of Time and Space for Reflection**

    Providing advisees with the time and space to reflect on their learning, growth, and lingering questions from the section allows them to synthesize the material in meaningful ways before being introduced to new themes and concepts.

2. **Prepare for a Big Paper Activity**

    Before the advisory meeting, write (or print and tape) each of the following questions on a piece of chart paper for a **Big Paper** silent discussion. Visit facinghistory.org/advisory-media to learn about this teaching strategy.

    - How do peer pressure, conformity, and fear affect the decisions students make about how they treat others in our school?
    - What does it feel like to be an upstander or to witness someone being an upstander?
    - What is one step you can take to help create more inclusive spaces at school where individuals and groups feel a sense of belonging?
    - What questions do you have about group membership, assumptions, stereotyping, or responding to injustice that you would like to discuss?

3. **Suggestion for an Alternative to Big Paper**

    If you prefer a more structured discussion format for the final reflection, you might start with small groups and then move into a larger circle, try the **Socratic Seminar** or **Fishbowl** strategy, or ask your advisees to respond to the Big Paper questions or the guiding questions on a **graffiti board**. Visit facinghistory.org/advisory-media to learn about these teaching strategies.

PROCEDURE

1. **Think about This Section's Themes and Questions**

   - Start by recalling the core texts (images, readings, videos) and activities from this section of advisory. It might help to create a list on the board.

   - Ask advisees to spend a few minutes quietly reviewing the materials from this advisory section in their folders and journals.

   - Then have them respond to the following prompt in their journals. Let them know that they will be sharing their responses with a partner or in threes.

     What was the most meaningful text (image, reading, video), activity, or discussion in this section of advisory for you? What makes you say that?

   - Have advisees turn and talk or meet in triads to share their responses. You might ask for volunteers to share with the whole group as well.

2. **Synthesize Key Concepts in a Silent Discussion**

   - Then explain the **Big Paper** strategy and give advisees time to address each question and respond to comments and questions that their peers raise (visit facinghistory.org/advisory-media to learn about this teaching strategy). Remind them that they should remain silent during this part of the activity. After they have finished responding to each question, they can circle back around and add comments to their peers' ideas and pose follow-up questions.

   - Divide your advisory into small groups around each paper and have them read and discuss their observations before summarizing them for the group as a whole.

   - Sit in a circle for a discussion of the Big Paper activity. You might start with the questions that advisees posed on the paper and then discuss their observations about the responses to the other questions and how they felt while engaging in the activity.

   - Finally, ask advisees to think about their response to the following sentence starter, which they will share in a **Wraparound** (visit facinghistory.org/advisory-media to learn about this teaching strategy). You might choose a different sentence starter (I am feeling/I wonder/I question/I am confused by/I wish/I hope) or give them a menu to choose from.

     After the Big Paper activity and our discussion, I am thinking about . . .

SECTION 4

SECTION 5:

Case Study: Ostracism and Bullying

ACTIVITIES

Revisiting Our Advisory Contract

The Roots of Bullying Behavior

My School's Climate

Introducing the Ostracism Case Study (Part 1)

Reading the Ostracism Case Study Transcripts (Part 2)

Connecting Choices to Outcomes (Part 3)

Understanding the Power of Ostracism and Bullying (Part 4)

Cyberbullying

Anatomy of an Upstander

Choosing to Be an Upstander

Case Study: Ostracism and Bullying Final Reflection

Purpose	Materials	Abridged Advisor Notes

53: Revisiting Our Advisory Contract — 30 min — page 210

Remind the group of its shared expectations, revise expectations as needed, and set the tone for difficult conversations. Draw connections between the factors that make a strong community and the norms that can help ensure it remains strong.	Advisory contract	You will be prompted to revisit your advisory contract at the beginning of each section of *Community Matters* to reflect on the ways the group has been honoring its contract and where they feel they can do better. This activity also provides the opportunity to add to or revise any of the norms and expectations before moving forward with this section of the Facing History advisory program.

54: The Roots of Bullying Behavior — 40 min — page 212

Explore the desire to belong, the range of responses to injustice, and the relationship between identity and choices. Practice perspective-taking by retelling a moment in a story from the point of view of the antagonist.	READING: **Fear**	None

55: My School's Climate — 40 min — page 216

Discuss ostracism, bullying, and cyberbullying at school and the responsibility of community members in the face of bullying.	HANDOUT: **Bullying and Cyberbullying Anticipation Guide** Your school handbook (specifically the bullying and cyberbullying policies) Four Corners signs Chart paper	If you would like to learn more about bullying and how it impacts students who are the targets of bullies before moving further into the case study section of *Community Matters*, we recommend that you download *A Guide to the Film "Bully,"* available at facinghistory.org/advisory-media, and read "What Is Bullying?" (pages 12–13). You will need copies of your school's anti-bullying and cyberbullying policies. The second part of this activity uses the Four Corners strategy. Visit facinghistory.org/advisory-media to learn about this teaching strategy.

56: Introducing the Ostracism Case Study (Part 1) — 40 min — page 219

Define ostracism and consider what factors influence our choices and decision-making process in the face of ostracism and bullying.	HANDOUT: **A Scene from a Middle School (Part 1 of 2)** HANDOUT: **A Scene from a Middle School (Part 2 of 2)**	The material in Activities 56–59 draws from "The Ostracism Case Study," a report on an incident that took place before middle school students took a Facing History course. In this case study, we hear the voices of eighth-grade students as they reflect on a particularly poignant social conflict among a group of friends that resulted in the ostracism of one of them.

57: Reading the Ostracism Case Study Transcripts (Part 2) — 40 min — page 224

Report on the perspective, choices, and role(s) played by one individual in the ostracism case study. Start to compare the perspectives of multiple individuals to arrive at a deeper understanding of the effects of ostracism on individuals and communities.	READING: **Interview with Sue** READING: **Interview with Rhonda** READING: **Interview with Jill** READING: **Interview with Lorna** READING: **Interview with Patty** READING: **Interview with Ms. Smith** HANDOUT: **Ostracism Case Study Group Activity**	Two of the six readings for this activity are longer than the other four, so you may need to modify the Jigsaw activity so "expert" groups finish around the same time. You will also need to modify it if you have fewer than 12 advisees in your group.

Purpose	Materials	Abridged Advisor Notes
58: Connecting Choices to Outcomes (Part 3)		40 min page 243
Examine the power dynamics in the ostracism case study and recognize that the outcome of the incident reflects the choices made by individuals and groups and was not inevitable.	Six signs for a modified Four Corners	The second part of this activity uses a modified Four Corners strategy (visit facinghistory.org/advisory-media to learn about this teaching strategy). Before the meeting, make six signs with the names of the individuals who were interviewed about the ostracism incident—Sue, Rhonda, Jill, Lorna, Patty, and Ms. Smith—and hang them around the room.
59: Understanding the Power of Ostracism and Bullying (Part 4)		40 min page 245
Reflect on and discuss the power of ostracism and apply new understanding from the case study to your school.	None	Depending on the size of your advisory group, you might have advisees discuss this activity's questions in a Socratic Seminar, Fishbowl, or circle discussion (visit facinghistory.org/advisory-media to learn about these teaching strategies).
60: Cyberbullying		2 x 40 min page 247
Analyze the Health and Human Services definition of cyberbullying, and discuss the range of responses to cyberbullying and how the choices we make online can impact members of our community.	HANDOUT: **Cyberbullying Scenarios**	This activity refers to the US Department of Health and Human Services definition of *cyberbullying*. Because it is long, if you can't project it during the activity, we recommend that you write it on the board or chart paper before the meeting or distribute it on a handout. If you would like to spend more time with this topic, you can extend this activity over two or more meetings.
61: Anatomy of an Upstander		30 min page 257
Examine specific qualities of upstander behavior and reflect on examples of witnessing upstander behavior.	None	None
62: Choosing to Be an Upstander		30 min page 259
Describe the steps that you can take before, during, and after an incident of ostracism, bullying, or cyberbullying has occurred.	HANDOUT: **Upstander Action Scenario Strips** HANDOUT: **Analyzing Upstander Actions**	In the first part of this activity, advisees will share bullying statistics from PACER's National Bullying Prevention Center, which you can access on PACER's website. Before the advisory meeting, make copies of and cut apart the handout Upstander Action Scenario Strips.
63: Case Study: Ostracism and Bullying Final Reflection		30 min page 263
Review materials from this section of the advisory program and reflect on new understanding and questions.	None	Providing advisees with the time and space to reflect on their learning, growth, and lingering questions from the section allows them to synthesize the material in meaningful ways before being introduced to new themes and concepts.

Case Study: Ostracism and Bullying

ACTIVITIES 53–63

OVERVIEW

After exploring themes of membership and belonging, advisees will embark on the next phase of the Facing History scope and sequence: the case study. In the first part of this section, advisees examine bullying behavior from different perspectives and then reflect on their own school's social climate and response to bullying and cyberbullying. Next, they analyze a real-life case study of an ostracism incident that occurred at a Boston-area middle school. This case study, which advisees explore over the course of four meetings, invites discussion of the roles that young people and adults can play in preventing and responding to these kinds of incidents. For a more in-depth exploration of ostracism and bullying, Facing History provides additional video and print resources for discussing these topics with your advisees. Our collection **Using Bully in the Classroom**, available at facinghistory.org/advisory-media, includes information about how to create safe classrooms and schools, strategies to combat bullying, and a resource guide to supplement clips from the film *Bully*. It is important that you preview all of these materials in advance of using them in your advisory to ensure that they are appropriate for your group.

NAVIGATING THE ACTIVITIES

Unlike with the other sections of the *Community Matters*, we recommend that you facilitate all of this case study section's activities in the order in which they are presented. The sixth and final section of the advisory program, Choosing to Participate, builds on the case study and provides your advisees with an opportunity to see examples of upstanders in action, both in schools and in communities, and to collaborate on planning and implementing their own project at your school site.

ACTIVITY **53**

Revisiting Our Advisory Contract

Purpose: Remind the group of its shared expectations, revise expectations as needed, and set the tone for difficult conversations. Draw connections between the factors that make a strong community and the norms that can help ensure that it remains strong.

APPROXIMATE TIME: 30 minutes

MATERIALS: NONE

ADVISOR NOTES:

1. **Reaffirm Advisory Norms**

   You will be prompted to revisit your advisory contract at the beginning of each section of *Community Matters* to reflect on the ways the group has been honoring its contract and where they feel they can do better. This activity also provides the opportunity to add to or revise any of the norms and expectations before moving forward with this section of the Facing History advisory program.

PROCEDURE:

1. **Reflect Individually in Journals about Your Advisory Contract**

   - Start by reading aloud your advisory contract, perhaps using the **Wraparound** strategy (visit facinghistory.org/advisory-media to learn about this teaching strategy).
   - Then ask advisees to respond to the following questions in their journals, citing specific examples from past meetings that support their thinking. Tell advisees that they will be sharing their responses in small groups.
     - What are examples from past advisory meetings where we did a great job of honoring one or more norms on our contract? What helped us do a great job?
     - What are examples from past advisory meetings where we struggled to uphold one or more of our contract norms? Why do you think we struggled? What might we do differently in the future to honor that norm?
     - What do you think, if anything, needs to be revised (reworded, added, deleted), and why?

2. **Discuss and Revise the Advisory Contract**

   - Divide the advisees into small groups and have them discuss the three journal questions one at a time. Then ask them to share highlights from their discussion, making a list on the board in three columns of their main ideas.

- Depending on their input, decide as a group whether or not your advisory contract needs to be revised and make the changes as needed. You might make changes on the original contract or create a new one.
- Then have everyone, including the advisor, sign the contract again.

3. **Commit to a Norm**
    - Finally, ask advisees to complete the following sentence starter in their journals. Revise the sentence starter as needed to fit what you think your group needs at this time:

        For the next month, I am going to work on _____ (choose a norm from the advisory contract). One way that I will work on it is by . . .

    - Then have each advisee share their completed sentence starter in a **Wraparound**.

ACTIVITY 54

The Roots of Bullying Behavior

Purpose: Explore the desire to belong, the range of responses to injustice, and the relationship between identity and choices. Practice perspective-taking by retelling a moment in a story from the point of view of the antagonist.

APPROXIMATE TIME: 40 minutes

MATERIALS:
READING
Fear

ADVISOR NOTES: None

PROCEDURE:

1. **Read and Discuss Gary Soto's "Fear"**

   - Let your advisees know that in this meeting, they will be reading and discussing a short story by Gary Soto from a book called *Living up the Street*, a collection of stories about a young boy coming of age in Fresno, California.

   - Pass out the reading **Fear** and read it aloud in small groups or as an advisory (visit facinghistory.org/advisory-media to learn about the Read Aloud teaching strategy). You might ask your advisees to underline words or phrases that help them understand the identities of the two main characters, the narrator and Frankie T.

   - In small groups or as a whole advisory, discuss the first four connection questions.

2. **See "Fear" from a Different Perspective**

   - Next, provide an opportunity for your advisees to practice perspective-taking by having them choose a moment in the story and retell it in the first person from Frankie's point of view. They might consider the following questions to help get them started:

     - What is Frankie thinking?

     - How is he processing what he is hearing, seeing, and feeling?

     - How does his perception of others and how he believes they perceive him impact his actions in that moment?

   - Give your advisees some time to write the section of the story from Frankie's perspective. Then you can ask advisees to share some or all of what they wrote with a partner. If they don't feel comfortable doing so, they can discuss how it felt to write from Frankie's point of view instead.

   - Finally, discuss the following questions:

     - How did it feel to write from Frankie's perspective?

     - What new insights, if any, did it give you about the scene you chose, a character, or the themes of identity, membership and belonging, or choices?

Community Matters: A Facing History and Ourselves Approach to Advisory

READING

Fear

Sometimes, feelings of embarrassment and humiliation about parts of our identities can influence the way we think about and act toward others. In a reflection titled "Fear," writer Gary Soto talks about how such feelings affected the way a boy he knew growing up treated others.

> A cold day after school. Frankie T., who would drown his brother by accident that coming spring and would use a length of pipe to beat a woman in a burglary years later, had me pinned on the ground behind a backstop, his breath sour as meat left out in the sun. . . . I stared at his face, shaped like the sole of a shoe, and just went along with the insults, although now and then I tried to raise a shoulder in a halfhearted struggle because that was part of the game.
>
> He let his drool yo-yo from his lips, missing my feet by only inches, after which he giggled and called me names. Finally he let me up. I slapped grass from my jacket and pants, and pulled my shirt tail from my pants to shake out the fistful of dirt he had stuffed in my collar. I stood by him, nervous and red-faced from struggling, and when he suggested that we climb the monkey bars together, I followed him quietly to the kid's section of Jefferson Elementary. He climbed first, with small grunts, and for a second I thought of running but knew he would probably catch me—if not then, the next day. There was no way out of being a fifth grader—the daily event of running to teachers to show them your bloody nose. It was just a fact, like having lunch.
>
> So I climbed the bars and tried to make conversation, first about the girls in our classroom and then about kickball. He looked at me smiling as if I had a camera in my hand, his teeth green like the underside of a rock, before he relaxed his grin into a simple gray line across his face. He told me to shut up. He gave me a hard stare and I looked away to a woman teacher walking to her car and wanted very badly to yell for help. She unlocked her door, got in, played with her face in the visor mirror while the engine warmed, and then drove off with the blue smoke trailing. Frankie was watching me all along and when I turned to him, he laughed, "*Chale*! She can't help you, *ese*." He moved closer to me on the bars and I thought he was going to hit me; instead he put his arm around my shoulder, squeezing firmly in friendship. "C'mon, chicken, let's be cool."
>
> I opened my mouth and tried to feel happy as he told me what he was going to have for Thanksgiving. "My Mamma's got a turkey and ham, lots of potatoes, yams, and stuff like that. I saw it in the refrigerator. And she says we gonna get some pies. Really, *ese*."

Poor liar, I thought, smiling as we clunked our heads softly like good friends. He had seen the same afternoon program on TV as I had, one in which a woman in an apron demonstrated how to prepare a Thanksgiving dinner. I knew he would have tortillas and beans, a round steak, maybe, and oranges from his backyard. He went on describing his Thanksgiving, then changed over to Christmas—the new bicycle, the clothes, the G.I. Joes. I told him that it sounded swell, even though I knew he was making it all up. His mother would in fact stand in line at the Salvation Army to come away hugging armfuls of toys that had been tapped back into shape by reformed alcoholics with veined noses. I pretended to be excited and asked if I could come over to his place to play after Christmas. "Oh, yeah, anytime," he said, squeezing my shoulder and clunking his head against mine.

When he asked what I was having for Thanksgiving, I told him that we would probably have a ham with pineapple on the top. My family was slightly better off than Frankie's, though I sometimes walked around with cardboard in my shoes and socks with holes big enough to be ski masks, so holidays were extravagant happenings. I told him about the candied yams, the frozen green beans, and the pumpkin pie.

His eyes moved across my face as if he were deciding where to hit me—nose, temple, chin, talking mouth—and then he lifted his arm from my shoulder and jumped from the monkey bars, grunting as he landed. He wiped sand from his knees while looking up and warned me not to mess around with him any more. He stared with such a great meanness that I had to look away. He warned me again and then walked away. Incredibly relieved, I jumped from the bars and ran, looking over my shoulder until I turned onto my street.

Frankie scared most of the school out of its wits and even had girls scampering out of view when he showed himself on the playground. If he caught us without notice, we grew quiet and stared down at our shoes until he passed after a threat or two. If he pushed us down, we stayed on the ground with our eyes closed and pretended we were badly hurt. If he riffled through our lunch bags, we didn't say anything. He took what he wanted, after which we sighed and watched him walk away after peeling an orange or chewing big chunks of an apple.

Still, that afternoon when he called Mr. Koligian, our teacher, a foul name—we grew scared for him. Mr. Koligian pulled and tugged at his body until it was in his arms and then out of his arms as he hurled Frankie against the building. Some of us looked away because it was unfair. We knew the house he lived in: The empty refrigerator, the father gone, the mother in a sad bathrobe, the beatings, the yearnings for something to love. When a teacher manhandled him, we all wanted to run away, but instead we stared and felt shamed. Robert, Adele, Yolanda shamed; Danny, Alfonso, Brenda shamed; Nash, Margie, Rocha shamed. We all watched him flop about as Mr. Koligian shook and grew red from anger. We knew his house and, for some, it was the same one to walk home to: The broken mother, the indifferent walls, the refrigerator's glare which fed the people no one wanted.[1]

Connection Questions

1. Make an identity chart for Frankie. Choose two phrases from the text that reveal something important about his identity. How might the identity chart you made for Frankie be different from the one he would make for himself?

2. What connection do you see between Frankie's identity and his choices?

3. What range of feelings does the narrator have for Frankie?

4. Why do you think Gary Soto called this story "Fear"? Who feels fear in the story, and what are they afraid of? How does fear affect their actions?

5. What is a bully? What motivations does this story suggest might be at the root of bullying behavior? What other factors might influence one to bully others?

1 Gary Soto, "Fear," in *Living Up the Street* (New York: Laurel-Leaf, 1985), 59–62. Reproduced by permission from Gary Soto.

ACTIVITY **55**

My School's Climate

Purpose: Discuss ostracism, bullying, and cyberbullying at school and the responsibility of community members in the face of bullying.

> **APPROXIMATE TIME:**
> 40 minutes
>
> **MATERIALS:**
> HANDOUT
> Bullying and Cyberbullying Anticipation Guide
>
> Chart paper

ADVISOR NOTES:

1. **Background Information about Bullying**

   If you would like to learn more about bullying and how it impacts students who are the targets of bullies before moving further into the case study section of *Community Matters*, we recommend that you download **A Guide to the Film Bully**, available at facinghistory.org/advisory-media, and read "What Is Bullying?" (pages 12–13).

2. **Your School's Bullying and Cyberbullying Policy**

   You will need copies of your school's anti-bullying and cyberbullying policy for this activity, so prepare copies in advance, project it, or ask advisees to bring their student handbooks to the meeting.

3. **Setting Up for "Four Corners"**

   The second part of this activity uses the **Four Corners** strategy, which you can learn about at facinghistory.org/advisory-media. We recommend that you set up the room for this activity in advance. Create four signs that read "Strongly Agree," "Agree," "Disagree," and "Strongly Disagree," and hang them in different corners of the room.

PROCEDURE:

1. **Define "Bully" and Reflect on Bullying Behaviors**

   - In their journals, ask advisees to respond to the following questions. Let them know that they will be sharing their responses with their peers.
     - What is a bully?
     - What motivations might be at the root of bullying behavior? You might think about Gary Soto's story "Fear," as well as other factors that could influence someone to bully others.

   - Have advisees share their responses in pairs or triads before coming together as an advisory to define "bully" and make a list on chart paper about the motivations at the root of bullying behavior. Save the chart paper because you will be referring to it later in this section of the advisory program.

Community Matters: A Facing History and Ourselves Approach to Advisory

2. **Explore Bullying at Your School and in Your Community**

    - Distribute the handout **Bullying and Cyberbullying Anticipation Guide** and ask advisees to complete it on their own by circling their responses to each statement (strongly agree, agree, disagree, strongly disagree) and briefly explaining their answers in the space provided.

    - After they have completed the anticipation guide, use the **Four Corners** strategy to discuss their responses (visit facinghistory.org/advisory-media to learn about this teaching strategy). Remember that advisees can change their positions in the room if they are persuaded by their peers. To ensure that you hear everyone's voice, try to create space for each advisee to share at least one idea with the group during the discussion.

    - Debrief the activity by leading a whole-group discussion based on the following questions:

        - What does this activity suggest about bullying and cyberbullying at your school?

        - How does this activity help you think about the choices you have if you witness or are made aware of an incident of bullying or cyberbullying at your school?

    - Then review your school's definition of bullying and the anti-bullying and cyberbullying policy with your advisees. Remind them where they can go for help and support if they or a friend are the target of bullying or witness bullying inside or outside of school or online.

3. **Reflect in an S-I-T Exit Card**

    Ask advisees to respond to the following question on an **exit card** that you will collect at the end of the meeting (visit facinghistory.org/advisory-media to learn about the Exit Cards teaching strategy):

    > What questions, ideas, and feelings did the activities in this meeting raise for you? If you would like to speak with me one-on-one about anything that came up in this meeting, please let me know on this exit card.

HANDOUT

Bullying and Cyberbullying Anticipation Guide

Directions: Read each statement in the left column. Decide if you strongly agree (SA), agree (A), disagree (D), or strongly disagree (SD) with it. Circle your response and provide a brief explanation of your opinion (on separate paper if needed).

Statement	Your Opinion
Bullying occurs at my school.	SA A SD D
Teasing is different from bullying.	SA A SD D
Cyberbullying is as harmful as bullying.	SA A SD D
Students who are the targets of bullying or cyberbullying should tell a trusted adult what is happening.	SA A SD D
There are clear consequences at my school for students who bully other students.	SA A SD D
The adults at my school have the power to prevent bullying from happening.	SA A SD D
The students at my school have the power to prevent bullying from happening.	SA A SD D
If I become aware of someone getting bullied or cyberbullied, I have a responsibility to help stop it.	SA A SD D
If I see someone getting bullied at school, I have a responsibility to offer support privately.	SA A SD D

ACTIVITY **56**

Introducing the Ostracism Case Study (Part 1)

Purpose: Define ostracism and consider what factors influence our choices and decision-making process in the face of ostracism and bullying.

APPROXIMATE TIME:
40 minutes

MATERIALS:
- HANDOUT
  A Scene from a Middle School (Part 1 of 2)
- HANDOUT
  A Scene from a Middle School (Part 2 of 2)

ADVISOR NOTES:

1. Background for the Facing History Ostracism Case Study

The material in Activities 56–59 draws from "The Ostracism Case Study," a report on an incident that took place in December 1996 and continued into 1998 at a middle school located in the suburb of a major US city. In this case study, we hear the voices of eighth-grade students as they reflect on a particularly poignant social conflict among a group of friends resulting in the ostracism of one of them. While the event itself occurred during seventh grade, the impact of this event could be felt in the eighth grade as well. The voices of these students bring us inside their world and provoke questions about issues of inclusion, exclusion, conformity, and belonging in adolescence and beyond.

PROCEDURE:

1. Reflect on Ostracism in a Journal Response

- Start by writing "ostracize" on the board and ask advisees to help you define it. Then provide the dictionary definition if you feel that your group would benefit from seeing it: "exclude by general consent from common privileges or social acceptance. [Example:] The other girls *ostracized* her because of the way she dressed."[1] As you discuss the definition together, note the difference between voluntarily leaving a group or being left out from time to time and ostracism, which is intentional, implies consent from the group, and is a form of bullying.

- Then ask advisees to respond to the following prompt in their journals. Let them know that they will not be sharing their responses unless they volunteer to do so.

    Write about a time when you were ostracized from a group or a time when you heard about or witnessed someone else being ostracized.

    - What happened and how did you feel?
    - What choices were available to you and/or to others?
    - What factors motivated your choices or the choices others made?

---

1 "Ostracism," Merriam-Webster.com, accessed June 2018.

- Ask for volunteers to share their responses to the second and third questions if they feel comfortable doing so.

2. **Read and Discuss the Introduction to a Real-Life Middle School Scenario**
   - Explain to the group that today and in upcoming meetings, they will read and discuss a seventh-grade middle school case study about an ostracism incident that happened in December 1996 and continued through 1997 and into 1998, when the students were in eighth grade.
   - Have advisees move into groups of four and pass out the handout **A Scene from a Middle School (Part 1 of 2)**. Invite advisees to read it out loud, with each advisee taking a role. After reading, they should discuss the questions and jot down notes to bring to a circle discussion.

3. **Read the Outcome of the Middle School Scenario**
   - Then move into a circle and ask each group to share a highlight from their discussion. It might be a point of disagreement that they would like the whole group to weigh in on, a new understanding about ostracism, a connection to their own lives or school community, or an interesting point they would like to share.
   - Pass out the handout **A Scene from a Middle School (Part 2 of 2)** and discuss the two questions as a group.
   - Let everyone know that in the next meeting, they will be hearing from the three students directly involved and other members of the school community who shared their reflections on this real-life incident in interviews.

HANDOUT

A Scene from a Middle School
(Part 1 of 2)

Directions: Choose roles and read aloud the following dialogue between three seventh-grade girls. The narrator can also read the setting section. Then discuss the questions on the second page together and record notes to share with your advisory group.

The Setting: The public school where this incident took place is located in a suburb bordering on a major city. Families living in the neighborhood surrounding the school range from working class to affluent, and a small percentage of students are bused to the school from the city as part of a longstanding desegregation program.

Narrator: In December 1996, Sue and Rhonda, seventh-graders in a public school, considered each other best friends. They belonged to a popular group of girls, which included another student named Jill. Most of these girls had known each other since elementary school.

Sue [*while writing a note*]: Hey Rhonda, what's up? Nothing much here. Did you hear about Jill? I can't believe it. She is breaking up with Travis. How could she break up with him? His mom just died. I think she's being really stupid. What do you think? Gotta go, Sue. P.S. Don't say anything to Jill about this. I haven't told her yet that I think she is stupid for breaking up with Travis.

Narrator: *Sue hands the note to Rhonda and walks away. Rhonda reads note. Then Jill walks by.*

Jill: Hey, Rhonda. What's up?

Rhonda: I was just reading a note from Sue.

Jill: What she'd say?

Rhonda: Well, she asked me not to tell you. I probably shouldn't say. But, you are my friend and you should know.

Jill: What is it?

Rhonda: Sue said you are stupid to break up with Travis.

Discussion Questions:

1. What feels familiar about this scene? What else would you like to know about the three students or the scenario?

2. Where do you see the students making choices in this scenario? What choices does each character—Sue, Jill, Rhonda—have? What factors do you think are motivating their decision-making processes?

3. Recall the range of responses to injustice that you have discussed this year: perpetrator, victim or target, bystander, upstander. What role(s) does each student adopt in this scene? Remember that the roles are choices and not parts of their identities, and that one person might choose different roles at different times within the same incident.

4. How might other students or members of the school community be impacted by this scenario?

HANDOUT

A Scene from a Middle School
(Part 2 of 2)

Narrator: When Jill found out about Sue's note, she confronted Sue after school, and they argued in front of a crowd of students. School staff heard the argument and broke it up. After this argument between Jill and Sue, Rhonda sided with Jill, and they influenced other girls to do the same. For the rest of seventh grade and almost all of eighth grade, these girls excluded Sue from her former group of friends, teased and put her down, avoided and ignored her, spread rumors about her, wrote hurtful letters, and made prank telephone calls to her home. Other students, including some boys who were not originally involved, joined in. Most students, if they did not participate directly, kept Sue at a distance and did not stand up for her. Sue went from being a very strong student to getting poor grades and not wanting to go to school.

Discussion Questions:

1. Why do you think this event turned out this way? How can you explain the actions of the three girls involved in this incident, the other girls, and the other students who got involved in the incident later in the year?

2. What about this situation feels familiar to you? This incident happened in 1996 and continued into the 1997–1998 school year. What might it look like in a school today?

ACTIVITY **57**

Reading the Ostracism Case Study Transcripts (Part 2)

Purpose: Report on the perspective, choices, and role(s) played by one individual in the ostracism case study. Start to compare the perspectives of multiple individuals to arrive at a deeper understanding of the effects of ostracism on individuals and communities.

APPROXIMATE TIME:
40 minutes

MATERIALS:

- **READING**
  Excerpts from the Interview with Sue
- **READING**
  Excerpts from the Interview with Rhonda
- **READING**
  Excerpts from the Interview with Jill
- **READING**
  Excerpts from the Interview with Lorna
- **READING**
  Excerpts from the Interview with Patty
- **READING**
  Excerpts from the Interview with Ms. Smith
- **HANDOUT**
  Ostracism Case Study Group Activity

ADVISOR NOTES:

1. **Creating Expert Groups for the Jigsaw Activity**

   There are six different readings representing six different perspectives about what happened during the ostracism incident that advisees were introduced to in Activity 56. Sue and Ms. Smith's transcripts are longer than the other four. For the **Jigsaw** portion of this activity, you might give stronger readers these transcripts, or, if you have random groups or let advisees choose groups, you might have them focus on certain sections so that everyone finishes the first half of the exercise around the same time. Visit facinghistory.org/advisory-media to learn more about the Jigsaw teaching strategy.

2. **Modifications for Advisory Groups Smaller than 12**

   If your advisory has fewer than 12 advisees, you will need to modify the jigsaw, which starts with six "expert" groups. For example, you can give some groups more than one short transcript. Alternatively, you could combine your advisory with another one so your advisees can discuss this case study with a wider range of students in your school.

PROCEDURE:

1. **Review the Scene from the Middle School Scenario (see Activity 56)**

   - In pairs or triads, ask advisees to discuss the following questions:
     - What happened in the middle school scenario you read about in the last meeting? Who was involved? What roles did they play?
     - What do you hope to learn in this meeting about the scenario or the students involved?

SECTION **5**

Community Matters: A Facing History and Ourselves Approach to Advisory

- Depending on how much time has passed since your last meeting and your advisees' recollection of the material, either spend time reviewing the scenario or move directly to the next part of the activity.

2. **Read and Discuss Firsthand Accounts of the Middle School Scenario**
    - Tell your advisees that they will now have an opportunity to read actual documents from the case study: firsthand accounts from the students involved in the incident, other students in the school, and a teacher. Review the **Jigsaw** strategy if needed (visit facinghistory.org/advisory-media to learn about this teaching strategy).
    - Explain that they will be working in groups. Each "expert" group will receive the transcript from one person who was involved in the ostracism incident in some way. After they read the transcript and discuss four questions, they will move into "teaching" groups to hear the perspectives of others who were involved.
    - Move advisees into six groups (see Advisor Notes for smaller groups), and pass out a different reading to each group and a copy of the handout **Ostracism Case Study Group Activity** to each advisee. Have them read their transcripts and discuss the four questions. They should record notes on side one of their handout to bring to their "teaching" groups.
    - After the expert groups have finished reading and discussing their questions, have advisees move into "teaching" groups where they will share their individual's perspective. Advisees should take notes on side two of their handout that help them capture all six perspectives.

3. **Reflect on New Understanding of the Incident**

    Let the group know that they will be discussing the case study further in the next meeting. To allow for a brief reflection, ask advisees to think about their response to the following question and then have them share in a **Wraparound** (visit facinghistory.org/advisory-media to learn about this teaching strategy).

    > How did hearing other perspectives about what happened confirm or change how you think about the ostracism incident?

READING

Excerpts from the Interview with Sue

Sue, an Asian American girl from a working-class family, was a leader among her friends until her argument with Jill. Below are word-for-word excerpts taken from interviews conducted in 1998 as part of a Facing History and Ourselves evaluation study. Please note that the names have been changed to protect the privacy of the students.

THE SUMMER AFTER EIGHTH GRADE
Sue's perspective on what happened and why

SUE: I used to be friends with a really cliquey crowd, a really, like, a really popular crowd too, and then like, um, last year, around December we got into a fight and then, like, I was like in a fight with, like, ten girls against me, and it was, like, really bad, and we had to go to mediation and I had to go to therapy and everything 'cause, like, the fight got really bad. And at one point it even got physical where like this girl came up to me and was like grabbing me and threatened me, and stuff.

It started because, like, Jill was going out with her boyfriend, and he liked her a lot, but, like, she didn't like him that much. She was afraid to get involved, like, into love or whatever, but like, um, I mean, this kid, his mother committed suicide and I felt really bad for him. And I thought how it was so sweet how he, like, liked someone after, like, all that happened to him, that's like so hard, and I just thought, like, Jill should be much kinder. Like, she didn't like him, and I mean . . . But like, I, like, said something in a letter that— we used to pass notes all the time, and I wrote something in a note like about how it was, like, wrong of Jill not to like Tony, or, like, ditch him like that kinda, 'cause like Tony liked her a lot and they were going out, but she didn't want to do anything with him. And then, like, Rhonda told Jill or something, and then, like, they both got mad. Jill got mad at me and then Rhonda got involved, and I don't know how Rhonda got involved, like, and I don't know how Tina got involved, but they all got involved. Like, the fight is so unclear how it started. I don't know how it turned into something that huge.

I know it's partly that the fight started as my fault and stuff, but it shouldn't have gotten as bad as it did with like ten girls against one.

Rhonda and Tina had all these girls to back them up. It was, like, caused out of fear, I mean the reason they have backup. Fear that, like, since other kids were picking on me, they were afraid to get picked on, so they backed them up and picked on me more.

It was, like, so gradual. I had never thought it would go that far. One day they had found out I told [a teacher] or something, and they got really mad. From that point on, they, like, hated me a lot because I had told. They just thought that telling—like, snitching—

was like the worst thing. So then, from then on it became, like, so bad. They would like, um, say stuff in class, like make comments or laugh at me if I made a comment in class or anything. From then on, I just, like, lost any self-esteem I had or anything. I mean, bit by bit I lost it, but, like, now I'm regaining it.

I think it was because Tina came in, it made it all worse . . . Because the girls I had been friends with, I had been friends with since fourth grade. That's a long time. And then after three years some girl comes with new views and everything, and a new attitude and stuff, and they start looking up to her and she changes everything. And so, she was able to do that, which is, like, powerful, I think.

When you have the ability to pick on someone, or like make fun of—like, that's power and stuff. But like, it's not good power, it's like, the worst kind of power you could have. It's like Hitler's power. You know how Hitler was able to, like, do everything—you know, like, make people do stuff—like, that's, like, bad power. And to kill that [many] people, that's like, powerful to be able to do that, but it's, like, bad. And Tina was, like, able to get everyone to gang up on me. But that's 'cause she caused fear, you know.

I think the fact that I am Asian has a lot, actually, to do with it. Not why I was being picked on, it was more to do with why the fight got as big as it did. I think, I mean, because I was a minority, it was easier for them to pick on me. Like, there [were] even, like, times, like my parents would always be like, um, "Yeah, um, the reason why, like, now you have to go to therapy and not them, the reason why the guidance counselor was saying that there's something wrong with you and not them, is because you were probably the minority, and stuff."

And the thing was, they were all rich. Which is also, like, the thing. I'm poor, I live in the projects and stuff, and . . . it's surprising to me now that I fit, I actually fit in that crowd, you know? I don't know how, like, I did. I don't know how that ever was, you know . . . I think it's surprising that I went from being at the top, . . . like starting from a low background or whatever, to getting to the bottom again, and now being in the middle, kind of.

THE SUMMER AFTER EIGHTH GRADE
Sue's point of view on the impact of the incident on her and its aftermath

SUE: I learned that you can't just trust everyone just because they say they're your friends. And, like, you have to be careful of what you say and you can't go around saying stuff just 'cause you feel like it. Now, like, when I make friends, I am more cautious. I am also, like, paranoid, 'cause I am afraid of this happening again, you know, and then just, like, before the fight I was . . . probably, like, so clueless, you know. Thinking I was, like, all that and, like, not caring about other people. And I was, like, always prejudice[d] against other people—it was just my crowd and no one else could come into it. And I would pick on other people too. I guess what goes around comes around. And it was probably partly one of the reasons it happened to me. Like, I would always pick on other people that were different, but, like, so I mean—now I wouldn't, you know. I think I understand more, like, why people get picked on and stuff.

I always hoped that I would have someone to talk to, and I didn't. And that was the thing that hurt the most.

Actually, I was so driven. 'Cause that was, like, the only way I could block my mind off and everything. And I actually got, like, good grades for a while, but then afterwards, everything just, like, was the pits. You didn't want to go to school, you didn't want to do homework, you didn't even see the point of like, living, it was just so bad.

When I came into the eighth grade this year, I was like: I'm gonna drop everything that happened last year. I'm gonna be as nice as I can. 'Cause I try to improve and try to change a lot because, I mean, and I try to be as not like I used to . . . I would always love to be the leader, you know. I used to love to be the leader, but now I wouldn't. I try to stay in the shadows more so people wouldn't notice me and stuff. But, like, this year, I didn't say anything. I never told a teacher if anything happened to me. I would try to ignore it.

I wanted to transfer—there were so many times that I wanted to transfer. There were actually some days when I would miss school just because I couldn't face it for that day.

THE SUMMER AFTER EIGHTH GRADE
Sue's perspective on the teachers' role in the incident

SUE: This isn't a fight you could ignore. And it wasn't a fight that you could confront, either, in a way.

You should be able to feel safe in a classroom, because there's a teacher, a supervisor, I mean, like, but now you can't. You don't feel, like, you can't feel safe at all even in the classroom. Cause they would say stuff to me inside of class.

I really had hoped—I wish that, like, I don't know, I wish, like, the teachers should have been able to stop it. But, I mean, I shouldn't have expected it, because they couldn't have.

I got mad at a teacher, kind of, because she couldn't keep the class under control. Like when they made snide remarks, even though it shouldn't, like, I should try to ignore it, it hurts, you know.

Teachers started putting into their lessons about friendships and fights and stuff. And they would always mention something about the fight, because the fight was so big, everyone knew it. Also because my guidance counselor emailed all the teachers and said, you know, to try to look out for me in a way. They mentioned it, but the thing was, like, partly it made it worse, because Rhonda's crowd or Tina's crowd . . . they hated the fact that they were all being ganged up on by teachers, but I hated the fact that they were ganging up on me, you know. And I was thankful so much for even like the least help, you know, that they could do. And the teachers would incorporate that into our lessons. Like, "You shouldn't do what you don't want others to do to you," but it never taught them anything. And the Facing History unit I related [to] a lot—like, from last year, I related [to] a lot of stuff, like the books we read and, you know, those surveys we took. I've been a bystander, a victim, and a perpetrator. In a lot of ways I can relate to a lot of those stories.

It [Facing History] helped me, like, know that I wasn't the only one who had gone through stuff like that, which helps a lot, to know that, you know? To know you aren't the only one and, like, that it happens. Like, reading [that] stuff was, like: it happened to teenagers, but it also—reading, like, the Facing History, learning about the Holocaust made me realize that what happened last year wasn't as—well, to me it was big, you know, 'cause it's my life—but there is so [much] other worse stuff that can happen in the world, you know, to kids my age, like what happened to Sonia Weitz at her age.

But now, like, there were two times when I really didn't want to live and stuff, and I would never think about, well, there's other worse stuff happening to people. I would just feel like I have to just show them that I am not weak. But now I feel like I have to because, look at—I mean, look at other situations. Why would you kill yourself over something like that, you know? Sometimes, like, you lose your perspective like that.

THE SUMMER AFTER EIGHTH GRADE
Sue's perspective on some positive outcomes from the incident

SUE: Before, I couldn't go anywhere by myself. I couldn't even walk down the street by myself, it was like, oh, I needed a friend . . . but now, like, I don't know, you know? It's like, I've learned to be more independent and stuff.

Back then, I probably would have just been, like—if I saw someone being picked on [by them], I'd probably go back them up, you know, like the . . . stronger people, but now, I mean, I try to stand up for the person.

READING

Excerpts from the Interview with Rhonda

Rhonda, an African American girl from an urban, working-class family, saw herself as a leader among her friends. Below are word-for-word excerpts taken from interviews conducted in 1998 as part of a Facing History and Ourselves evaluation study. Please note that the names have been changed to protect the privacy of the students.

THE FALL OF EIGHTH GRADE
Rhonda's perspective on the original incident

RHONDA: Last year, it was a real big thing from like December to the end of the year, where this girl named Sue, like, she said some stuff to me about my, like, best friend, and, like, Sue was my best friend at the time. But then she was good friends with the other people too, but she went behind . . . Sue was talking about people behind their backs, 'cause, you know, there's a boy named Tony, and Jill used to go out with Tony. And Sue and Jill were, like, really good friends. And Jill didn't like Tony and she wanted to break up with him. And Sue was, like, helping her break up with him. But then she wrote me a letter saying that Jill was ignorant to break up with Tony. And so I showed Jill that, and Jill got mad. And then Sue got mad at me because she said in the letter don't show this to anybody, but I showed it anyway, 'cause I felt obligated to show it to her because it wasn't, like, right for Sue to do something like that. Then we all got mad at each other.

THE FALL OF EIGHTH GRADE
Rhonda's perspective on the aftermath of the original incident

RHONDA: All these people started taking sides and, like, the teachers took Sue's side because they thought we [were] being, like, really mean to Sue when she really was . . . What they did was they, they always said, "Sue what happened?"—they never said, "Okay, Tina, Jill, and Rhonda, what happened?" . . . The teachers never heard our . . . They heard her side, but they didn't, like . . . They felt sorry for Sue . . . During that time period, from December to June, the teachers [were] mean to us and they didn't, like, listen to us. And they held grudges against us . . . The teachers, like, they held grudges against us because Sue told them, or Sue was crying about this, Sue was doing that—never, they never [said] "Sue did things to us and we did things back to Sue," but Sue never seemed to tell them what she did to us . . . Everybody who was part of our group, everybody who was on our side, got degraded. Everybody who was on Sue's side got, like—they [were] sympathizing [with] Sue, so they . . . [were] more lenient towards them.

The groups changed significantly. There was more people on our side than on Sue's side, but the teachers was on Sue's side. So then it seemed like teachers were, like—the teachers together would probably be more than as many kids as was on our side. So that the teachers had more, they have more power than us, so they can do whatever they want. Not whatever they want, but they would do a lot of things. But there were still people who, like, wasn't even in it that got into it anyway, and so . . . it just, it . . . It was a real big problem last year and we had, like, mediation and all these other things.

What they [were] doing is putting parents into it, and our parents had nothing to do with it and like I got in trouble because the guidance counselor called my father and told him that I was helping in part of this little grudge held against Sue or stuff like that, and she never said anything about what Sue did, which really made me mad, and I got in trouble for that. And, like, I guess everybody else, like, got talked to by their parents about whatever, and nobody never, nobody never said anything about what Sue did, so that's how we figured everybody was on Sue's side. And people . . . I still don't talk to her now, 'cause I don't like to forgive and forget, I don't like to forgive something that wasn't resolved at all . . .

THE SPRING OF EIGHTH GRADE
Rhonda's point of view on the incident and its aftermath

RHONDA: What we did was really, really wrong. I regret it now . . . because I think it was stupid . . . Well, I treated Sue really, really bad. And I don't think it's right now, but I can't do anything to change that. But we're friends now. So, it's kind of changed how it was. I didn't change it, really, but I kind of made it better . . .

And, 'cause we were good friends before, and, so, we shouldn't have wasted a good friendship just because of that. . . . We're friends. I don't know, we just started talking . . . we just talked in the classes together . . . I don't know. I can't really explain it. It's just, we're friends now.

INTERVIEWER: Did you and Sue ever talk about what happened?

RHONDA: Yeah. It's funny now. We find it pretty funny. We laugh at it now, but it wasn't funny then.

THE SPRING OF EIGHTH GRADE
Rhonda's perspective on the adults' role in the incident

RHONDA: There was no need to have parents involved. So you might as well—that made me, at the time, made me more, like, I would say, it made me mad again. . . . Because teachers got parents into it. And parents had nothing to do with it. And at the time, it just made me go—like it just made me go and do stuff. Worse.

READING

Excerpts from the Interview with Jill

Jill, a white girl from an upper-middle-class family, did not see herself as having much influence on others. Below are word-for-word excerpts taken from interviews conducted in 1998 as part of a Facing History and Ourselves evaluation study. Please note that the names have been changed to protect the privacy of the students.

THE FALL OF EIGHTH GRADE
Jill's perspective on the precursor to the incident and the incident itself

JILL: Sue and I were friends, and Rhonda and Tina were all friends with Sue, and then she started being really rude to me, and just, like, I didn't like it anymore. Like, she would try and tell me what to do and everything, and when I wouldn't, she'd get mad.

INTERVIEWER: What kinds of things did she try to tell you?

JILL: Like, to go out with certain people, and, like, if I didn't, she'd be mad. And, like, she'd talk about me behind my back, and she'd try and make me, like, do things for her or whatever. So, when I stopped, like, talking to her and stuff, Rhonda showed me letters that she'd written about me and stuff.

She was kinda controlling, like she would write letters to me, and if I didn't write back in time, she'd get upset, and it was like—it was all focused on her. And it was . . . I just didn't like it. And she would, like, talk about me behind my back, and then say I was her best friend and stuff like that. And she read my diary, and so I really didn't like her anymore.

THE SPRING OF EIGHTH GRADE
How Jill's perspective changed

JILL: Yeah, that was basically a gang-up against Sue and stuff, like, you know. But now, I mean, she has different friends, and we're not like enemies but we're not friends, we don't talk to each other. I mean, like, we say hi, but, um, everyone—everybody got mad at her. She—I mean, she had a couple friends . . . but hardly anybody. But there was a good reason for it. When she was really rude to all of us, she treated me very badly. So as a friend, I stopped liking her. And it didn't have to do with anyone else not liking her. It was just that I didn't like her and then everyone else stopped liking her.

I think a lot of people stopped because no one else did. No one else liked her.

INTERVIEWER: Do you think you were the first to stop liking her?

JILL: Yeah, no, I really do. I think that, like: I remember the day that it started, and I was the one that told her that I was mad at her. And, like, then everybody else stopped liking her.

INTERVIEWER: And do you think that had to do with—because you were mad at her?

JILL: No, I think—no, I just think people started to realize how, how rude she was.

I think, like—I realize how mean we were to her, but at the time I didn't think that it was that big of a deal, because she was mean to me, and she had been mean to me, she was getting what she deserved. But now it's just, like—I was childish.

INTERVIEWER: What happened over the course of the year, do you think, to make you change about what you thought about that?

JILL: Well, she really felt I didn't—I left her alone and I [stopped] talking about her behind her back and just like let things cool off. It was like—it was like she wasn't there, kind of, and so I [stopped] being angry and everything just calmed down. And then this year, um, I think we had to work together on a project in a group, and I just, like, forgot it all. I just, like, talked to her, you know, we had to work together, and I didn't feel like going through that.

INTERVIEWER: Were there any apologies made?

JILL: No, no.

INTERVIEWER: And now how would you summarize the way you feel about her?

JILL: She's nice. I really don't want to be friends with her anymore. I think it would be too weird. And she's just not my type, I guess. She's just not anyone I want to hang around with.

READING

Excerpts from the Interview with Lorna

Lorna, an African American student from an urban, working-class family, was not close friends with the other girls in the case study. Below are word-for-word excerpts taken from interviews conducted in 1998 as part of a Facing History and Ourselves evaluation study. Please note that the names have been changed to protect the privacy of the students.

THE FALL OF EIGHTH GRADE
Lorna's perspective on the incident and its aftermath

LORNA: I saw something happen to another girl in the school that I didn't really approve of.

INTERVIEWER: What happened?

LORNA: Well, there was, like, a lot of people—Sue, she was like a center for a target, or whatever. People like to make fun of her because of past things that happened, like in the sixth grade. So, I just—like, she didn't do anything to me. She said—people said that she said something about me, but she didn't say it to my face. So, I just, like, I mean, I'm friends with her—it's nothing—but she's not, like, buddy-buddy, she's just, like, we're just friends or whatever.

I think it was because of, like, not a survey—like, a rumor that happened. People said that she had said something about them, and that she had started saying something, she had told everybody, and that she wasn't really a good friend, she was a liar and stuff like that.

INTERVIEWER: Do you know what she said?

LORNA: No. Whatever it was, it had to be pretty bad, because everybody's mad at her still, and it's eighth grade now.

Well, they probably made her feel like she was, I don't know, she had some, like, incurable disease that she would die from, and that if anybody would come near her, they would die, too. I mean, a lot of people are just that mean that they would just make somebody feel like that, 'cause a lot of people prank-called her house—I mean, they wrote mean letters to her and stuff. . . . I have an idea of who was doing it, but it was mostly boys—like, the girls would say something nasty about her or whatever, like, behind her back, but they wouldn't go to that extreme, to call her up or write letters or whatever like that.

People are just still, like, making fun of her, and they're just still not hanging around with her. Well, she has friends, but they've been her friends all along, so I think that's pretty good.

THE FALL OF EIGHTH GRADE
Lorna's perspective on her role in the incident and its aftermath

LORNA: I didn't really know her, so I, like, kind of stayed away from her, but, like, this year I just got sick of all the stuff that was happening to her. So I just, more or less, became more of a friend than I was last year.

INTERVIEWER: And did you do anything about what happened?

LORNA: No, I just wasn't a part of it.

INTERVIEWER: Okay. And how do you feel about that?

LORNA: Well, if I had been a part of it, then I know that a lot of rumors would have been said about me, that she would have probably not have said, but other people might have said that she had said.

THE SPRING OF EIGHTH GRADE

LORNA: Like, nobody thinks about it. Well, they think about it, but it's like they laugh it off or something. So, like, everybody's friends now. So, she, like, sits at our table sometimes. And, like, I mean, everybody's friends now.

INTERVIEWER: So, everyone who was against her before is friends with her now?

LORNA: Yeah.

INTERVIEWER: It sounded like, from what you said, a lot of kids were against her. But you came forward and you were friends, so I wondered: What was going on for you? Why did you make that decision?

LORNA: Why not? I mean, she didn't do anything to me—didn't say anything about me.

INTERVIEWER: Yes.

LORNA: Just because she said something about my friend doesn't mean I'm going to jump in every time they have a problem. Like, I don't think it's fair for, like, a whole group of people just to pick on one person. That's just not fair.

READING

Excerpts from the Interview with Patty

Patty, a white girl from a middle-class family, did not see herself as a leader among her friends. Below are word-for-word excerpts taken from interviews conducted in 1998 as part of a Facing History and Ourselves evaluation study. Please note that the names have been changed to protect the privacy of the students.

PATTY: Also, it's sort of weird, 'cause you'd never expect somebody who was as popular as she was to, like, be sort of, like, shunned from the group by everyone else, but we sort of, like, we all just went against her.

She talked about people behind their back . . . but I think other people did that, too. . . . I really don't know . . . why we were so willing to jump on her and attack her more than anyone else. People were breaking the confidence. . . . She had told them stuff in confidence, and people sort of forgot that was one of the reasons why they didn't like her. And they just sort of, like, started doing it to her.

It sort of seemed like it was a cool thing to do . . . to be mean to her. And I guess it felt good to be able to get your anger out on a person, regardless of whether or not they really deserved to be the person. . . . It sort of seemed, like, sort of exciting, like it was something you could talk about.

I figured if I stuck by her, I would probably be her friend or be friends with all the other friends that I have, and I guess I, sort of, like, chose them over her because, like, they were more important to me.

If I sort of, like, became her like good friend—like started hanging out with her and doing stuff with her—I would definitely sort of, like, be not as close to the friends I have now. I don't know how far it would go, but it definitely would have an effect on it.

People still . . . might say something [like], "Oh, look at what she's wearing today," or whatever, but, like, I mean, I know I don't say—I try not to say mean stuff about her anymore, but it's sort of become a habit.

What they've done has left a permanent effect on Sue. She'll never get over it. Though people feel remorse, it's too late now.

THE SPRING OF EIGHTH GRADE

PATTY: Once we had started, it was sort of like you couldn't stop. . . . It builds and builds and builds until the point where you can't . . . turn back and say we're not going to do this to her anymore.

The Holocaust, or whatever: I think it started out with little things like that. Like, it didn't all happen at once. And so, I mean, that's what I think about how it connects to me personally. 'Cause it's like we allow people to be hurt for no reason. Or because if we're there every, like, every day. And, that's on like a much, a much smaller scale [than] what happened in the Holocaust. And that's how I connect [to] it myself, really. I think probably because you feel, like, if they are picking on her, they are going to leave me alone.

Some people who make fun of other kids, I think that one of the reasons they do it is out of fear that if they don't, someone would make fun of them for how they are. . . . I think the people who are actually the ones making fun are also afraid of what might happen if they don't make fun of people. Because then other people would make fun of them.

INTERVIEWER: Knowing the things that you know now, that you've learned this year, do you feel like you would have acted differently now? That you would act differently if this happened?

PATTY: I'm not sure it would have happened. I mean, I think . . . it makes you realize that these things happen every day and you just can't sort of say, like, "Oh, this isn't a big thing." . . . I'm not sure it would have happened. Some people would have realized this isn't right, which I don't think we did at the time.

When you realize it could happen to her, you realize it could happen to you. I think that was one point [at] which I lost a lot of trust for my friends. 'Cause it was like: You say the wrong thing or you do the wrong thing and it could happen to you.

I started to be a lot more careful about . . . what I say and what I [do]. I guess everybody knows it's been, like, a lot harder . . . to stand up and say what you believe or say what you want to say.

There's a lot of pressure to act a certain way. To be a certain way. And since there's all that pressure, you're, like, afraid to say things, you know, you want to say. You—you don't know what necessarily it is that's going to happen to you once you say them.

READING

Excerpts from the Interview with Ms. Smith

Ms. Smith taught a ten-week Facing History and Ourselves unit as part of her eighth-grade language arts course at the school where the conflict took place. The students involved in this case study were in her class. Below are word-for-word excerpts taken from interviews conducted in 1998 as part of a Facing History and Ourselves evaluation study. Please note that the names have been changed to protect the privacy of the students.

A teacher's perspective on the ostracism incident and its relation to her teaching

MS. SMITH: This eighth grade is a class that has gone through a lot of social/friendship upheavals. There's been a lot of—especially last year, but it's flowed over a little bit to this year—some tension in the breakup particularly [of a] girls' group of friendships that kind of broke apart last year . . . It was very painful for some girls, and there was definitely victimizing and the victim and all that sort of thing going on, and so in that case it's been a very interesting class to watch. And yet that seems to have leveled off and that seems to have pretty much taken care of itself, so now, again, it's interesting to watch the different groups as they move around, making friends, that sort of thing. It's a fascinating group.

INTERVIEWER: The incident that happened last year—do you think it influenced the kids in this class in particular, in terms of the kinds of discussions you are having, at all?

MS. SMITH: Um, I think, um, when we talked about *The Crucible*—when we talked about victimizing, there are a number of times in the discussion, without saying outright, you know, using the example of what happened last year, because it would have been too painful or too personal. I did talk a lot about why certain people in certain situations seem to have a power over other people, and it's a really—for me, anyways, it's something that we will talk about as we do more of Facing History, but we've talked about it as a group, how people get a certain amount of power. And kids, through the discussion of *The Crucible*, they were very aware that sometimes the totally incorrect person has the power. And with *The Crucible*, we did talk about it a bit, and it's something we are going to pursue more, and when I do that I really am definitely hoping some of them—and I think they are—are making the connection to what happened in the school.

INTERVIEWER: Yeah, I was going to ask you: Did you get a sense that they did make that connection?

MS. SMITH: I—yes, again, I—yes, I did. I got a sense that they kind of knew what I was talking about without stating it, 'cause I never would, because it's just too, too close to home.

INTERVIEWER: Did anyone raise their hand and say, "Wait a minute. This sounds a lot like . . . "?

MS. SMITH: No, no. But I think, again, it's too—I think, partly because there's still a person in that room with power—or, not in that room, but in that class—with power who kids are still afraid to go against.

INTERVIEWER: Really?

MS. SMITH: Yeah. I think kids—I think that one thing that happened last year, and I think it's kind of a negative, a sad thing, is that kids realized how quickly . . . you could be isolated, how powerful a group, in this case a group of girls, can be. And, in fact, when I was filling out the questionnaires, I said a lot of kids have had the experience of standing by and not getting involved with someone else who was a victim. And this was the class: that because of that, there were very few kids who tried to jump in and help out in that situation. They all, I think, were afraid that they would be the next victim. It was really an interesting situation.

INTERVIEWER: Can you just outline it? You don't need to name names, but . . .

MS. SMITH: It was basically a friendship, a very intense, close friendship of a few girls who had been friends down through the years. A few things happened, and, again, I don't think any of them were major, but enough different things happened amongst the girls, and then there was a new girl that came into the school. This is part of it, too, and when that happens, you know, people are kids—other girls are curious. For whatever reason, this girl tends to wield a lot of power.

INTERVIEWER: The new girl?

MS. SMITH: The new girl. And all of the sudden—not all of the sudden, but slowly but surely—one of the girls that used to be a very close member of this girls' group became isolated. She couldn't understand quite why. Um, there was a lot of cruelty, a lot of back-stabbing, a lot of just meanness. And . . . definitely shut-off: this girl is not any longer a part of this group. And it eventually involved teacher intervention. Not myself—I mean, I was concerned about it, but it was really something that the counselor really had a part in, and the principal and some parents were called in, and even then it wasn't resolved because some kids just couldn't see it. They just couldn't see that this was, you know, something that teachers should be involved in, or parents should be involved in. Some parents thought it was silly and foolish that, you know . . . It was really an interesting situation, and yet one girl was tremendously hurt by it.

This happened last year. I mean, this girl is very bright, the one who was isolated, um, very talented, always gets A's, although a few of the other girls who were doing this to her are pretty much in that same bracket, so I think there might have been some of the jealousy issue. She might have, you know, she might have turned them off in some ways and maybe her attitude was a little—she might have come across a little too sure of herself, a little too, you know, sort of cut-her-down-a-little-bit sort of thing. But . . . you know, I'm not the only teacher who thinks the, um, the idea of this new young woman coming to the seventh grade and just, again, having the kind of personality that draws people to her, and then she can do things with that personality that, you know . . . It's really fascinating. We'll talk more about it as time goes on. It may come out in some of the discussions with the Facing History [unit] . . . I hope it will, you know: some of the issues surrounding what happened last year.

INTERVIEWER: So that's definitely in the room?

MS. SMITH: Oh, yeah. That's part of this class's history. It's a big part. And what breaks my heart is some of the brightest, some of the most insightful, some of the most mature students in the class still seem to need her approval. Still seem to . . . It's just fascinating. And, you know, they will kind of, there is a little adoration there that I would've thought wasn't necessary for them. That they were self-assured enough not to have to do that. But I think everyone is afraid of not being on her right side. Because if you're not on the right side, you could be isolated, or you could be not one of the "in" crowd. It's pretty interesting. She is also the kind of kid who will tease other kids. She'll be supportive of other kids and she'll also tease.

. . . So, you don't want to do anything to jeopardize your position in the group. You don't want to be one of the kids who doesn't have a group. You don't want to be one of the outsiders. We're taking a great leap here: when we talk about what happened in Germany—how willing are you to go against what your neighbors are doing, what your neighbors are joining, you know . . . ? I mean, how many of us are willing to take a stand against that, even if we feel morally that, you know, we should—and then you bring that down to in our school. How many of us would be morally willing to take a stand against some of our friends if they were doing something that we think is wrong? And I hope to get into that discussion with the girls and the boys. So, we'll see.

HANDOUT

Ostracism Case Study Group Activity

"Expert" Group Directions: Read your transcript with your group, and then record your answers to the following questions. You will be using this information to help others understand your individual's perspective. Do not start side two of this handout yet.

Individual's Name: _____

1. What stands out for you about your individual's perspective on the incident? Record three to five details that help you capture her perspective.

2. What role or roles did your individual play in this incident (victim of injustice, bystander, perpetrator, upstander)? What makes you say that? (Remember, someone can move between different roles over the course of the same incident.)

3. If you were this individual's peer (either another student or another teacher, if you have Ms. Smith), what would you want her to consider that was not apparent in her perspective on the incident?

4. What questions does this perspective on the ostracism incident raise for you? Who might be able to help you answer your questions?

"Teaching" Group Directions: Use the bull's eye graphic organizer to record notes from your expert group discussions. First, each person should share one or two key ideas from each question on side one of this handout. Next, in the inner circle, write each individual's perspective. In the outer circle, write the role(s) they played in the incident.

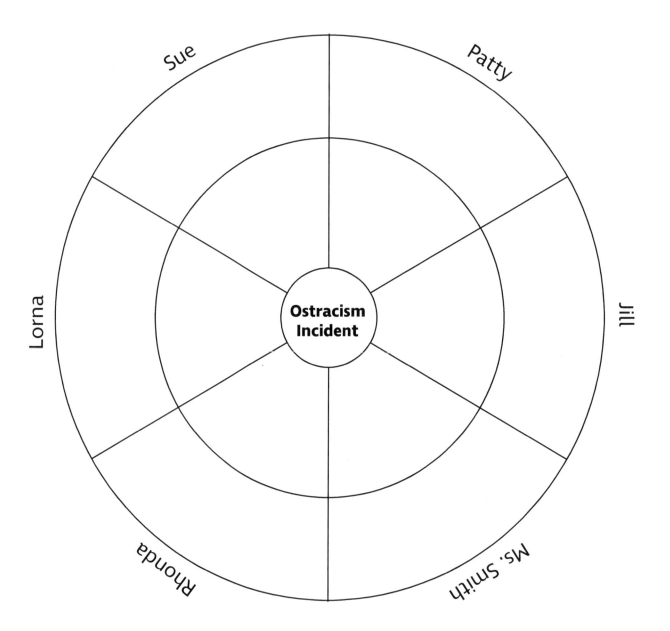

ACTIVITY **58**

Connecting Choices to Outcomes (Part 3)

Purpose: Examine the power dynamics in the ostracism case study and recognize that the outcome of the incident reflects the choices made by individuals and groups and was not inevitable.

APPROXIMATE TIME: 40 minutes

MATERIALS: Signs for modified Four Corners (see Advisor Notes)

ADVISOR NOTES:

1. **Set Up for a Modified Version of Four Corners**

   The second part of this activity uses a modified version of the **Four Corners** strategy. To learn about this teaching strategy, visit facinghistory.org/advisory-media. Before the meeting, make six signs with the names of the individuals who were interviewed about the ostracism incident—Sue, Rhonda, Jill, Lorna, Patty, and Ms. Smith—and hang them around the room.

2. **Choose Final Discussion Questions in Advance**

   The activity that follows this one includes a Socratic discussion of the ostracism incident. There is some overlap between this activity's final discussion questions and what you will find in the next activity. If you plan to do the next activity with your group, choose which questions you will use for each advisory meeting.

PROCEDURE:

1. **Review Notes from Activity 57**

   Depending on how much time has passed since your last meeting, advisees may need to review their notes on the Ostracism Case Study Group Activity handout. Divide into groups to review their handouts and add to their notes as needed.

2. **Reflect on the Power to Change the Course of a Conflict**

   - In their journals, ask advisees to respond to the following question:

     Who had the most power to change the conflict in the ostracism case study (Sue, Rhonda, Jill, Patty, Lorna, Ms. Smith)? What makes you say that?

   - Debrief the activity using a modified version of the **Four Corners** strategy (visit facinghistory.org/advisory-media to learn about this teaching strategy). Ask advisees to move to the sign of the individual they feel had the most power, and have advisees explain their choices to others in their group. Then have them share across groups. Remember that they can change places if they are swayed by the discussion.

3. **Consider Alternative Choices and Outcomes**
   - Working in the groups they ended in after the Four Corners discussion (you can divide groups of four or more into smaller pairs and triads as needed), ask advisees to consider a different choice that their individual could have made and the potential outcome of that choice.
   - Invite advisees to role-play these choices for each other or for the advisory group. Alternatively, they can write a dialogue on chart paper or in their journals, or, if you have time or want to spend an additional meeting on this activity, create a **storyboard** (visit facinghistory.org/advisory-media to learn about this teaching strategy).
   - Time allowing, facilitate a circle discussion that draws from the following questions:
     - What can we learn about the power of our choices in the face of bullying and ostracism from this case study?
     - What might this incident look like if it happened in our school today?
     - What choices can we make when we notice that a student or group of students is starting to be singled out in a way that is hurtful or harmful?
     - What choices can we make if we realize that an individual or group in our school community is being ostracized and that the situation shows no sign of stopping?
     - What factors make it challenging to be an upstander when we witness someone being ostracized or bullied?
     - What are big and small ways that you can help when you witness someone being ostracized or bullied?

ACTIVITY **59**

Understanding the Power of Ostracism and Bullying (Part 4)

Purpose: Reflect on and discuss the power of ostracism and apply new understanding from the case study to your school.

APPROXIMATE TIME: 40 minutes

MATERIALS: NONE

ADVISOR NOTES:

1. **Choose a Discussion Format**

   Depending on the size of your advisory group, you might have advisees discuss this activity's questions in a Socratic Seminar, Fishbowl, or circle discussion. Visit facinghistory.org/advisory-media to learn about these teaching strategies. If there are other advisory groups at your school that have been working with the case study, you can also combine your advisory groups, which would allow advisees to hear other voices and perspectives. It might be interesting to have them work with students in their own grade, or try a cross-grade discussion.

PROCEDURE:

1. **Prepare for the Discussion with a Journal Reflection**

   To provide time for reflection, ask your advisees to respond to the following questions in their journals. Encourage them to use their journal reflections and handouts from this section of *Community Matters* to formulate their responses. Let them know that they will be participating in a Socratic Seminar or Fishbowl discussion that focuses on ostracism and bullying.

   - Why is ostracism so powerful? Why is bullying so powerful? How are they similar and different?
   - What can you learn about ostracism and bullying from the case study?
   - What can we do at our school to combat ostracism and bullying?
   - What question(s) would you like to bring to the discussion?

2. **Discuss the Power of Ostracism and Next Steps**

   - Before the discussion, you might review the advisory contract with a focus on any norms related to listening, respect, and participation.
   - Using the Socratic Seminar or Fishbowl discussion strategy, have advisees share their responses to the journal prompts, as well as their own questions about ostracism and bullying (visit facinghistory.org/advisory-media to learn about these discussion strategies).

3. Reflect on New Understanding

In their journals or on an **exit card**, ask advisees to respond to the following question (visit facinghistory.org/advisory-media to learn about the Exit Cards teaching strategy):

> What new, different, or deeper understanding about ostracism or bullying do you have after reading and discussing the case study with your peers?

ACTIVITY **60**

Cyberbullying

Purpose: Analyze the Health and Human Services definition of cyberbullying, and discuss the range of responses to cyberbullying and how the choices we make online can impact members of our community.

APPROXIMATE TIME:
2 x 40 minutes

MATERIALS:
HANDOUT
Cyberbullying Scenarios

ADVISOR NOTES:

1. **Preparing Materials for This Activity**

   - First Advisory Meeting: This activity uses the US Department of Health and Human Services definition of cyberbullying. The definition is long, so if you can't project it, you can write it on the board or chart paper before the meeting or distribute it on a handout.

   - Second Advisory Meeting: If your advisory has fewer than 12 advisees, remove one or more of the scenarios or combine your group with another advisory. You need at least two advisees per scenario for the Jigsaw.

2. **Your School's Cyberbullying Policy**

   If your school has a cyberbullying policy in the student handbook, bring a copy to read aloud or project during the first meeting. If your school does not have a cyberbullying policy, consider asking your advisory group to draft one as an extension to this activity. They could draft, revise, and edit their policy and then invite members of the administration to a future meeting where they present and discuss it with them.

3. **Recommitting to the Advisory Contract**

   We recommend that you review your advisory contract in the second meeting before the cyberbullying scenario activity. Because one or more scenarios may feel familiar to your advisees, it is important that they feel safe and can engage in the activity. Remind advisees that they should focus on the discussion questions and not personalize the scenarios with comments like, "Oh! I remember when that happened to _____!"

4. **Digging Deeper into Cyberbullying: Extending This Activity**

   If you would like to spend more time with this topic, you can visit StopBullying.gov to learn about laws and policies that states have adopted to prevent bullying and cyberbullying. If your advisees have access to computers, they can click on, read, and discuss the interactive map and policies for their state in small groups. Alternatively, you can project the map and explore it together. You can also click on your state and then print the information.

PROCEDURE:

First Advisory Meeting

1. **Reflect on Cyberbullying in a Journal Response**

   - To help advisees connect this activity to the ostracism case study, remind them that the ostracism incident took place in December 1996, before it was commonplace for students to have cellphones. A lot has changed since then! While ostracism and bullying are still prevalent in schools, in some ways, they might look and sound different today, when students spend so much of their time interacting with each other online.

   - Ask advisees to reflect on the following questions in their journals. Let them know that they will be sharing their responses with a partner.
     - How can people use social media to ostracize or bully others?
     - Have you seen examples of your friends or other students at your school bullying each other online? If so, on which apps do you think cyberbullying occurs the most?
     - What is the difference, if any, between "joking around" online and cyberbullying?

   - Have advisees turn and talk with a partner. Let them know that they should focus on their school's climate rather than individual experiences with cyberbullying. Then see if any volunteers would like to share their responses with the group.

2. **Define and Discuss Cyberbullying**

   - As a group, define *cyberbullying*. Create a web on the board or chart paper with the following question in the center: *What is cyberbullying?* Then have advisees share their ideas and record them on the web.

   - After your group has created its web, project or pass out the following definition from the US Department of Health and Human Services:
     - "Cyberbullying includes sending, posting, or sharing negative, harmful, false, or mean content about someone else. It can include sharing personal or private information about someone else causing embarrassment or humiliation. Some cyberbullying crosses the line into unlawful or criminal behavior. The most common places where cyberbullying occurs are:
       - Social Media, such as Facebook, Instagram, Snapchat, and Twitter
       - SMS (Short Message Service) also known as Text Message sent through devices
       - Instant Message (via devices, email provider services, apps, and social media messaging features)
       - Email"[1]

---

1 "What Is Cyberbullying?" StopBullying.gov, accessed June 16, 2018.

- Next, compare the US Department of Health and Human Services definition with your group's cyberbullying web. You might draw a Venn diagram on the board or chart paper to help advisees organize the ideas and discuss the similarities and differences they see.
- If your school has a cyberbullying policy in its student handbook, read it aloud, project it, or hand it out and discuss it as a group by comparing it to the Health and Human Services definition and your advisory's web.
- In pairs, small groups, or in a circle, discuss the following questions:
    - What are the similarities between in-person and online bullying?
    - What are the differences between in-person and online bullying?
    - Why do you think so many people choose to bully others online?

3. **Capture Understanding and Questions on an Exit Card**
    - To get a sense of your group's understanding of cyberbullying, have them complete an **exit card** in which they finish the following sentence starters (visit facinghistory.org/advisory-media to learn about the Exit Cards teaching strategy):
        - After today's cyberbullying activities, I am thinking about . . .
        - A question that I have about cyberbullying is . . .

Second Advisory Meeting

1. **Share Some Responses from the Exit Cards**

    Without revealing the identities of the writers, share some observations about any patterns you noticed in the exit card responses. You might discuss one or two of the questions or save them for the circle discussion at the end of the meeting.

2. **Apply the Definition of *Cyberbullying* to Scenarios**
    - Now is a good time to revisit your advisory contract. Some advisees in your group might find that one or more of the scenarios feels familiar, and it is important that everyone feels safe and can fully engage in the activity, share their perspective, and feel heard.
    - Let your group know that in this activity, they will be reading and discussing scenarios that involve teenagers interacting on social media. Divide your advisory into six groups for a **Jigsaw** (see Advisor Notes for smaller groups and visit facinghistory.org/advisory-media to learn more about the Jigsaw teaching strategy). Pass out one scenario from the handout **Cyberbullying Scenarios** to each "expert" group and explain to advisees that they will read and discuss their scenarios together. Then they will move to a new "teaching" group, where they will share their scenarios with each other and discuss some new questions together.

- After the expert groups have finished discussing their scenarios, "jigsaw" your advisory into "teaching" groups. Each advisee should give a brief summary of their scenario and an overview of their group's discussion. Then have the "teaching" groups discuss the second set of questions on their handouts.

- Move into a circle to discuss the following questions as a whole group:
    - What solutions do you have that would encourage students to choose to be upstanders when they witness cyberbullying?
    - What responsibility, if any, do the companies who own social media platforms like Instagram or Twitter have to prevent cyberbullying on their sites? What other solutions do you have to prevent cyberbullying?
    - What lessons can you learn from these scenarios about the choices you make online or what you can do if you witness or are a target of cyberbullying?

3. **Reflect on Cyberbullying**

   Ask advisees to respond to the following questions on a **3-2-1 exit card** (visit facinghistory.org/advisory-media to learn about these teaching strategies):
    - What are **3** things that you learned about cyberbullying?
    - What are **2** questions that you have about cyberbullying?
    - What is **1** specific action that you can take if you are the target of cyberbullying or witness cyberbullying online?

HANDOUT

Cyberbullying Scenarios

SCENARIO 1

Jasmine and Tanya, friends since seventh grade, are texting about a new boy named Dwayne in their tenth-grade class. What starts as a back-and-forth conversation becomes more heated when they each realize that the other one likes Dwayne and has been talking to him online. Name-calling quickly escalates to put-downs. Then Tanya threatens to send an ugly selfie from Jasmine's Finsta to Dwayne. Jasmine replies with a warning that Tanya had better watch her back after school the next day if she knows what's good for her. Then she signs off with two emojis: an angry face and an ambulance. Tanya tells her mother that she feels too sick to go to school the next day.[1]

Read your scenario together and discuss the following questions. You should refer to the Health and Human Services definition of cyberbullying to guide your discussion.

1. What makes or doesn't make this scenario an example of cyberbullying?
2. What role does each student choose in your scenario (perpetrator, bystander, upstander)? What factors motivate their choices?
3. Where do you see students making choices in this scenario? What other choices are available to them?
4. Are there any examples of upstanders in your scenario? If not, what are some ways that an upstander could respond?
5. How might this scenario be resolved?
6. What questions does this scenario raise for you?

After you move into your new group, have each person share a brief summary of their scenario and discussion. Then discuss the following questions together:

1. What patterns, if any, do you notice across multiple scenarios?
2. What factors motivate the students' choices to be perpetrators, bystanders, or upstanders? What solutions do you have that would encourage students to choose to be upstanders when they witness cyberbullying?
3. What responsibility, if any, do the companies who own social media platforms like Instagram or Twitter have to prevent cyberbullying on their sites? What other solutions do you have to prevent cyberbullying?
4. What can you learn from these scenarios about the choices you make online?
5. What can you learn from these scenarios about what to do if you witness or are a target of cyberbullying?

---

1 Scenarios 1–4 in this handout have been adapted from scenarios published by the Cyberbullying Research Center as well as accounts of cyberbullying in schools and on the news.

SCENARIO 2

Magda is a new girl at school. She is attractive, outgoing, and instantly popular with the "in" group, and many boys want to ask her out. Sara, a member of the "in" group, is concerned about Magda stealing away her boyfriend. With the help of her friends, Sara creates a "100 Reasons Why We Hate Magda" group chat, and her friends start to fill in the list. Girls include other students at the school on the chat, and soon boys and girls begin to post lies and hurtful messages about Magda. Magda's grades slip, she becomes depressed, and she asks her parents if she can transfer to a different school at the break.

Read your scenario together and discuss the following questions. You should refer to the Health and Human Services definition of cyberbullying to guide your discussion.

1. What makes or doesn't make this scenario an example of cyberbullying?
2. What role does each student choose in your scenario (perpetrator, bystander, upstander)? What factors motivate their choices?
3. Where do you see students making choices in this scenario? What other choices are available to them?
4. Are there any examples of upstanders in your scenario? If not, what are some ways that an upstander could respond?
5. How might this scenario be resolved?
6. What questions does this scenario raise for you?

After you move into your new group, have each person share a brief summary of their scenario and discussion. Then discuss the following questions together:

1. What patterns, if any, do you notice across multiple scenarios?
2. What factors motivate the students' choices to be perpetrators, bystanders, or upstanders? What solutions do you have that would encourage students to choose to be upstanders when they witness cyberbullying?
3. What responsibility, if any, do the companies who own social media platforms like Instagram or Twitter have to prevent cyberbullying on their sites? What other solutions do you have to prevent cyberbullying?
4. What can you learn from these scenarios about the choices you make online?
5. What can you learn from these scenarios about what to do if you witness or are a target of cyberbullying?

SCENARIO 3

Dominic, a tall, skinny teenager, feels embarrassed when he has to change in the boys' locker room at school because he is not very muscular. Other boys notice Dominic's shyness and discomfort. One of the boys secretly takes a picture with his cell phone of Dominic wearing only his boxer shorts and posts it to Snapchat. One of his friends records the image on his brother's phone, adds a face filter, and posts it to his Snapchat story. The picture quickly goes viral and spreads to other members of the student body. Soon enough, boys and girls mock Dominic as he walks down the halls, calling him names and moving away from where he is sitting in class and the cafeteria. Dominic becomes distracted in his classes, fails a French quiz, and starts getting headaches.

Read your scenario together and discuss the following questions. You should refer to the Health and Human Services definition of cyberbullying to guide your discussion.

1. What makes or doesn't make this scenario an example of cyberbullying?
2. What role does each student choose in your scenario (perpetrator, bystander, upstander)? What factors motivate their choices?
3. Where do you see students making choices in this scenario? What other choices are available to them?
4. Are there any examples of upstanders in your scenario? If not, what are some ways that an upstander could respond?
5. How might this scenario be resolved?
6. What questions does this scenario raise for you?

After you move into your new group, have each person share a brief summary of their scenario and discussion. Then discuss the following questions together:

1. What patterns, if any, do you notice across multiple scenarios?
2. What factors motivate the students' choices to be perpetrators, bystanders, or upstanders? What solutions do you have that would encourage students to choose to be upstanders when they witness cyberbullying?
3. What responsibility, if any, do the companies who own social media platforms like Instagram or Twitter have to prevent cyberbullying on their sites? What other solutions do you have to prevent cyberbullying?
4. What can you learn from these scenarios about the choices you make online?
5. What can you learn from these scenarios about what to do if you witness or are a target of cyberbullying?

SCENARIO 4

Felix and Cyrus go to different schools but play on the same soccer team. One afternoon on the bus ride home from a game, they create a list on the back of a napkin of girls they think are hot. Their teammate and friend, Anthony, finds the list and posts it on a private soccer-team Facebook page, titling it "Sluts that Felix and Cyrus Dream About." The list then spreads via social media, and soon students at both schools and even some parents find out about it.

Read your scenario together and discuss the following questions. You should refer to the Health and Human Services definition of cyberbullying to guide your discussion.

1. What makes or doesn't make this scenario an example of cyberbullying?
2. What role does each student choose in your scenario (perpetrator, bystander, upstander)? What factors motivate their choices?
3. What role does language, specifically Anthony's word choice, play in this scenario?
4. Where do you see students making choices in this scenario? What other choices are available to them?
5. Are there any examples of upstanders in your scenario? If not, what are some ways that an upstander could respond?
6. How might this scenario be resolved?
7. What questions does this scenario raise for you?

After you move into your new group, have each person share a brief summary of their scenario and discussion. Then discuss the following questions together:

1. What patterns, if any, do you notice across multiple scenarios?
2. What factors motivate the students' choices to be perpetrators, bystanders, or upstanders? What solutions do you have that would encourage students to choose to be upstanders when they witness cyberbullying?
3. What responsibility, if any, do social media companies like Facebook or Twitter have to prevent cyberbullying on their sites? What other solutions do you have to prevent cyberbullying?
4. What can you learn from these scenarios about the choices you make online?
5. What can you learn from these scenarios about what to do if you witness or are a target of cyberbullying?

SCENARIO 5

Richard, Julian, and Nadia are exchanging texts late Friday night. They start to talk about how annoying Mia, a girl in their World History and English classes, is, especially when she raises her hand to volunteer to read and answer every question that the teacher asks. Richard jokes that they should create a fake Twitter account to let her know how annoying she is. Julian sends three "thumbs up" emojis. Five minutes later, Nadia sends a screenshot of an anonymous Twitter account with the following tweet: "@miagram thinks shes all that and more #tryhard #nerd #teacherspet." Richard responds: "LMAO." Over the course of the weekend, Nadia posts more mean tweets about Mia, which get retweeted around the school. Richard and Julian don't retweet Nadia's posts. The following week, Mia stops raising her hand in class, and when teachers call on her anyway, she says she doesn't know the answer. After two weeks, one of Mia's friends shows a counselor the thread on Twitter.

Read your scenario together and discuss the following questions. You should refer to the Health and Human Services definition of cyberbullying to guide your discussion.

1. What makes or doesn't make this scenario an example of cyberbullying?
2. What role does each student choose in your scenario (perpetrator, bystander, upstander)? What factors motivate their choices?
3. Where do you see students making choices in this scenario? What other choices are available to them?
4. Are there any examples of upstanders in your scenario? If not, what are some ways that an upstander could respond?
5. How might this scenario be resolved?
6. What questions does this scenario raise for you?

After you move into your new group, have each person share a brief summary of their scenario and discussion. Then discuss the following questions together:

1. What patterns, if any, do you notice across multiple scenarios?
2. What factors motivate the students' choices to be perpetrators, bystanders, or upstanders? What solutions do you have that would encourage students to choose to be upstanders when they witness cyberbullying?
3. What responsibility, if any, do social media companies like Facebook or Twitter have to prevent cyberbullying on their sites? What other solutions do you have to prevent cyberbullying?
4. What can you learn from these scenarios about the choices you make online?
5. What can you learn from these scenarios about what to do if you witness or are a target of cyberbullying?

SCENARIO 6

Jayme, an openly gay senior, is in the student lounge talking about who has asked whom to the upcoming junior/senior prom and who is wearing what. Jayme says that she is bringing her girlfriend, who goes to a different school, and is planning to wear a tux. The next afternoon after lunch, Jayme receives an anonymous message on her Tumblr stating that she will ruin the prom if she shows up in a tux with her girlfriend. Similar comments follow, escalating to include homophobic slurs. Then someone threatens physical harm and posts that they would all be better off if Jayme and her girlfriend were dead. Not wanting to return to what once felt like an open and progressive school, Jayme tells her parents what is happening. The next morning, they bring Jayme's laptop to school and request a meeting with the administration.

Read your scenario together and discuss the following questions. You should refer to the Health and Human Services definition of cyberbullying to guide your discussion.

1. What makes or doesn't make this scenario an example of cyberbullying?
2. What role does each student choose in your scenario (perpetrator, bystander, upstander)? What factors motivate their choices?
3. Where do you see students making choices in this scenario? What other choices are available to them?
4. Are there any examples of upstanders in your scenario? If not, what are some ways that an upstander could respond?
5. How might this scenario be resolved?
6. What questions does this scenario raise for you?

After you move into your new group, have each person share a brief summary of their scenario and discussion. Then discuss the following questions together:

1. What patterns, if any, do you notice across multiple scenarios?
2. What factors motivate the students' choices to be perpetrators, bystanders, or upstanders? What solutions do you have that would encourage students to choose to be upstanders when they witness cyberbullying?
3. What responsibility, if any, do social media companies like Facebook or Twitter have to prevent cyberbullying on their sites? What other solutions do you have to prevent cyberbullying?
4. What can you learn from these scenarios about the choices you make online?
5. What can you learn from these scenarios about what to do if you witness or are a target of cyberbullying?

ACTIVITY **61**

Anatomy of an Upstander

Purpose: Examine specific qualities of upstander behavior and reflect on examples of witnessing upstander behavior.

ADVISOR NOTES: None

APPROXIMATE TIME:
30 minutes

MATERIALS:
Chart paper and markers

PROCEDURE:

1. **Reflect on Upstander Behavior**
   - Ask advisees to respond to the following prompt in their journals. Let them know that they will be sharing their responses with a partner.

     Write about a time when you were (or witnessed someone being) an upstander. Describe the situation. Then describe what it felt like to be an upstander or to see someone being an upstander.

   - Have advisees turn and talk to share their stories of being or witnessing upstanders. Then ask them to work together to make a list in their journals of the words or phrases they used to describe what it felt like to be or to witness an upstander.

   - Ask each advisee to share one word or phrase, and write a list on the board. Time allowing, you might have a quick discussion about how it felt in the moment versus after some time had passed to see if there are any differences.

2. **Discuss the Anatomy of an Upstander**
   - Divide your advisory into groups of three to four and let them know that they will be brainstorming ideas about what an upstander looks, sounds, and feels like when they choose this response to an injustice. They should record their ideas on chart paper and be ready to share them with the group.

   - After groups have finished brainstorming, have them post their chart paper on the wall. You might have each group present their ideas or have them do a **gallery walk** (visit facinghistory.org/advisory-media to learn about this teaching strategy).

   - It is important that advisees understand that an upstander can act in small or large ways. For example, reaching out privately to someone who is the target of bullying can help that individual feel less alone.

3. **Apply Upstander Behavior to Past Readings**
   - In their small groups or in a circle discussion, have advisees apply ideas from the upstander brainstorm to four previous advisory readings: **The "In" Group, The Silent Pact, Fear,** and the **Ostracism Case Study**. Invite advisees to find the readings in their folders.

- Then ask advisees to apply the following question to each text:

  What would an upstander have looked like, sounded like, and felt like in the instance described in the text?

They can discuss the main individual in each scenario as well as other individuals and groups in each story, such as those listed below. You might have groups tackle all four scenarios or assign one text per group, in which case they will present before moving to the next part of the activity.

- Eve Shalen and the diary
- Eboo Patel and the antisemitic slurs and graffiti at his school
- The narrator and the other children in "Fear"
- A student at Sue's school in the Ostracism Case Study

- After groups have shared their responses to the question, invite them to add new ideas from their discussions to their upstander posters.
- Finish the activity by having members of each group share their new insights in a quick circle reflection.

ACTIVITY **62**

Choosing to Be an Upstander

Purpose: Describe the steps that you can take before, during, and after an incident of ostracism, bullying, or cyberbullying has occurred.

> **APPROXIMATE TIME:**
> 30 minutes
>
> **MATERIALS:**
> - **HANDOUT** Upstander Action Scenario Strips
> - **HANDOUT** Analyzing Upstander Actions

ADVISOR NOTES:

1. **Prepare Statistics for the Opening Part of the Activity**

   In the first part of this activity, advisees will share bullying statistics from PACER's National Bullying Prevention Center. You can access these statistics by going to pacer.org/bullying, selecting "Resources," and choosing "Stats." One way to share data from this website is to choose a group of statistics to print and cut into strips before the meeting. You can give each advisee one to three strips and then have them stand in a circle and read their statistics using the **Wraparound** strategy. Visit facinghistory.org/advisory-media to learn about this teaching strategy. Because this activity focuses on upstander behavior, it is important that one student has the ninth statistic: "More than half of bullying situations (57%) stop when a peer intervenes on behalf of the student being bullied (Hawkins, Pepler, & Craig, 2001)."[1]

2. **Prepare Upstander Action Strips for the Second Activity**

   Before the advisory meeting, make copies of and cut apart the handout **Upstander Action Scenario Strips**. For this activity, your advisees will work in small groups, and each group will need one strip.

PROCEDURE:

1. **Read Some Statistics about Bullying and Cyberbullying**

   - Share some or all of the bullying statistics from PACER's National Bullying Prevention Center at pacer.org/bullying (select "Resources" and then "Stats"). Let advisees know that they will be responding to the statistics in an **S-I-T** journal response to help activate their listening (visit facinghistory.org/advisory-media to learn about the S-I-T teaching strategy).

   - Ask advisees to respond to the following questions in a S-I-T journal response:
     - What statistic did you find surprising?
     - What statistic did you find interesting?
     - What statistic did you find troubling?

---

1 PACER Center, National Bullying Prevention Center, "Bullying Statistics," accessed June 19, 2018, http://www.pacer.org/bullying/resources/stats.asp.

Section 5: Case Study: Ostracism and Bullying

2. Brainstorm Upstander Actions in the Face of Bullying or Ostracism

- Divide your advisory into three groups. Pass out the handout **Analyzing Upstander Actions** and one scenario strip to each group. You will most likely have multiple groups working on each scenario.

    - Scenario 1: What actions can an upstander take when they become aware (hear gossip, see a post on Snapchat, etc.) that someone may become the target of ostracism, bullying, or cyberbullying?
    - Scenario 2: What actions can an upstander take when they witness someone being ostracized or bullied in person or online?
    - Scenario 3: What actions can an upstander take when they become aware that someone they know is the target of ostracism, bullying, or cyberbullying?

- Explain that the groups will be discussing the actions that an upstander can take when they witness ostracism, bullying, or cyberbullying. They should record their ideas for three possible actions, as well as the possible consequences (both good and bad) for each action, and on the **Analyzing Upstander Actions** handout.

- When they have finished their discussions, have each group share their answers and ideas for how to be an upstander. Look for similarities and differences across groups and discuss the consequences of taking certain actions.

- Remind advisees where they can get help and support at your school if they or someone they know is the target of ostracism, bullying, or cyberbullying.

3. Reflect on How You Can Be an Upstander

- In their journals, ask advisees to finish the following sentence starter.

    One small step that I can take to be an upstander at _____ (school's name) is . . .

- Have advisees share their completed sentences in a **Wraparound** (visit facinghistory.org/advisory-media to learn about this teaching strategy).

HANDOUT

Upstander Action Scenario Strips

Directions for the Advisor: Make copies and then cut apart the scenario strips before the advisory meeting. Your advisees will work in small groups, and each group will need one scenario strip.

Scenario 1

1. What actions can an upstander take when they become aware (hear gossip, see a post on Snapchat, etc.) that **someone may become the target** of ostracism, bullying, or cyberbullying?

2. What are the possible consequences for each action?

Scenario 2

1. What actions can an upstander take when **they witness someone** getting ostracized or bullied in person or online?

2. What are the possible consequences for each action?

Scenario 3

1. What actions can an upstander take when **they become aware that someone they know is the target** of ostracism, bullying, or cyberbullying?

2. What are the possible consequences for each action?

HANDOUT

Analyzing Upstander Actions

Directions: Write your group's question in the scenario box and then discuss possible actions an upstander might take and consequences of those actions. Record your ideas in the spaces below.

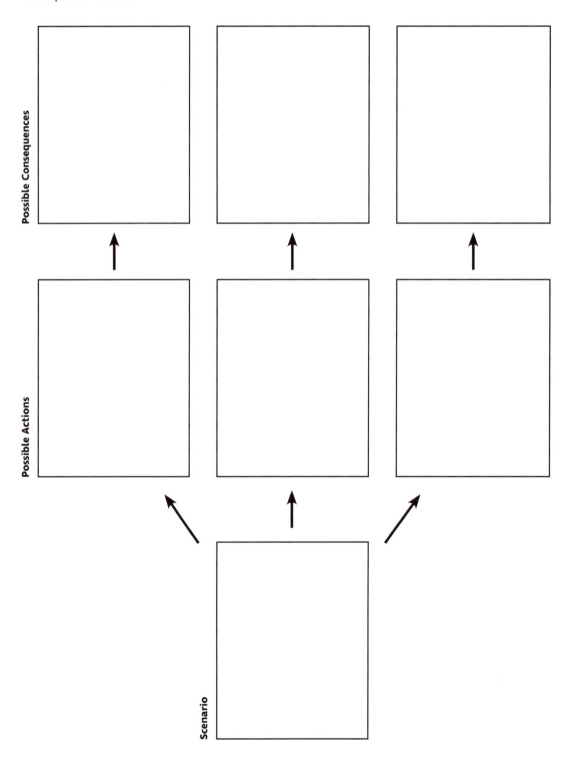

ACTIVITY **63**

Case Study: Ostracism and Bullying Final Reflection

Purpose: Review the overarching themes, questions, journal responses, and work from this section of *Community Matters* and reflect on new understanding and lingering questions.

APPROXIMATE TIME: 30 minutes

MATERIALS: NONE

ADVISOR NOTES:

1. **Creating Time and Space for Reflection**

   Advisees will repeat this activity at the end of each section of *Community Matters*. Providing them with the time and space to reflect on their learning, growth, and lingering questions about the central themes from the section allows them to synthesize the material in meaningful ways before being introduced to new themes and concepts.

2. **Choosing a Discussion Format**

   Before the advisory meeting, decide how you would like the group to engage in the final discussion. You might start with small groups and then move into a larger circle, or you might try the **Socratic Seminar** or **Fishbowl** teaching strategies, which you can learn about at facinghistory.org/advisory-media.

PROCEDURE:

1. **Reflect on Individual Identity**

   - Tell advisees that for this reflection, they will need their journals and materials from this section. Advisees should first review their journals, handouts, and texts from this section of the advisory program and then do the following:

     - Place a star by two or three places where you arrived at a new insight or understanding of ostracism, bullying, cyberbullying, or the roles we can play and the impact of our choices when we witness these events.

     - Place a question mark by one or two places that raise questions for you about ostracism, bullying, cyberbullying, or roles (target, perpetrator, bystander, upstander).

   - Then ask advisees to spend some time writing a new journal entry in which they elaborate on a new understanding and/or question. If you feel like they would benefit from some structure, invite them to respond to one of the following questions:

- What new insights and understanding do you have about ostracism, bullying, cyberbullying, or the range of responses in the face of injustice? What questions do you still have?

- I used to think _____ about _____ (a theme from this section of advisory), but now I think _____.

2. **Reflect on Advisees' Understanding of Ostracism and Bullying in a Group Discussion**

    - In small groups and then in a circle or using the **Socratic Seminar** or **Fishbowl** strategy, ask advisees to discuss their journal responses (visit facinghistory.org/advisory-media to learn about these two teaching strategies).

    - You might record the questions they still have on chart paper to refer to in the final section of *Community Matters*, Choosing to Participate.

    - Let advisees know that in upcoming meetings, they will be learning about and discussing specific actions they can take to help make their school community stronger.

SECTION 6:
Choosing to Participate

ACTIVITIES

Advisory Community-Building Project Guidelines

Revisiting Our Advisory Contract

The Bully Zones Project

Leaving a Positive Footprint Project

The Hazleton Integration Project

Take a Seat, Make a Friend Project

End-of-the-Year Closing Activities

Culminating Project: Advisory Community-Building Project Guidelines • page 269

Time	Purpose	Materials	Abridged Advisor Notes
Multiple advisory meetings	Work collaboratively to design and implement a school-based project that impacts the community in a positive way.	HANDOUT: **Project Planning Guide** HANDOUT: **Project Storyboard Template** Other materials will vary depending on the project	Students are given the opportunity to work collaboratively on a project that benefits the school community. The projects will vary depending on school, students' interests, what they perceive as the school's needs, and the resources and materials available to you.

Activities 64–69

Purpose	Materials	Abridged Advisor Notes

64: Revisiting Our Advisory Contract — 30 min — page 277

Remind the group of its shared expectations, revise them as needed, and set the tone for difficult conversations. Draw connections between factors that make a strong community and norms that ensure it remains strong.	Advisory contract	This is the last time that you will be prompted to revisit your advisory contract. This activity provides the opportunity for your advisees to reflect on the ways they have grown as a community, where they have improved over the course of the year at upholding their contract, and where they feel they can still do better.

65: The Bully Zones Project — 30 min — page 279

Reflect on inclusion and exclusion in your school community and explore how students at one high school took action to educate each other about bullying and create more inclusive spaces.	VIDEO: **Bully Zones** (see facinghistory.org/advisory-media) READING: **Bullying at School** (optional)	This activity is designed to help advisees think about and respond to the video "Bully Zones." If you have time, you might also read the first half of the reading "Bullying at School," available at facinghistory.org/advisory-media, and choose one or more discussion questions.

66: Leaving a Positive Footprint Project — 30 min — page 283

Explore how a class of elementary school students took action to stop bullying and spread positive messages to encourage their community to create an inclusive and welcoming environment.	VIDEO: **Leaving a Positive Footprint** (visit facinghistory.org/advisory-media)	This activity ends with a personal exit card reflection (visit facinghistory.org/advisory-media to learn about this teaching strategy). You might share excerpts from some of the exit cards as part of the opening routine in your next meeting.

67: The Hazleton Integration Project — 30 min — page 285

Discuss the ways that members of the school community should treat each other, and propose ways in which the group can help to make the school a more inclusive and welcoming space.	VIDEO: **Joe Maddon in Coal Country** (see facinghistory.org/advisory-media)	None

68: Take a Seat, Make a Friend Project — 30 min — page 286

Explore how conversations between strangers can create connections and help break down stereotypes.	VIDEO: **Take a Seat, Make a Friend** (see y2u.be/HfHV4-N2LxQ)	After watching the video, pairs will discuss some of life's big questions together. Write each prompt on a piece of paper that you or an advisee will choose randomly from a bag, hat, backpack, or box.

69: End-of-the-Year Closing Activities — One or more advisory meetings — page 288

Reflect on personal growth and learning over the year and appreciate individuals in the school community.	Varies depending on the number of activities you choose	This activity includes suggestions for different ways you can close the year with your advisory group. You might choose to have one closing activity or devote multiple meetings to final reflections and sharing.

Section 6: Choosing to Participate

Choosing to Participate

CULMINATING PROJECT + ACTIVITIES 64–69

OVERVIEW

In the final section of *Community Matters*, advisees encounter stories of individuals and groups who "choose to participate" in positive ways in their school and local communities. One of the aims of Activities 64–69 is to open advisees' eyes to the different ways of participating—big and small—that are happening around them, and to help them realize that even though they are young, they still have the power to shape their communities through their choices and actions. Encountering these real-life examples offers an opportunity for your advisees to reflect on who they are as individuals and members of their school community, who they want to be, and what kind of school and world they want to help create. Then advisees will work together to envision, design, and implement their own project, one that will have a positive impact on their school community in a small or large way.

NAVIGATING THE ACTIVITIES

The activities in this section fall into four categories: the final project, revisiting the contract, learning about community-based projects, and the final days of the year.

- The section starts with the *Community Matters* final project guidelines. Here you will find a framework, menu of activities, reflection and discussion questions, and handouts to support a school-based advisory project.

- The videos in Activities 64–68 highlight different school and community projects that share the goal of bringing people together to create a more welcoming space. The activities include questions to prompt discussion about how advisees might apply lessons from each project to their own school and lives. You can decide whether or not to show and discuss all four videos.

- Activity 69 has suggestions for end-of-the-year rituals that spark reflection and provide ways for your advisees to express gratitude to those individuals who supported them along the way.

Advisory Community-Building Project Guidelines

CULMINATING PROJECT OVERVIEW

> **MATERIALS:**
> - HANDOUT
>   Project Planning Guide
> - HANDOUT
>   Project Storyboard Template

Now that your advisees have seen examples of upstanders of all ages creating projects that have positively impacted their communities, it is time for them to take the lead and create their own school-based project. The goal of this final project is for the advisory to have the experience of working collaboratively on a project that benefits the school community. It is best to find a project that is realistic and doable, so that your advisees can have a sense of accomplishment and get a chance to "flex their muscles" by doing something together for their community. If this is the first time implementing an advisory project, it is more important to have a small success than to take on a major project and fall short. Regardless of the scope of the final product, it is important that everyone in the group plays a role in its planning and execution and that you build in time to allow the group to reflect on how they worked together to conceive of, implement, and present their project.

The projects can be on any scale and at any level of visibility and will vary depending on your school, your advisees' interests, what they perceive as the school's needs, and the resources and materials available to your advisory group. In the past, advisories have done a variety of different *Community Matters* projects. Some examples include making posters to hang in the school to create a more welcoming environment; designing a museum of learning for others to visit on a topic advisees deemed important for the community to know about and understand; writing and delivering a performance about bullying to help others in the school recognize the signs of bullying behavior; planting a garden to learn more about sustainable living and provide vegetables to the school community; holding an assembly with featured speakers; creating a Facing History student council to implement restorative justice practices; and nominating and interviewing members of the community who they deem to be "upstanders."

ADVISOR NOTES

1. **Tips for Navigating the Project Guidelines**

   The project guidelines provide a range of activities and resources that you can use with your advisees to support a student-driven project that they design and implement in their school or local community. Depending on how much time your group has for the project, you can select some or all of the activities listed in the Procedure section and arrange them in an order that fits your group's needs. There is also a section titled Questions to Support an Advisory Community-Building Project that aligns with the steps outlined in the Procedure section and helps provide your advisees with some structure and guidance through the process.

2. Steps for Brainstorming and Implementing a Project

The steps we recommend for a successful project are the following: personal reflection, brainstorming a need, brainstorming a way to respond to the need, and then planning, implementing, and reflecting on the project itself. There are two separate brainstorming steps. The first is for the advisory to answer the question: "What does our community need?" Any of the brainstorming strategies listed below can be used with that step. It is up to you to decide if you want your advisory to end this step with consensus on the need they have decided to address OR if you want smaller groups or individual advisees to choose different needs to address in their project. The second step is to brainstorm ways to respond to the need. Again, any of the brainstorming strategies listed below can support this step.

3. The Importance of Ownership

The following activities help support a school-based project. While you might be overseeing the timeline and facilitating the activities, is important that your advisees feel ownership of the process and product. They might feel passionate about working together to take on an issue in their local community rather than in their school. They might want to work on a project together, or small groups might have their own ideas. The process of coming up with a project and getting started is messy and probably can't be achieved in one or even two advisory sessions. However, if advisees feel like they have ownership of the project, they will be more excited by, invested in, and committed to the process and the outcome.

4. Additional Resources to Generate Ideas and Support Student-Led Projects

Facing History's **10 Questions for Young Changemakers** unit, available at facinghistory.org/advisory-media, includes lesson plans and resources to help students reflect on the values and actions that will help strengthen their communities. The final lesson provides explicit guidance to assist students' civic participation, helping them transfer the knowledge gained from their unit of study into tangible opportunities to take action in their community. While that unit is designed for 50-minute class periods, you could adapt its lessons and materials to fit within shorter advisory sessions or just focus on Lesson 1 and Lesson 4, which introduce a framework for enacting change and then provide materials to support the planning process.

If you feel like you and your advisees would benefit from seeing other examples of student-led projects, you can show additional Not in Our School project videos and draw ideas from their lesson plans and classroom resources, available at www.noit.org.

PROCEDURE:

1. **Reflect on a Quotation by Toni Morrison**

    - In their journals, ask advisees to answer the following questions in response to a message that author Toni Morrison tweeted in 2013. Let them know that they will be sharing their ideas with their peers.

        "If there's a book that you want to read, but it hasn't been written yet, then you must write it."[1]

        - In your own words, what message is Morrison trying to convey?
        - How can you apply Morrison's message to your own life?

    - In pairs or triads, have advisees share their thoughts about Morrison's message, as well as how they would apply her message to their own lives. Ask for a few volunteers to share with the group.

    - Let your advisees know that they will be putting Morrison's message into action at their own school. They will have an opportunity to write their own book, one that benefits their school community in some way.

2. **Brainstorm What Your School Community Needs and Ways to Respond**

    While you and your advisory group might already have ideas for a project, choosing one of more of the following activities can help provide some structure for the brainstorming process. You can use these strategies to help your advisees first brainstorm ideas for their project(s) and then brainstorm different ways they can respond to the need that they have identified.

    - **Guiding Questions:** Start by choosing one or two guiding questions to anchor your project. While the guiding question(s) for the project should align with your school's mission and goals for advisory, the following ideas can help get you started:

        - What do I have to offer my community that can help make it a more inclusive space for everyone in our school?
        - What does our community need to bring us together? Why is this need important to me?
        - How can we help to create inclusive and welcoming spaces (or focus on one space) for everyone in our school?
        - What are some themes we discussed in advisory this year? How can we address a theme through a school-based project?

    - **Graffiti Board:** Brainstorm project ideas on a graffiti board (visit facinghistory.org/advisory-media to learn about this teaching strategy). Don't edit ideas at this point. Think big. Think small. Encourage creativity. Then discuss the results as a group. Invite advisees to share their visions for projects and desired outcomes.

---

1 Toni Morrison, Twitter post, October 30, 2013, 5:26 p.m, https://twitter.com/tonimorrrison/status/395708227888771072.

- **Sticky Blast:** Give each advisee a stack of sticky notes and explain that they will spend ten minutes brainstorming ideas for a project that addresses the guiding question(s). Encourage them to think creatively and not edit their ideas. Tell them to write one idea per sticky note.
  - Then have your advisees post their notes on the board and, as a group, read them out loud, asking advisees to explain their ideas in two sentences or less. Then have them start to group their ideas into categories that they create. Once they have finished, see if there is a category that they want to use as a starting place to develop a final project.
  - Alternatively, you might create a web or map from the sticky notes. Write "Advisory Project" in the center of the piece of chart paper and then start to create groupings of notes. Draw lines between notes and groupings, write connections and questions over the lines, and draw images to represent new ideas.

- **Idea Pass-Around:** Sit in a circle and give each advisee a piece of lined paper. Have them write a guiding question (see the first bullet point for ideas about guiding questions) at the top, and then have them explain one or more project ideas. Remind them that they don't need to edit their ideas! Then have them pass their papers to the right. They should read the new paper and write any ideas that their peer's paper generates for them. They might expand on an idea, pose a question, or draw an image or map. Keep passing and writing until everyone has their original paper. Advisees should read their peers' comments and questions and then share new insights with the group.

- **Calling on a Hero:** Sit in a circle and have advisees respond to the following prompt in their journals: *Who is your hero or alter ego?* (Real people, past or present, or fictional characters from books, films, or comics are all fair game!) *What would your hero or alter ego do to make a positive impact on your school community?* Have advisees share their ideas in pairs or trios and then discuss what they can learn from how their heroes or alter egos would take on this project.

3. **Create a Project Storyboard Outline**

   Note: Your advisory group can design and implement one project or work in small groups on different projects. You may need to adapt the storyboarding activity accordingly.

   Pass out the handouts **Project Planning Guide** and **Project Storyboard Template**. Divide your advisory into groups of three or four to choose one idea that they would like to develop into a project. Have the groups complete the storyboard outline process, circulating to answer questions and offer encouragement. Note that the template asks them to envision and articulate their project's end point first before they consider the steps they will need to take in order to reach their goal. If your advisees are working on different projects, each group can present its storyboard to the advisory in order to share ideas and receive feedback. If your group is doing one project together, your advisees can vote on one proposal to implement or, alternatively, combine multiple ideas into a single project.

Depending on how much time your advisory can devote to its project, have advisees revisit their storyboards periodically. They may encounter roadblocks along the way, and taking time to reflect in their journals and revise their plan will help them develop problem-solving skills and resilience.

4. **Implement the Project**

   After your group has identified its project(s), discuss the desired outcome(s), create a schedule, and assign roles (as needed). Then encourage advisees to work together as a whole group or in their smaller groups, helping them build in time to reflect on the process, asking questions to help them troubleshoot issues, and providing materials as needed.

5. **Reflect on the Project**

   It is important that your advisees have time and space for individual and group reflections. They can start their reflections in their journals and then share their thoughts in small- or whole-group discussions. Discussion strategies like **Fishbowl**, **Save the Last Word for Me**, and **Learn to Listen, Listen to Learn** can help provide structure to these discussions. Also, in addition to individual journal responses, you can also use the **Big Paper** teaching strategy or "Small Paper" variation for a silent discussion of some reflection questions. Visit facinghistory.org/advisory-media to learn about these discussion and teaching strategies.

QUESTIONS TO SUPPORT AN ADVISORY COMMUNITY-BUILDING PROJECT

Choose from the following menu of questions or create your own to help support your advisees through the process of brainstorming, planning, implementing, and reflecting on their project.

Brainstorm What Your School Community Needs

1. What do I have to offer my community that can help make it a more inclusive space for everyone in our school?
2. What does our community need to bring us together? Why is this need important to me?
3. How can we help to create inclusive and welcoming spaces (or focus on one space) for everyone in our school?
4. What are some themes we discussed in advisory this year? How can we address a theme through a school-based project?

Consider How to Respond to a Community Need

1. Why does this issue matter?
2. What might we do to respond to this particular need in our community?
3. Who should we talk to in order to better understand this issue?
4. What research should we do to better understand this issue (interviews, surveys, data analysis, online research)?
5. What would a successful response look like?

Develop a Plan of Action

1. What would success look like, sound like, and feel like?
2. What steps do we need to take to complete our project?
3. What steps are you most interested in being involved in? What skills and talents can you bring to these parts of the project?
4. What challenges might we encounter while we implement our project?
5. What are some strategies we might use to overcome these challenges?

Respond to Challenges and Make It Happen

1. Are we making progress? Are we moving through the steps we identified on our storyboards?
2. Do we need to change course or plans? How might we need to modify our original project?
3. Are we uncovering additional or different needs as we implement our project?
4. Who can help us address additional needs?

Reflect on the Project

1. What did you learn about yourself during this project?
2. What did you learn about your school during this project?
3. What new knowledge or skills did you develop during this project? How did you learn or develop them?
4. What is one challenge that you faced in doing the project? What strategy did you use to overcome this challenge? How was the strategy effective or not effective? What might you do differently if you face a similar challenge in the future?
5. Did your project achieve the desired outcome? If so, how do you know? If not, what work still needs to be done?
6. What is an example of your group collaborating effectively during the project? What factors contributed to this success?
7. What is an example of your group not collaborating effectively during the project? What factors contributed to this breakdown?
8. What advice would you give to an advisory group doing this project next year?

HANDOUT

Project Planning Guide

Directions: The following questions will help you make a plan for implementing your project. For each step listed below, discuss the questions with your group and then follow the instructions as you outline your project using the **Project Storyboard Template** handout.

Step 1

Discuss the following questions as a group. Then, starting with the **last square** on the storyboard, use text and images (simple sketches are fine) to represent what you envision the end of your project looking like.

1. What will the end of your project look like?
2. Because of this project, what will have changed in your classroom, school, or community? Write your answer under your image.

Step 2

Fill in the rest of the storyboard. Include information that helps you answer the following questions:

1. In order to get to our final vision, what steps do we need to take?
2. What people are needed at each stage?
3. What role will different members of our advisory or project group play? Write the names of people and their roles on the lines below each picture.
4. What materials do we need? At what stage in the process do we need them? Draw and highlight the materials in each part of the storyboard.

Step 3

Review your completed storyboard, and then make a list of "Things We Need." Include materials, support from school administrators or community members, a mentor you can go to if/when you hit a roadblock, and any other people you might consult to get ideas, support, or materials.

Remember that your project storyboard is a starting point. You will have opportunities to revisit and revise it once you start implementing your project.

HANDOUT

Project Storyboard Template

Directions: Outline each step of your project using words and images. Remember to start with the last box to capture your vision of a successful finished project.

ACTIVITY **64**

Revisiting Our Advisory Contract

Purpose: Remind the group of its shared expectations, revise expectations as needed, and set the tone for difficult conversations. Draw connections between the factors that make a strong community and the norms that can help ensure that it remains strong.

APPROXIMATE TIME: 30 minutes

MATERIALS: NONE

ADVISOR NOTES:

1. **Reaffirm Advisory Norms**

   This is the last time that you will be prompted to revisit your advisory contract. This activity provides the opportunity for your advisees to reflect on the ways they have grown as a community, where they have improved over the course of the year at upholding their contract, and where they feel they can still do better in the final section of the Facing History advisory program.

PROCEDURE:

1. **Reflect Individually in Journals about Your Advisory Contract**

   - Start by reading aloud your advisory contract, perhaps using the **Wraparound** strategy (visit facinghistory.org/advisory-media to learn about this teaching strategy).
   - Then ask advisees to respond to the following questions in their journals, citing specific examples from past sessions to support their thinking. Tell advisees that they will be sharing their responses in small groups.
     - What are three examples of ways that our group has gotten better at upholding our advisory contract this year? What factors contributed to our growth?
     - What norm do you think we should work on as a group, and why? What are two concrete steps that we can take as a group to get better at upholding this norm?

2. **Discuss and Set Goals**

   - Divide the advisees into small groups and have them discuss the two journal questions. Then ask them to share highlights from their discussion, making a list on the board of their main ideas.
   - Focus on the second question and the list of concrete steps that advisees brainstormed. You might ask groups to rank them and decide which one or two

they are committed to focusing on moving forward. Write these on chart paper along with the concrete steps, have advisees sign the paper, and then hang it alongside the contract. Refer to and reflect on this commitment during some opening and closing routines in the upcoming weeks.

3. **Commit to a Norm: Closing Activity**

   - Conclude the meeting by asking each advisee to complete the following sentence starter in their journals. They might choose a norm that the group highlighted as one they want to focus on, or they might choose a different norm that challenges them as individuals:

     For the next month, I am going to work on _____ (choose a norm from the advisory contract). One way that I will work on it is by . . . You all can help me by . . .

   - Then have each advisee share their completed sentence starter in a **Wraparound**.

ACTIVITY **65**

The Bully Zones Project

Purpose: Reflect on inclusion and exclusion in your school community and explore how students at one school took action to educate each other about bullying and create more inclusive spaces.

> **APPROXIMATE TIME:**
> 30 minutes
>
> **MATERIALS:**
>
> VIDEO
> Bully Zones
> (see facinghistory.org/advisory-media)
>
> READING
> Bullying at School (optional)

ADVISOR NOTES:

1. **Choosing Materials for This Activity**

   This activity is designed to help advisees think about and respond to the video **Bully Zones**, available at facinghistory.org/advisory-media. If you have time in this meeting or a future meeting and would like to read another example of how two Canadian students chose to be upstanders when they learned about a freshman who was bullied for what he wore to school, read the reading **Bullying at School** and choose one or more discussion questions.

2. **Find Additional Resources to Combat Bullying and Intolerance**

   For additional resources, such as lesson plans and videos, to help inspire your group to be upstanders when they witness bullying or intolerance, explore the "Not in Our School" program at niot.org.

PROCEDURE:

1. **Reflect on Inclusion and Exclusion in Your School**

   - Ask advisees to respond to the following question in their journals. Let them know that they will be sharing their ideas with their peers.

     What do inclusion and exclusion look like at your school?

   - Have advisees debrief in pairs or triads and then as a group. Create a T-chart on the board or chart paper and make a list of their ideas for what inclusion and exclusion look like at your school.

2. **Learn How Students at One School Raised Awareness about Bullying**

   - Let your group know that they will be watching a short video called "Bully Zones." Ask them to predict what they think it might be about, based on this activity's journal prompt and the video's title.

   - Then play the video **Bully Zones** (08:08) at facinghistory.org/advisory-media.

- In small groups or in a circle discussion, discuss the following questions:
    - What lessons can you learn from this video?
    - What questions does this video raise for you?
    - What might a Bully Zones project look like at your school?
    - Is bullying an accepted behavior in your school? Is being an upstander an accepted behavior? What steps can a community take to change its social norms (the behavior and language that a community considers acceptable)?
    - What strategies does your school use to address bullying? Which strategies are most effective? Which are least effective? What do you do in your school to help combat bullying? In what areas do you need more support from your peers, teachers, parents, or administrators?

READING

Bullying at School

A bullying incident in school is often the first time a teenager is confronted with the decision of whether to be an upstander or a bystander. In a world full of injustice, suffering, and other social problems, the choice to participate can actually originate very close to home.

The following stories highlight the power of students to make positive change by taking seemingly small actions in response to bullying in their own school communities.

In Canada, two students responded this way when a classmate was taunted because of what he wore:

> Two Nova Scotia students are being praised across North America for the way they turned the tide against the bullies who picked on a fellow student for wearing pink.
>
> The victim — a Grade 9 boy at Central Kings Rural High School in the small community of Cambridge — wore a pink polo shirt on his first day of school.
>
> Bullies harassed the boy, called him a homosexual for wearing pink and threatened to beat him up, students said.
>
> Two Grade 12 students — David Shepherd and Travis Price — heard the news and decided to take action.
>
> "I just figured enough was enough," said Shepherd.
>
> They went to a nearby discount store and bought 50 pink shirts, including tank tops, to wear to school the next day.
>
> Then the two went online to e-mail classmates to get them on board with their anti-bullying cause that they dubbed a "sea of pink."
>
> But a tsunami of support poured in the next day.
>
> Not only were dozens of students outfitted with the discount tees, but hundreds of students showed up wearing their own pink clothes, some head-to-toe.
>
> When the bullied student, who has never been identified, walked into school to see his fellow students decked out in pink, some of his classmates said it was a powerful moment. He may have even blushed a little.
>
> "Definitely it looked like there was a big weight lifted off his shoulders. He went from looking right depressed to being as happy as can be," said Shepherd.

And there's been nary a peep from the bullies since, which Shepherd says just goes to show what a little activism will do.

"If you can get more people against them . . . to show that we're not going to put up with it and support each other, then they're not as big as a group as they think they are," he says.[1]

---

[1] "Bullied student tickled pink by schoolmates' T-shirt campaign," CBC News Canada, last modified September 18, 2007, accessed July 12, 2016.

ACTIVITY **66**

Leaving a Positive Footprint Project

Purpose: Explore how a class of elementary school students took action to stop bullying and spread positive messages to encourage their community to create an inclusive and welcoming environment at their school.

> **APPROXIMATE TIME:**
> 30 minutes
>
> **MATERIALS:**
> VIDEO
> Leaving a Positive Footprint
> (see facinghistory.org/advisory-media)

ADVISOR NOTES:

1. **Collecting the Exit Cards**

    This activity ends with a personal exit card reflection. Visit facinghistory.org/advisory-media to learn about the Exit Cards teaching strategy. You might share excerpts from some of the exit cards as part of the opening routine in your next meeting. Because these are personal reflections, it is important that you do not reveal the writers' names or identities when sharing unless you receive permission in advance to do so.

PROCEDURE:

1. **Reflect on Upstanders at Your School**
    - Ask your advisees to respond to the following prompt in their journals. Let them know that they will be sharing their responses with their peers.

        Make a list of upstanders at your school. Include a brief description of what makes each one of them an upstander.

    - In pairs or triads, have advisees share their responses. See if any volunteers would like to share with the group.

2. **Learn How Students Worked to Create an Inclusive School Culture**
    - Let your group know that they will be watching a short video about a project at a Northern California elementary school, where students learned about the impact of bullying, shared their personal stories, and led a cross-grade project to create a more inclusive and welcoming school community.
    - Then play the video **Leaving a Positive Footprint** (05:43) at facinghistory.org/advisory-media.

- In small groups or in a circle discussion, discuss the following questions:
    - What lessons can you learn from this video?
    - What questions does this video raise for you?
    - What might a Leaving a Positive Footprint project look like at your school?
    - What would your school look like if all the students committed themselves to being upstanders in more situations? What action can your advisory group take to help create a culture where students at your school choose to be upstanders rather than perpetrators and bystanders?

3. **Reflect on What Being an Upstander Feels Like at Your School**

    On an **exit card** that you collect at the end of the meeting, ask advisees to respond to the following question:

    Do you feel comfortable making the choice to be an upstander at your school? Why or why not?

ACTIVITY **67**

The Hazleton Integration Project

Purpose: Discuss the ways that members of the school community should treat each other, and propose ways in which the group can help to make the school a more inclusive and welcoming space.

APPROXIMATE TIME: 30 minutes

MATERIALS:
VIDEO
Joe Maddon in Coal Country
(see facinghistory.org/advisory-media)

ADVISOR NOTES: None

PROCEDURE:

1. **Think Creatively about Your School Community**

   - In pairs or triads, have advisees answer the following question using the **Alphabet Brainstorm** strategy (visit facinghistory.org/advisory-media to learn about this teaching strategy). They should record their lists in their journals. You might model the first two or three letters with the group (accepting, brave, compassionate . . .).

     How do we want the members of our school community to treat each other?

   - Depending on the size of your advisory, have each pair share their list with the whole group or combine groups one or two times to have them share with each other. Comment on similarities, as well as unique ideas, that emerge.

2. **Watch Joe Maddon's Efforts to Strengthen His Hometown Community**

   - Let advisees know that they will now see how former Chicago Cubs manager Joe Maddon answers the questions they just discussed and the efforts he has made in his hometown of Hazleton, Pennsylvania, to make it a more inclusive and welcoming place for its diverse community.

   - Play the video **Joe Maddon in Coal Country** (07:18) at facinghistory.org/advisory-media.

   - In small groups or in a circle discussion, discuss the following questions:
     - What words might Joe Maddon include on his alphabet brainstorm to express how he wants members of the Hazleton community to treat each other?
     - What lessons can you learn from this video?
     - What ideas from this video can you apply to your school community?
     - What questions does this video raise for you?
     - What divisions exist at your school? How can you work together to overcome these divisions so it is an inclusive and welcoming space for everyone?

ACTIVITY **68**

Take a Seat, Make a Friend Project

Purpose: Explore how conversations between strangers can create connections and help break down stereotypes.

> **APPROXIMATE TIME:**
> 30 minutes
>
> **MATERIALS:**
> VIDEO
> Take a Seat, Make a Friend
> (see y2u.be/HfHV4-N2LxQ)

ADVISOR NOTES:

1. **Prepare Discussion Materials in Advance**

   After watching the video, pairs will discuss some of "life's big questions" together. You might use the topics from the video for the discussion, which are listed in the second part of this activity, make up your own topics, or ask advisees to suggest topics after they watch the video. Write each topic on a piece of paper that you or an advisee will choose randomly from a bag, hat, backpack, or box.

PROCEDURE:

1. **See What Happens When Strangers Tackle Life's Big Questions**

   - Explain to the group that they will watch a short video in which strangers discuss some of life's big questions. You might ask your advisees to predict what they think will happen during the discussions.

   - Play the video **Take a Seat, Make a Friend** (04:52) at y2u.be/HfHV4-N2LxQ.

   - Next, challenge your advisees to pair up with someone in the group that they do not feel like they know well. Perhaps they don't have classes together, belong to the same clubs, teams, or activities, or live near each other. Have them sit side by side, away from other pairs as much as possible. Then you or an advisee should pick the first prompt (see Advisor Notes), and pairs can discuss it together. Then have someone else pick the next prompt, simulating the discussion format in the ball pit from the video. Topics might include:

     - Share three things on your bucket list.
     - Describe the first time you fell in love.
     - Talk about someone who inspires you.
     - Find something that you share in common.
     - Talk about the experience that changed your life.
     - Create a secret handshake.

2. Discuss New Understanding from the Video

Move into a circle to discuss the following questions as a group:

- What is something new that you learned about your partner during your discussion?
- What lessons can you learn from this video?
- What questions does this video raise for you?
- How can you apply the lessons from this video to your own school community?

ACTIVITY **69**

End-of-the-Year Closing Activities

Purpose: Reflect on personal growth and learning over the year and appreciate individuals in the school community.

> **APPROXIMATE TIME:**
> One or more advisory meetings
>
> **MATERIALS:**
> Dependent on activities

ADVISOR NOTES:

Choosing Your Closing Activities

This activity includes suggestions for different ways you can close the year with your advisory group. You might choose to have one closing activity or devote multiple meetings to final reflections and sharing. Regardless of whether you have one or many end-of-the-year activities, it is important that your advisees feel a sense of closure before heading off for the summer.

SUGGESTED ACTIVITIES:

1. Notes of Appreciation (2 meetings)

- Spend one advisory meeting creating notes of appreciation for members of the group and school community. You might have each advisee make three notes: one for an advisee in the group, one for a teacher, and one for a staff member.
  - Have each advisee choose an advisee's name from a hat and then write that person a note that expresses something they appreciate about them, a positive contribution they made to advisory, a time they helped cheer up the writer, etc.
  - Choose a teacher to thank in writing, maybe for spending extra time tutoring or for helping the advisee learn something important about themself or their world.
  - Make a list on the board of staff members to thank—the often unsung heroes of schools—and have each advisee choose one to appreciate with a note. Remember to consider the nurses, counselors, maintenance and custodial staff, cafeteria staff, librarians, the registrar, and security team.
- Provide supplies such as white and colored paper, glue sticks, and markers. Use an advisory meeting to sit in groups and create the notes. Encourage advisees to hand-deliver their notes to the teachers and staff members in the building so they can also shake hands and say "thank you" in person.
- Then, in the next meeting, have a circle discussion where each advisee gives their note to their peer and tells the group one of the things they appreciate about this person.

2. Goodbye Graffiti Board (1–2 meetings)

- Create a Goodbye **Graffiti Board** with memories, stories, and reflections from the year (visit facinghsitory.org/advisory-media to learn about this teaching strategy). If possible, use a long piece of butcher paper and supply your advisees with colored markers. You can pass out or project a list of prompts, or write them on the butcher paper in advance so your advisees can move from prompt to prompt during writing time. You can also brainstorm a list of prompts with your advisees at the outset of the meeting. Regardless, make sure there is enough space on the graffiti board so they can all stand and write at the same time. Prompts might include:
    - This group helped me . . .
    - My favorite moment in advisory this year was when . . .
    - I appreciated learning . . .
    - I appreciated it when . . .
    - I use to think . . . but now I think . . .
    - Advisory helped me think about . . .
    - One thing I learned how to do well this year was . . .
    - I enjoyed learning about . . .
    - I was challenged by . . .
    - This group helped me overcome . . .
    - Thanks for . . .

- After advisees have had time to reflect on the Goodbye Graffiti Board, read it together and comment on what you notice. If you are allowed to give permission for cell phone usage, invite advisees to take photos of the graffiti board to remember the community they built together.

3. Final Journal Reflection (1 meeting)

- Ask advisees to reflect in their journals using one or more of the Goodbye Graffiti Board sentence starters. Let them know that they will be sharing their ideas in a circle discussion.
- Sitting in a circle, invite advisees to share one or more ideas that they wrote about in their journals in a closing group discussion.

APPENDIX

Designing Your School's Advisory Program

This section highlights some of the choices that administrators and advisory coordinators should consider carefully when designing and launching their advisory program. These choices include

- where and how advisory fits into your master schedule,
- where advisory groups will meet,
- who on the staff will serve as advisors,
- how you will group students into advisories,
- how you will structure the advisory program around other programs, such as assemblies and class meetings, and
- who will oversee the advisory program, provide professional development, and tailor the activities to fit the mission of your advisory program and needs of your student body.

For more guidance about launching an advisory program at your school, we recommend *The Advisory Guide: Designing and Implementing Successful Advisory Programs in Secondary Schools* by Rachel Poliner and Carol Miller Lieber. In addition to chapters about professional development and resources for your advisors, many of the points outlined below are explained by Poliner and Lieber in greater depth in this excellent resource for administrators and advisors alike.

Placing Advisory in the Master Schedule

How much time you need for advisory each week depends on your goals for advisory and how many advisees are in each group. Larger groups and more goals require more advisory meetings built into the master schedule. No matter the goals, you need frequent enough meeting times to have a sense of continuity in order for groups to develop strong relationships and interact with activities in meaningful ways, for advisors to provide support and feedback, and for advisees to have time for self-assessment, goal-setting, and reflection.

Scheduling advisory at the beginning or the end of the day can increase skipping, especially in high schools. Scheduling advisory in the middle of the day sends the message that advisory is as important as academic classes. Athletes (and teacher/coaches) leaving campus early for games and students arriving late to school will be less apt to miss meetings. In contrast to many high schools, some middle schools choose the beginning or the end of the day for advisory to help advisees get settled and prepare for the day, check in on their homework routine, and address topics for the day, week, or month.

If you are using the same period in the master schedule for advisory as you are for assemblies, grade-level meetings, and/or tutorial or study halls, it is important to map out where in the master calendar each meeting falls so you know approximately how many periods you can devote to advisory versus other kinds of meetings and school-wide events. From there, you can start to plan the advisory activities for the first six weeks of the year (see **Sample Advisory Meeting Maps for the Opening Weeks** on page 19). You can set aside meetings for *Community Matters: A Facing History and Ourselves Approach to Advisory*, as well as intersperse other activities that address personal, social, and academic goal-setting, mini-conferences to review grade reports, and other topics like study and time-management skills.

Coordinating and Sustaining the Advisory Program

Your academic departments likely have department heads and/or district curriculum directors. Your teaching teams likely have lead teachers. Your school has adult leaders for clubs and sports. Advisory, too, needs one or more staff members to take the lead. Most successful advisory programs have a coordinator or committee who are given the role as part of their school job or are paid a stipend as they would be if they were coaching a team or teaching an extra class. The coordinator or co-coordinators plan and conduct all-staff advisory professional development throughout the year, help administrators schedule advisory into the master calendar, assign advisees to advisors, oversee the scope and sequence of the activities and communicate the information to advisors, order supplies, identify rooms, coach struggling advisors, arrange the logistics for special project days, and assess effectiveness and improvement needs.

Deciding Who Will Serve as an Advisor

When launching an advisory program, we recommend involving all members of the faculty and professional staff. Doing so sends a message that all adults in the school care about the students. It gives all adults a common role in the school community, making professional development about advisory-related topics relevant to everyone. It also allows you to have smaller groups. Certain adults might be co-advisors, such as the principal (so they can tend to emergencies when necessary) and novice teachers (so they can share the responsibility as they acclimate to their teaching load).

Establishing Advisory Meeting Spaces

Since advisory is about the young people in the group, it is important to have the group size be as small as possible while still having workable meeting spaces. There are often more adults in school than there are good spaces for advisory groups to meet, so it doesn't always work to take the number of students and divide it by the number of adults. The administrator or advisory coordinator should walk the building and create a map of the suitable meeting spaces. Some unusual spaces can work well, such as conference rooms, backstage, or large offices. Some classrooms are difficult to make work, like computer or science labs, unless there is a way to arrange the space for circle discussions and for paired and small-group activities. Certain areas of the library might feel contained and private enough. The cafeteria and gym, however, are almost always problematic—too public, too noisy, and even the most skillful facilitation can't compensate for the expectation of playing, eating, and hanging out.

It is important that you have a plan for advisors in spaces that do not have a board or way to project videos. One workaround is to create pairs of advisors who combine their groups for meetings that require them to use technology. You can also have plenty of chart paper, butcher paper, and markers on hand to help advisors compensate for the lack of a board.

Providing Materials for Advisors

In addition to handouts, many *Community Matters* activities require specific materials, such as advisory journals, sticky flip-chart paper, and colored markers. You can support your advisors by making sure the necessary materials are readily available on meeting days in a central location. The materials for each activity are included on the overview chart at the start of each section, as well as in the written description of each activity.

Grouping the Students into Advisories

Advisory is an intentional group, so the composition of groups deserves special attention. Advisory groups can be comprised in any number of ways that serve different goals and outcomes. Consider the following factors when deciding how to group students into advisories:

- Single grade versus mixed-grade groupings of students
- Advisories that remain together with the same advisor for multiple years versus new groups every year
- Dedicated grade-level groups at key points, such as ninth or twelfth grade, with advisors who specialize in those years
- Single-gender, ELL, or special-interest groups versus mixed groupings of students
- Advisors who teach or coach their advisees versus advisors who may or may not have advisees in class or on teams

Planning Advisory Meetings: Consistency versus Tailoring

There is often a tension that arises in advisory planning and implementation: Should all advisory groups do the same thing at the same time so groups have shared experiences that help support students and promote school culture? Or should advisors tailor what they are doing to meet the needs of their particular group on a particular day?

There are compelling arguments for both approaches. Some community-building experiences are crucial for group development, such as name games and contracting, and should be done by everyone within the same time frame. Also, there are experiences unique to advisory that every advisee deserves to have, like the individual attention, coaching, and support they receive from their advisor during mini-conferences. Finally, in *Community Matters: A Facing History and Ourselves Approach to Advisory*, there are important concepts and skills, such as following the scope and sequence, key activities like identity charts, and strategies like journaling designed to establish a sense of belonging and connectedness to school and each other.

On the other hand, groups gel at different speeds, and an advisory group of seniors that has been together with the same advisor for three years has different needs in the first two weeks of the school year than a new group of freshmen. Or one advisory group might be boisterous while another is naturally more introspective. Opening routines like "mindfulness minutes" can help the former transition from the passing period into advisory, while the latter group might benefit from a kinesthetic opening routine. Members of the first group might feel confident early in the year having individual mini-conferences, while members of the latter group might prefer to start their mini-conferences in pairs or trios until they establish a sense of trust with their advisor.

The following strategies can help administrators and advisory coordinators find a middle ground between consistency and supporting each group's needs:

- Create a master advisory calendar for the first year of the program.
    - Record key benchmarks, such as mini-conferences, in the middle and end of each term.
    - Schedule advisory, class meetings, and whole-school assemblies for the year.
    - Identify faculty meetings or other times for advisory-specific professional development and list potential topics for each session.
- Using the **Sample Advisory Meeting Maps for the Opening Weeks** as a guide, create agendas for the first six weeks of the academic year. We recommend that you leave some space for flexibility in the sequence of events to allow for pacing adjustments.
- For the remainder of the year, the advisory coordinator or committee can schedule six to eight weeks' worth of activities and lead professional development to help advisees prepare for each new section of the program.

- Support individual groups' needs by encouraging advisors to choose their own opening and closing routines for each meeting while keeping the content between the routines consistent across advisories.
- Decide when/if you will include "open choice" days for advisors and advisees to create their own agendas, and record these days on the master advisory calendar.

Advisory as a Go-To Structure When Troubling Events or Crises Arise

In the event of a school, community, national, or global crisis, advisory can provide a comforting space where advisors and advisees gather to process the event together. In these cases, school administrators might bring everyone together for an assembly to deliver a singular message about the tragedy or crisis and then have adults and students move into advisory groups, with counselors available in a central location to meet with students who need immediate professional support. When tragic events occur, it is important that the advisory coordinator and administrative team work together to provide advisors with some materials, such as a set of questions to prompt reflective journal writing and discussion.[1]

---

1 Rachel Poliner, a national leader and author for advisory programs, contributed to this section.

CPSIA information can be obtained
at www.ICGtesting.com
Printed in the USA
BVHW021001160820
586497BV00003B/100